# New Approaches in Sociology
## Studies in Social Inequality, Social Change, and Social Justice

*Edited by*

Nancy A. Naples
University of Connecticut

A Routledge Series

# New Approaches in Sociology
## Studies in Social Inequality, Social Change, and Social Justice
### Nancy A. Naples, *General Editor*

# No Place Like Home

## Organizing Home-Based Labor in the Era of Structural Adjustment

David E. Staples

Routledge
New York & London

Routledge
Taylor & Francis Group
711 Third Avenue
New York, NY 10017 (US)

Routledge
Taylor & Francis Group
2 Park Square, Milton Park
Abingdon, Oxon OX14 4RN (UK)

First issued in paperback 2013

*Routledge is an imprint of the Taylor & Francis Group, an informa business*

International Standard Book Number-10: 0-415-97797-5 (Hardcover)
International Standard Book Number-13: 978-0-415-97797-5 (Hardcover)
International Standard Book Number-13: 978-0-415-65575-0 (Paperback)

---

**Library of Congress Cataloging-in-Publication Data**

---

Staples, David E.
   No place like home : organizing home-based labor in the era of structural adjustment / David E. Staples.
      p. cm. -- (New approaches in sociology: studies in social inequality, social change, and social justice)
   Includes bibliographical references and index.
   ISBN 0-415-97797-5 (alk. paper)

   1. Home-based businesses. 2. Women--Employment. 3. Minority women--Employment. 4. Sexual division of labor. 5. Small business. I. Title.

HD2333.S82 2006
331.4--dc22

2006018039

---

# Contents

# List of Figures

# Acknowledgments

There are many intellectual debts that I wish to acknowledge, and you will see them noted here and there throughout the book. In particular, however, Patricia Clough and Dan Moshenberg both offered and inspired new intellectual directions at various points, and for this and much else I am forever indebted. From beginning to end, I am grateful to colleagues at Tenants & Workers United (TWU). We've shared so much time and struggle, I really don't know how to say (or whether to say) thank you. For helpful comments and suggestions on portions of this book, and especially for the principled collaboration over the years, I am most indebted to Jon Liss, executive director of TWU. Former TWU organizers Gyula Nagy, Megan Macaraeg, and Kathleen Henry shared background information during the research phase. Members of the TWU Unity Campaign permitted me to attend their meetings and events and document, at least in part, their actions and statements. Others who shared their time and knowledge of child-care worker organizing in the United States were Judy Victor of the Home Daycare Justice Cooperative in Rhode Island and Keith Kelleher of SEIU Local 880 in Illinois. Jane Tate showed me great hospitality on a visit to Homenet in Leeds and shared her knowledge and insight about homeworker organizing worldwide. Stanley Aronowitz, Hester Eisenstein, and Cindi Katz supported the project from the beginning and provided critical suggestions during the formative stages. Amit Rai and Ioanna Laliotov provided helpful and timely readings of the manuscript. Thanks to Ben Holtzman at Routledge and Nancy Naples, series editor, who invited and supported publication of the book. Special thanks to Brook Pieri, whose intelligent caring and strength inspired me every day as I completed the book. Finally, I wish to acknowledge: Virginia Johnstone; the Center for the Study of Women and Society; the Center for Place, Culture and Politics; the Graduate Center of the City University of New York; Tenants &

Workers United; and the Women's Studies program at George Washington University for their financial and institutional support of this work. Portions of Chapter Six are reprinted by permission of Duke University Press.

Introduction
# The Invisible Threads of Homeworker Organizing

My interest in the subject of home-based work, or homework, derived initially from learning about cross-border organizing of maquiladora workers in Texas and Mexico in the late 1990s. I was especially interested in the work of community-based labor organizations such as La Mujer Obrera in El Paso, which had achieved some success through a "home-based" strategy of worker organizing. Home-based in two respects: one, because home was where, under the intensifying conditions of maquiladorization and structural adjustment, including the North American Free Trade Agreement, more and more "factory" work was taking place (again); and two, because home was where La Mujer Obrera intentionally encountered many of the women workers it was organizing. This double movement from factory to home, of both work itself and worker organizing, launched me in a particular way on the trail of homework, and more specifically, the organization of home-based labor.

"Labor" entered the picture once it became clear that despite what many were saying (and not saying), homework looked more and more not like a transitory phase of capitalism, or an old kind of "new contingent work," as some scholars (including some Marxists) have claimed over the years; rather, it looked more and more like a continuous and long-term strategy of capitalist accumulation and social organization. What I came to learn is that far from an isolated or contingent situation, home-based work, variously referred to as homeworking, homework, or home-located work (among other terms), constitutes minimally an extension of the workday worldwide—the workday in particular of several hundred million women and an uncertain number of children. In a different register, homework also constitutes a reshaping of "workforces" and national and international working classes. Far from an informal or irregular type of employment, homework is, from the perspective of capital, both a necessary and highly profitable form of work, so much so that homeworking has become tightly interwoven with national and international economic policies, including local and national micro-economic development strategies and the so-called structural adjustment programs sponsored by the International Monetary Fund and World Bank. As activists and researchers have noted, these strategies and programs, which I'm loosely combining under the heading of "structural adjustment," have as a central focus not only the relationship of capital to labor across the borders of the nation. They are also centrally concerned with breaking down the borders of public and private, formal and informal production, and work-time and lifetime.

My interest in home-based labor issues developed gradually into an interest in the ways that the binary divisions of labor and social organization—formal and informal, productive and reproductive, public and private, home and work—were being exposed (both critically and uncritically), and how especially the binary divisions of home-based labor were crisscrossed with other, even more powerful divisions, including sexual, ethno-racial, and international divisions of labor. Labor or worker "organizing" struck me as a particularly important component of the critical exposure of the multiple divisions of homework. Research on and thought about home-based organizing appealed to me for other reasons. One of these was that in my ongoing work as the principal fundraiser for a grassroots, racial and economic justice organization based in Alexandria, Virginia, the Tenants' and Workers' Support Committee[1] (TWSC), I was in touch with a group of organizers and workers who had already started to learn a lot about a particular kind of homework and homeworker organizing: home-based child-care. In addition to writing grant proposals for the TWSC's Unity Campaign of child-care providers and other projects, I began spending time (very little compared to the organizers with whom I spoke and consulted often) following the public activities of home-based child-care workers in Alexandria, a city of 130,000, starkly divided by race and class, located several miles from Washington, DC.

Combined, these interests formed one basis for my research, which is reflected more or less in the first half of *No Place Like Home*. In chapter four, for instance, I discuss the TWSC's Unity Campaign of home-based child-care providers, as well as other cases of home-based worker organizing, including that of Direct Action for Rights and Equality, in Rhode Island. Although my conceptual frame for this home-based worker organizing was to relate it and the situation of home-based workers to the top-down changes resulting from local and global structural adjustment (including so-called welfare reform in the United States), it didn't take long to realize that homework, no matter how one configures it ideologically or analytically, evokes a historical perspective to which such framing doesn't accurately or adequately respond. The deeply gendered bias and racialized divisions of homework, alongside the expanded state control and capitalist exploitation of the labor of subordinate female workers, required a more theoretically specific, if not trans-historical, analysis than much sociology or political economy—even critical political economy—typically utilized.

Thus, the second basis for my research was a kind of threading of textual and theoretical sources around questions arising from the crossing of home, labor, and the state; around the sexual, ethno-racial and international divisions underlying, and in many ways, undergirding these crossings; and the interests of and in the *long-range* politics of organizing *this* labor at *this time*.

One of the less visible threads running through *No Place Like Home* is the place of home-based labor and home-based work in organizing and advocacy associated with the "gender gap," the "glass ceiling," labor segmentation, and the sociological studies these subjects attract. Put quite simply, the growing body of research on the vast range of home-based work indicates that the continuing location of work at home undermines efforts to achieve gender/wage parity elsewhere. Lourdes Benería and Marta Roldán (1987) argued this point in the late 1970s, in their groundbreaking work on women's home-based labor in Mexico City. The growing field of studies inspired in part by their research finds that homework, by its apparently contingent but actually continuous and expansive nature, offers a kind of illusory freedom to women (and to men somewhat differently), often in exchange for the dubious status of "independent" or "self-employed" worker. The dynamic described by many researchers of home-based work includes apparent, but rarely actual, work process control; apparent (and actually) higher costs borne by the home-based worker; as well as virtually always lower wages than the already unequal wages of the modern factory and office. The effect, or success, of the homework strategy, however, isn't simply to reproduce in practice the *ideological* divisions that confine women to the family and women's work to the sphere of reproduction and consumption—and thus obscure the expansive field of home-based work from the interested gaze of researchers, feminist advocates, and labor organizers, among others. Because we know historically (that is, both before and during the emergence of industrial capitalism) that labor, writ large, is predominantly *women's* labor, the effect of home-based work is also, more importantly, to fragment and isolate the progressive resistance and power of labor *tout court*. While such a conclusion may strike even sympathetic readers as over-generalized, the systematic relation of sex and gender to class remains a cultural and economic hypothetical that stands up to scrutiny.

Indeed, "women's work" and women's labor are buried deep in the heart of the capitalist social and economic structure, and these dual subjects underwrite, in a critical and deconstructive sense, the new and continuing location at home of low-waged work of virtually all kinds. One of the ways of exposing these subjects is to see how the organization of home-based work taps into and maps onto the *unpaid* home-based labor of women as a source of expanded (surplus) value and (affective) energy. That is to say, the structure of home-based work is drawn cannily to what Marxist feminists called for a contentious period of time in the 1970s and early 1980s, domestic or reproductive labor, including the labor of cleaning, cooking, child-care, home maintenance, "caring"—and sex, some have argued. Part of the capitalist and neoliberal state rationale for homework is that it provides "flexibility" for *women* workers who prefer to be or otherwise must be at home to take care of children, husbands, relatives, families, households and others. What researchers of home-based work note with increasing frequency, however, is the reversal of this ideological frame: the call of domestic work, of service to family and community, isn't so much the cause of home-based work as the effect. Indeed, many women have indicated to researchers that as home-based workers, they end up doing more housework than they ever did working outside the home.

What some researchers call the transfer or shifting around of value via the home, isn't simply a question of gender, ideology, or the pendulum swings of family normalization, however. Nor is it simply a product of the increasing reliance on subcontracting and outsourcing in capitalist "globalization," or an intensifying social division of labor. It is also a question of governmental strategy in the field of social organization. As Ursula Huws (2003) has argued, the privatization of public and state-subsidized goods such as health-care, child-care, elderly-care, and education occurs as more of the paid labor of women is de-commodified through its transformation into unpaid domestic labor. Thus, neo-liberal programs of structural adjustment, including welfare reform, both engender and enjoin the sexual and racial definitions and divisions of labor—with the effect of situating more low-paid and unpaid work at home through the de-valorization of specifically women's labor. Unfettered, such a process has demonstrated the potential to make the home at once a more apparently desirable and a more actively controlled place of work for women, and mothers, in particular. The home remains a powerful nexus, then, for governmental strategies of simultaneous class, gender, and ethno-racial control.

With the crossing of home-based work and housework, or what Marxist-feminists term production and reproduction, I began to look at a set of political considerations that was forced to draw on what researchers of home-based work have repeatedly referred to as the "invisibility," "hidden-ness," or "secret" of work at home. To anyone reading the literature, invisibility is without a doubt the most frequent and significant trope of home-based labor studies. The untangling or unhitching of invisibility from its literal referent, I argue in a variety of ways in *No Place Like Home*, is a paramount political and theoretical task for critical studies of race, gender and labor, especially home-based labor and work. What exactly is invisible? To whom? What is being kept hidden or secret? By whom? The answers to these questions are not obvious—situated as they are in the long history of "women's work," as well as slavery. Indeed, in turning to some of the theoretical sources, it becomes apparent that both in classical and Marxist political economy, the feminine subject of home-based labor is only partially predicated in historical material terms. In *Capital*, Karl Marx referred to home-based labor as the "army set into motion by capital by means of invisible threads." The capitalist socialization of other, more "visible" forms of labor—forms thought to be more central, if not more prone to centralization (and therefore common "organization"?), than homeworkers for instance—is in part the history I am attempting to dislodge here. For Marx, with the advent of capitalism on a social scale, women and children would henceforth be "cheap labor" for capital. But what would they be for labor? In theory, it seems, as well as practice, so-called "women's work," including what we call housework, child-care, and homework, were subsumed, but not in an invisible way, in the formation of the "working-class" and labor subject. The supposed invisibility of "women workers" at home today is not about their invisibility to capitalists—it's about their invisibility to those who are opposed, in one way or another, to capitalists.

Like many researchers of home-based work today, Marx's formulation mistook a key turning point, or point of crossing. For, as feminist scholars of Marx noted several decades ago, Marx also considered "women's work"—the labor of reproduction—to be part of the "natural," or *given*, force of "total social labor" (the latter a critical concept for Marx, then, and Marxists today.) "Total social labor," much as theorists might like it to be, is not an undivided perspective. And what researchers of home-based work literally all over the world have established is that the organization of home-based work is drawn inexorably to the historically distinct, subsumed structure of unpaid domestic labor; and therefore, more properly speaking, home-based work is drawn to the ethno-racially distinct laboring bodies of women of all ages in metropolises, cities, suburbs, towns, and villages in virtually every country of the world on a massive scale. This division in Marx's critique, of specifically female (as well as child) labor that is paid and unpaid, visible and invisible, valuable and valueless—all at the same time—is a "closed" opening, an "aporia" to use a more technical term, through which the home-based worker, and home-based work researcher, must continue to pass.

## THE FORCE OF HOME-BASED LABOR

Part of the attraction of home-based labor for local and global capital and their institutional allies, is that the structure of paid and unpaid domestic labor is given to a kind of value-production that appears to be infinite, or what some theorists have termed "zero-work." This constitutes another aporia for the researcher of home-based work, for while the work of domestic and home-based labor has generally appeared in popular culture and political economic theory as non-work, its productivity is nevertheless always taken for granted. The somewhat simplified paradox is that while homework and housework are "work," they are "not work," too. Within this apparent contradiction lies a turbulent and confusing space that is expanding on a global scale. There are numerous studies of homework, for instance, which find that the earnings of home-based women workers, while they typically are applied to major household expenses such as rent and utilities, are just as often referred to, by both official and casual observers, as "extra income" or "discretionary money" for work that is defined formally and informally as household chores, "housework," "mother's work," etc. The sex/gender definitions of labor that feminist historians and theorists have explored at length explain much, but not all, of this phenomenon. For at the same time, structural adjustment programs such as micro-lending launch women's home-based work as work, but in the context of a debt structure premised on a dubious self-employment status; critical investigation of this arrangement has found that micro-lending earnings from women's home-based work typically are controlled not by female workers, but by husbands, subcontractors, and bankers. In the example of home-based child-care that I explore in chapters three and four, in the United States, one sees how the struggle to define this work as work meets with both external (state) and internal (worker) resistance. These and other findings from the homework field do raise the question of the gendered divisions and definitions of work, but they also raise the "biopolitical" problem-question, following Michel Foucault (1978, 1979), of "governmentality" in the circuits of institutional and subjective force, which I come to shortly.

The growing field of home-based labor studies notes these and similar tendencies rather implicitly. There has been a somewhat more explicit attempt made to bring homework scholarship into theoretical dialogue with earlier research and debate on so-called "reproductive" or domestic labor, as well as the growing body of research on "domestic workers" such as maids, housekeepers, nannies, home health assistants, etc. I address the former research in *No Place Like Home* considerably more than the latter, an unevenness that becomes obvious at certain points. Theoretical arguments appear throughout the book, making this a somewhat unusual entry in home-based labor studies. I am also purposely polemical at times. Those who write in this and related fields risk becoming what Antonio Gramsci (1971) called capital's "organic intellectuals": consciously or unconsciously in service to a moral and political economy which continues to exploit and deepen sexual, racial, and international divisions of labor in the name of "freedom," economic "opportunity," and individual "choice." While a small number of home-based labor studies have begun moving towards explicitly theoretical approaches, usually around the so-called "gendering" and "globalizing" of such work, much of the field is dominated by positivist approaches which generally avoid choosing to see how home-based labor draws on given or existing structures of gender division or ethno-racial subordination, much less the historical nature and given-ness of those structures and strategies. Even more important, in the much-discussed conjuncture of globalization and structural adjustment, many studies fail to examine how the expansion of home-based work reasserts women's practical place in the home as domestic labor that underwrites (that is, that politically and economically insures) broader social organization strategies, including the privatization of public jobs, health care, education, energy resources and other public works and goods. Whether we like it or not, these are the dynamic structural conditions for what we think of as global capitalist class, or neoliberal, hegemony today, and to ignore them risks not only obfuscation, but a more obvious kind of unacknowledged complicity. In this respect, globalization does not proceed just through continuous improvements in productivity, technology, and trade agreements, unless we understand that higher productivity and technology investment depend in multiple ways on the subcontracted labor of female workers—many, possibly the majority of them, home-based. In this overarching political and theoretical context, I note Gayatri Chakravorty Spivak's extended argument (1999) that Eurocentric culture does not permit the unfashionable appearance of the home-based female worker, even as the financialization of the globe finds a convenient alibi and political conduit through micro-lending to the "woman in development."

At the same time, I join many in arguing that structural adjustment has been led by the United States not merely globally but "at home," where it is well documented that welfare reform legislation of the mid-1990s had the effects of eliminating the jobs, income, welfare, and, to a lesser extent, public education of millions of women and children. In the process, it had the effect as well of expanding the field of home-based work across the board, including the home-based work I look at most closely, child-care. What this leads me to argue in *No Place Like Home*—this being the political, if not sociological interest of the work—is that home-based work is not only a strategy for global and local capitalist and state control; it is also a key arena for political and social contestation and counter-organizing. Resistance, as Gilles Deleuze (1986) noted, comes first. This points both critically and hopefully to the "invisible," "hidden," privatized nature of home-based labor organizing as well as home-based work in general. The community and labor organizing among home-based workers that I discuss in chapters three and four exposes not only the super-exploitation of black and immigrant female workers in, and through, the home. It also exposes the potential of homeworker organizations, grassroots lobbying groups and networks, and trade unions, among others, to organize the otherwise divided labor of the home to locally and globally counter-hegemonic ends. It exposes the power of organizing, advocacy and lobbying for multi-scaled legislative and regulatory changes that enhance or improve the power, status and position of ethno-racially subordinate female workers in a wide variety of low-wage, home-based work. And it exposes the power specifically of home-based "women workers" to alter the relationship between the force of their subsumed domestic labor and the state that, arguably, modulates and controls it.

Before (and in a definitive way, confronting) its own power to alter the course of international capitalism, home-based organizing exposes, as I examine in the case of home-based child-care worker organizing in the United States, the powerful neoliberal mechanisms of what Michel Foucault termed governmentality—of social policing and control at the sub-individual level. Savvy labor organizers recognize what Foucault called the technologies of governmentality in the state-regulated treatment of the African American and multinational immigrant women who make up a large portion of the urban child-care labor force in the United States. Viewing home-based work and organizing through the prism of governmentality takes us to the limits of the politics of recognition and redistribution of the value of child-care labor, which some might wish to argue is, or should be, the strategy for "care workers" across the board. The cases I discuss from Rhode Island and Virginia highlight a turbulent politics of control, where the political power of organized homeworkers depends not so much on gaining recognition for their work or higher rates of reimbursement, or even employment benefits such as health insurance—all of which are vital, and all of which are being sought. Power depends more on altering the racist and paternalist violence flowing from state apparatuses which seek to de-value and disrupt the organized force (the "society") of home-based labor—i.e., on resisting and transforming the pervasive governmentalist forces that seek to control home-based labor once it has been recognized and once social redistribution and efforts for social justice and human rights are well underway. In the place of (home-based) labor organizing, a nuanced politics of control and counter-control is emerging, and I must say I continue to learn a great deal from the kinds of "bottom-up," home-based organizing that understand that the starting point for organizing is always what the next strategy of hierarchical re-insertion, especially of women and ethno-racially marked worker-populations, is becoming.

Given these cases and findings, I argue in the latter part of the book that more thinking is required to address the political dangers or risks identified by Lourdes Benería and Marta Roldán nearly two decades ago in their work on home-based labor in Mexico. Where feminist sociologists, researchers, policymakers and advocates, particularly (although not exclusively) in the United States and Europe, are concerned to address the problems of wage inequality between male and female workers, studies of home-based work demonstrate that even when and where progress is being made, there is a counter-movement taking place below. This movement is formal and informal at the same time, and it both subverts the gains being made elsewhere, as well as subtly alters the deep-rooted sexual and racial divisions of labor—divisions that we might understand better as control operating via culture—which undergird the politics of equality and inequality in *other* parts of the economy. What one finds is that for launching and modulating this not so hidden, not so invisible, not so underground work which researchers of homework so often refer to, there is no place like home, a phrasing and a framing which I have intended throughout this work to draw on the (paid and unpaid, formal and informal, productive and reproductive) labor and political experience of women who are always positioned "at home," as well as (less directly) on the subjective experience of "internalized gendering" that revolves in and around the laborious "gifts" of family, sex, community, and personal life (and time).

Building on arguments that I begin in chapter two, I explore in the concluding chapters how historical developments of state, capital and labor have also sought, sometimes in cooperation, other times in conflict, to manage and control the turbulent relation of home to political economy. The generalized economy of home does not have a definitive or conclusive end for human labor. Rather, it draws on the "gratuitous" gifts of socialized surplus labor time—including material and immaterial labor as diverse as information production and child care—for ever-expanding forms of neo-liberal governmentality which are simultaneously attempting to modulate and control these sub-divided labor forces. The organizing I have sought to highlight, organizing both within and against neoliberal governmentality, reveals these layers of modulation and control to be "biopolitical"—Foucault's descriptive term for the management of relations at the *sub-individual* level. I take the latter to be those forces which induce subjective and material linkages between work and life, exchange and "gift" economies, paid and unpaid labor time, sex and race, etc. In the context of homework, one might also add linkages between the home as a site of sexual, racial and familial reproduction and the home as the historic site of the social and economic circulation of "values." In this theoretical juncture, I occasionally reference philosopher Jacques Derrida's (1992) notion of the "gift" where gift is understood, following the sociologist Marcel Mauss and others, as a giving of time that launches duty, obligation and debt in such a way that the possibility of return is by definition forgotten (and one may suppose, in a related sense, hidden or invisible). The gift (if it is that) of what feminists of the 1970s and 1980s called "domestic labor" is the one, decades on, that keeps on giving. By this I mean neither to trivialize nor romanticize the reality or perspectives embodied in "women's work." Quite the contrary. How, indeed, is domestic labor, especially the various forms of care of others, to be socialized? I leave to readers to determine how well I attend to the risk of calling the labor of home, essentially, a "gift" to neoliberal, patriarchal capital.

The implications of such an approach to home-based labor, as well as to the politics of home-based labor organizing, are the ultimate concern of this work. For some of this discussion, I turn to Foucault in particular, to understand neoliberalism as a two-sided strategy of positioned (theoretical and political) critique of the state as such as well as the ever-intensified policing and biopolitical control of social, economic, and political life. Foucault referred to this combined strategy as governmentality. I attempt to show that there is a double-bind in the view of neoliberal capitalist governmentality which is especially appropriate to the revision of neo-Marxist theories of class formation and value production. With Antonio Negri, in particular, one can see the movement in neo-classical and critical political economy away from the calculable and measurable terms of value in exchange-driven capitalism, to the incalculable, "immaterial" forms of value associated with the so-called "affective labor" of producers in high-tech, information-driven capitalism. Feminists rightly reel at any notion of affective labor that doesn't theorize or expand on gender and race-based claims for labor and cultural politics (not to mention the black hole of "policy"). In this context,

I note how women's work in the home and other place-based "care" and service sectors, haunts any political economy, Marxist or otherwise, insofar as this labor is both so institutionally-based (in capitalist enterprise and the public sector) and affectively inscribed in capitalist historicity.

As a variety of late-twentieth commentators on the revolutionary displacement of human labor in machines, information and other technologies have noted, Marx's labor theory of value was deeply informed by both the social and technoscientific developments of his own day. In the mid-nineteenth century, questions ranged from whether machines theoretically could (and politically should) produce value, to what the place of women and children in production morally should (and politically could) be, to the physical limits of abstract labor's capacity to work and produce value infinitely. As Anson Rabinbach (1990), George Caffentzis (1992), and others have noted, nineteenth century studies of thermodynamics—the exchange of heat between energy-producing machines—were as deterministic for Marx as supply and demand were for classical political economy. And for better or worse, Marx did not apply ideology critique to the physical sciences. His critique of bourgeois political economy, on the other hand, with its dialectical insistence on the human-centered (and androcentric) production of value, has remained a powerful, if techno-scientifically challenged, source for thinking about the dualistic dynamics of home-based work. Marxist-feminist deconstructive thought is a resource for thinking through the binary relationships of paid to unpaid labor, of productive to reproductive work, of formal to informal sectors of labor, of public to private, and of culture to class. Today in particular, there is growing evidence (which I realize is what the neo-liberal versions of social science must always be seeking, and so risk repeating from time to time) of the crossing of these binary oppositions in a way that exposes, in both industrial and low-waged service work in the home, the definitive force of unpaid labor (which one might also think of as reproductive or domestic labor) in the politics of structural adjustment, as well as in the ongoing dividing and defining of work, along sexual, racial, and international lines.

For the politics of class composition, the historic province of Marxist political analysis, this perspective may be especially relevant, for here once again, the sexual, racial and international divisions of labor return in unpredictable ways to confound both the categories of what Negri, diverging somewhat from Foucault's use, also terms "biopolitics," as well as of everyday practical politics, when representatives are chosen to stand in for the "new working-class," or the "grassroots," or the new "revolutionary subject" or the new "proletariat." I suggest in *No Place Like Home* that home-based organizing seeks to make those interested in counter-biopolitics more attentive to these everyday politics. This is not an altogether easy task. Even more difficult to come to terms with in the neo-Marxist-feminist frameworks that I partially argue for and with, is the relative dynamism of the all-too-important "divisions" of "biopower" in the strategic organizing as well as theory-building taking place today in far-flung places such as Porto Alegre, Quito and Mumbai (i.e. the World Social Forum), in the International Labor Organization, which sets international rules on labor (and thus in a restricted way sets rules for class formation), and in localities and regions where home-based female workers, among many others, are organizing towards a variety of turbulent, but not necessarily "revolutionary" (in the old sense), changes in capitalist sociality.

Home-based labor, in the words of Sheila Rowbotham (1993), "confuses the categories," and it does so literally and in incalculable ways. I argue that it would be a mistake to believe that the categories could be defused, or that the confusion is anything other than what Derrida (1992) has called the "experience of the impossible." With Gayatri Spivak (1999), I argue that the figure of the impossible doesn't refer to things that can't or won't be done politically or otherwise, or to the possibility that with the right informants we can finally enter into the domain of the political-culture game knowing the score. On the contrary, much is being done all the time, in diverse and conflicting names and registers, and often with a nod to "native informancy"—including "democratic" or "grassroots" "consultation," and indeed, as Julia Elyachar (2002) has critically shown, "grassroots organizing"—as the legitimating practice of cultural control. And it is the task of deconstructive, Marxist-feminist analysis to provide an opening to the ethico-political foreclosures of and within much well-meaning political organizing, policy advocacy, and cultural analysis, while noting the continuous formation of debts to divided labor and organizing elsewhere. In the case of organizing home-based labor, it is important to see not only how global capital reaches out to and depends on the sweating of home-based labor of all kinds to launch its cycles; it is also important to see how this labor draws on another figure, that of the home-based worker, for whom, as Spivak has written in a number of places, "internalized gendering perceived as ethical choice" remains a key obstacle. As one distinguished researcher of home-based work has noted, the question of how the technology and labor of home are to be socialized remains little asked by anyone these days (Huws 2003). To the above two perspectives, we would also have to counter-pose ethno-racial subjection perceived as "autoaffection" (Clough 2000). Understanding these varying obstacles—and as Swasti Mitter put it, the "common fate" and "common bond" in them—is essential to understanding "gendering" and "race" as a linked site (a "non-place like home") of culture and control which is biopolitically, that is to say, systematically linked to capital via a political ethics, or governmentality, that extends into the home, into the life of the mother, the caregiver, the provider, the nurturer, the domestic partner—and then back out into the *more familiar* areas of social policy, change-oriented philanthropy, and politically motivated research.

In the case of "progressive social change" organizing in the homework field (with child-care as a principal example), the figure of the "responsible woman" or "mother" assumes a many-sided importance and power, not only to control, via her biopolitical gendering and ethno-racial subjection, her and others' labors, nor merely to auto-valorize her labors by resisting or refusing elements of responsible motherhood. The worker at home, by practical definition a woman or a child, redefines the boundaries of economy in general; this practical redefinition is experienced as much in the street-level organizer's sense of building power, as it is in the full-blown global and local divisions of labor which capital seeks to exploit. And in between the structured research perspectives and systematic political perspectives of "bottom-up" and "top-down" organizing that I explore in these pages, there is the turbulent and confusing world of work at home.

Chapter One

# The Turbulent World of Home-Based Work

> . . . capital also sets another army in motion, by means of invisible threads: the outworkers in the domestic industries . . . (Karl Marx, *Capital, vol. 1*)

> Home based workers are presently invisible. There are no official or even unofficial records of their existence, their conditions and their contribution to the national economy. (Ela Bhatt, "The Invisibility of Home-Based Work . . .")

> Homework confuses the categories. (Sheila Rowbotham, *Homeworkers Worldwide*)

## HOMEWORK AND CAPITALISM

For the past two centuries, low-wage work conducted in workers' own homes, so-called homework or outwork, alongside unpaid housework, child-care, and other domestic labor, has been a *formal* feature of capitalist production and services on a global scale.[1] Such a notion goes against the grain of commonsense thought that homework is a dying vestige of the nineteenth century—as well as against contemporary social scientific thought that industrial and other kinds of homework, though representing a vast sector of production, nevertheless should be considered part of what economists term the "informal sector." While it is assumed, especially in the Northern hemisphere, that low-paid homework no longer exists, or that it exists on a very small scale, social scientists (who should know better) continue to assert that after 150 years of observed presence, homework isn't really an integral or formal part of capitalism.

While low-paid home-based work has been eclipsed in American and European popular consciousness by the advent of high-paid professional work at home and telework, its disappearance in fact remains a question for labor organizers, advocates, feminists, and critical social scientists. In many ways, things have not changed much for the home-based worker in 150 years. In *Capital*, Marx analyzed the introduction of machinery into manufacturing as the cause of a dissolution not just of the work process, but of the entire social division of labor. Henceforth, he wrote, the social division of labor would be:

> based, wherever possible, on the employment of women, of children of all ages and of unskilled workers, in short of 'cheap labour' as the Englishman typically describes it. This is true not only for all large-scale production, whether machinery is employed or not, but also for the so-called domestic industries, whether carried on in the private dwellings of the workers, or in small workshops.[2]

Several things are still at stake in Marx's expert formula for capitalism: industrial labor divided as much by the combined forces of sex, generation and empire, as by skill; specifically capitalist production based on women's and children's home-based labor; and, as we shall see, and as noted by Marxist feminists for some time, a patriarchal, or at very least androcentric, conceptualization of the home and economic production that in turns defines what does and does not count as work.

Home-based industry, Marx wrote, once characterized by "independent urban handicrafts, independent peasant farming and, *above all, a dwelling-house for the worker and his family* . . . has now been converted into an external department of the factory. . . ."[3] That is to say, things had already changed in Marx's time: the deskilling and dissolution of the old division of labor; the emergence of homework on a large industrial scale, where previously it had existed on a more or less independent or decentralized scale; and the emergence of sexually and generationally divided labor in capitalist production. Sexually divided home-based production had gone on before, to be sure, and would continue "for the worker and his family." But for Marx, the devaluation of *this* labor, set in motion "by means of invisible threads" in capitalism, represented a loss not merely of value in the "collective labourer," but a loss of the women's and children's labors that had traditionally maintained the home. Yet contrary to appearances, what had changed was not the specifically sexual division of labor of the home.

Far from inexorable progress, then, the ensuing labor struggle for a "family wage" under capitalism would be marked in years to come by efforts to return the sexual division of home-based labor "back to the future." Much as Dorothy intoned on her return from the multiply sexualized and gendered dream of Oz, "there's no place like home."

Even farther from progress, in a sense that Marx also didn't recognize, were the inexorable cycles of decentralization of capitalist production. Homework never has given way to centralized production: far from it (Benton 1990; Portes, Castells, and Benton 1989). In the United States for example, officially counted work that is done for pay in people's own homes, including manufacturing, assembly and literally hundreds of different personal and business services, increased more or less steadily in the last three decades of the twentieth century (Bureau of Labor Statistics 1998). Telework, clerical, personal service homework, and child-care, in particular, emerged quickly over the last two decades (Christensen 1988). As I have indicated, the full extent of home-based work, alongside underground and informal economic activity in general, are impossible to know with statistical certainty, much as researchers will continue to try.[4] Estimates of unlicensed home-based child-care providers in the United States, for instance, range from several million to tens of millions (Smith 2002). Neighbors, friends, parents, grandparents, siblings—all provide various forms of child-care in their own homes, many for pay, many for exchange of one sort or another, many for free, many because they don't conceive of not doing it. That these forms of homework are not counted—literally don't count as work—is part of the problematic, defined by the intersection of sex, race, home and work, which the politics of home-based worker organizing, together with theory, are forced, one way or another, to account for and strategize within.

So what are the forces propelling the increase in home-based work in the U.S., where in recent decades it is the increasing number of hours people, especially married women with children, are spending or being forced to spend at work outside the home, that has garnered more academic and political attention than work inside the home?[5] This is a deceptively empirical question: knowing the causes or factors of the current increase may not matter all that much historically. For homework, as we know from Marx and labor historians, has been around since the first belching mills of capitalism were outsourcing different parts of the production process, from carting or carrying in raw materials to taking out products for overnight processing to final assembly or finish work.[6] Belief in the expectation that home-based work would wither away as a vestige of pre-modern modes of production is our own calculated theoretical and empirical mistake. In fact as a number of critical scholars have shown, "sweated" labor—which historically was inaccurately associated only with women's home-based work—is a very "modern" phenomenon.[7] Why liberals and conservatives alike should think that homework is outmoded, I will show, has as much to do with the conceit of globalizing capitalism as being the most scientifically advanced way (and in a eugenic sense, the *only* way) of doing things in the world, as with the need to continually forget that work—most of it unpaid, most of it by women—goes on in the home all the time, from the wealthiest sites of capital accumulation to the poorest sites of economic pillage and capital flight.

In this context, it must be remembered that there are alternative (and not just oppositional) forms of social and economic organization, and that the alternatives are (at certain moments) up for grabs. In a fragmented political culture, the protracted struggle for moral and political control of the transnational home involves both the creation of a common cultural sense of what the home should be, as well as consent to what it actually is, that is to the conditions of control over and within the class politics of the "household." In this context, it remains important to highlight how the home has always been multiply divided, socially networked, and productively integrated in an expansive "general" (and in this sense, libidinal) economy.[8] The stakes of community and labor organizing in the twenty-first century depend in part, I argue, on such an understanding of the home and home-based work.

What does this argument about the relationship of the home and home-based labor to political hegemony imply for gender and labor studies? In classical Marxist terminology, who owns and controls the product of, for instance, the self-employed homeworker's labor? Does the home-based child-care provider whose labor and organization I look at in chapter four, own or control her own means of production? Is she in fact self-employed, as most experts insist? Who controls her work process? The worker? The contractor for services? The family? The state? Is there ever uniquely one source of ownership or control? The turbulent situation in which one works at home, frequently with the support of child and spousal labor—"in science" not only to self, "home" and family most if not all of the time, but to the state and capital as well; or selling a service on the formal or informal market, being subcontracted as a self-employed producer, and being made available for work, so to speak, as part of state-led economic development and structural adjustment policies—the worker of these increasingly common scenarios, inasmuch as she hardly ever exists simply as "worker" (in that old masculinist, factory-floor kind of way), is interpolated by a series of powerful forces that "overdetermine" the time and space of home-based work and production and relegate millions of predominantly female workers to a degraded and highly exploited economic and cultural status.[9]

The literature of homework reveals the home, "home bodies" and home-based labor to be "privileged" sites of ongoing economic globalization, structural adjustment, commodification, informalization as well as colonization: privileged in the sense that the home and the labor it is expected to offer comes without rules, laws, treaties or negotiations. The rules that govern the home are altogether different from the standard workplace, and though related, derive from social processes and cultural formations which stem from "everyday life" and "deep" bio-relations (Petersen 1996; Bourdieu 1977). The promise of "work at home," built on the drive and desire for "flexibility" in the circulation of labor, familial reproduction, and productive value, hinges on ethics and politics that precede and underwrite the exchanges and antagonisms of capital and labor, men and women, and parents and children—to name only the most obvious and generic players. Hegemony, in this context, is built up not so much in the supply and demand of home-based laboring bodies, although this cannot be underestimated. Rather, cultural and political analysis of home-based labor helps to reveal how hegemony gathers force in the tri-partite organization of laboring "affects," regimes of sexual and ethnoracial autonomy and difference, and "standards of living" (and, one might add, measures of dying). I return in a variety of ways to this hegemonic organization of the home and home-based labor in the chapters that follow.

## THE GLOBALIZATION AND STRUCTURAL ADJUSTMENT OF WOMEN'S HOME-BASED LABORS

The scale of homework is global and local, or to use a more dissonant amalgam, "glocal." The much heralded technological revolution of the past thirty years in the post-industrializing, now glocalizing, North has been premised both strategically and materially on shifts to decentralized production, "flexible" and casualized employment, massive technological investment and tremendous capitalization in its own highly industrialized countries. It has been equally premised on a range of super-exploitation and accumulation strategies, including offshore assembly and export processing zones, financial deregulation and informal sector economic development in the industrializing postcolonies of the global South (Moody 1997). Part and parcel of this shift to a so-called post-Fordist regulation of labor (and consequent deregulation of capital) has been an intensified multinational capitalist push for higher rates of profit based on favorable trade agreements, strategic international financial dominance, and the super-exploitation of women's very-low-wage labor (Mitter 1986; Piore and Sabel 1984). Such strategies were themselves premised on already existing and manipulable local and global divisions of labor (Nakano Glenn 1992; Phizacklea 1984; Sassen 1988).

There is an abundance of studies which have documented the impact of foreign and national investment in export-based production on sexually- divided labor in maquiladora and other on- and offshore assembly work around the world, often with a focus on U.S.-led industrialization in the Americas and Carribean, as well as East Asia (see, e.g., Fuentes and Ehrenreich 1983; Fernandez Kelly 1983; Fernandez-Kelly and Garcia 1989; Tiano 1994). Backing up these enormous shifts of sexually-divided labor, the so-called structural adjustment policies of the U.S. and European-controlled International Monetary Fund and World Bank—hailed at the turn of the twenty-first century as the "Washington Consensus"— forced industrializing countries in the Southern hemisphere to restructure internal markets and domestic economies as preconditions for continued international loans, economic assistance, and capital investment (see, Bello 1994; Chang 1999). However, the casualization of labor in the "global South," including the creation of massive informal economies and forced migration, as well as export-oriented economic restructuring, cannot be explained as mere appurtenances of "economic globalization" (Sassen 1988). Even as the "globalization" thesis held sway in the popular media and misnamed "anti-globalization" social movements at the turn of the century, the rapid diffusion of "globalization" as a multi-valent signifier of local, national, and international structural change has become more controversial, and the extent of changes which "globalization" is purported to explain are now receiving much closer scrutiny (Aronowitz and Gautney 2002; Moody 1997; Panitch and Leys 1999). Behind economic "globalization," there was certainly abundant evidence for major shifts after the 1950s in capitalist enterprise, towards, for example, longer chains of production through subcontracting—which is important for understanding the glocal scale of home-based work (Carr, Chen and Tate 2000). Yet compared to a century ago, the proportion of global trade and investment isn't significantly different today and worldwide labor remains deeply divided.

What is different from a century ago is multinational commodity production—production of a line of clothing or furniture that begins in a design department of a US-based company, for instance, then make its way through a chain of managers and subcontractors based in different countries to a home-based assembly shop in yet another country, and returns ultimately for distribution and sale back in the US, or in Europe or Japan.

But truly multinational production still isn't such a vast percentage of total production on a global scale (Moody 1997). In the colonial period, the typical demand by the dominant national economies was for raw materials, as well as manufactures such as cloth and agricultural productions. In the neo-colonial and post-colonial periods, this hasn't changed much. The difference from the perspective of the international division of labor, important as it is, isn't exactly phenomenal. There was compelling evidence in the post-1973 period of an intensified (although not qualitatively different) international division of labor and sex (Mies 1986; Heyzer 1986; Midnight Notes Collective 1992). The creation of so-called free trade zones, "manned" almost entirely by women, was the direct and explicit effect of structural adjustment policies imposed by international finance agencies of the North (as well as of other forms of international-state complicity) in *producing* low-wage labor and low-wage labor migrants. Far from *searching* for "cheap" labor, as today's globalization-friendly story tells us, structural adjustment policies and other international trade agreements effectively *commanded* developing nation-states to make ever cheaper labor present (and present labor cheaper) in exchange for loans, capital, military aid and a place in the "family of nations" (Fuentes and Ehrenreich 1983; Mitter 1986). In this broad, global economic and international political context, women's increasing presence as devalued and degraded labor in free-trade zones, maquiladoras, sweatshops, multinational telework offices and other paid labor outside and inside the home, has been viewed both as the intended effect of economic and social liberalization, as well as a discrete (though often quite explicit) form of local and global sex trafficking (Chang 1999; Enloe 1989).

While this may not differ so much from previous epochs, what is phenomenally different today in globalizing terms—and this may be the signature effect of structural adjustment—is the emergence of global financialization and indebtedness, as well as the enormity and speed of multinational financial transactions, all of which have ultimately changed the nature and stakes of global capitalism. The 1997 Asian financial crisis, the 2001–02 Argentina financial (and subsequent political) crisis, and the ongoing debt crisis in the global South are telltales of the changes wrought by global financialization and IMF structural adjustment programs. With the deregulation of state controls on capital movement, part and parcel of a broader liberalizing strategy to force newly industrializing markets under multinational corporate ownership and control, capital in the 1990s became increasingly secure in knowing that it could flow, while rebellious and redundant labor would still be subject to strict controls on international movement. So when the bottom dropped out in Thailand in 1997, capital pulled out, freely and quickly, from the countries in the region where it had wrested control.[10]

This freedom of capital mobility, as well as multinational corporate ownership and control (with increased focus on intellectual property rights and royalties), could not have proceeded, however, without the political and economic force of structural adjustment policies; and this, I argue, is what defines "globalization" from the perspective of internationally divided sexual labor. "Structural adjustment programmes, designed to reorient economies to the advantage of foreign investors, typically through the wholesale privatisation of state-owned industries and services, the liberalisation of rules on trade and investment, a reduction in wages and social spending, a tight monetary policy and related measures, have generated widespread condemnation among affected citizens' groups around the world," reports 50 Years is Enough, a leading political network for global debt cancellation. "It is generally acknowledged that adjustment programmes have been devastating for the poor and have increased income inequality and social instability. Just as importantly, they have wrecked the national productive capacity of many countries."[11] The sell-off of state-owned or controlled property and industry, as well as natural resources, has meant massive unemployment in these sectors, weakening of existing trade union power, lower wages, and the informalization of much of this previously public, formal and state-sector employment (Elyachar 2002). And informalization, in turn, reinforced what Maria Mies termed "housewifization": the hand-in-glove process of "ex-territorialization of costs which otherwise would have to be covered by the capitalists" and the "total atomization and disorganization of these hidden workers" (Mies 1986, 110).

Theoretically, seeing "housewifization" conjoined to informalization of labor and structural adjustment policies and outcomes (that is to economic and political "ex-territorialization of costs") helps to fill in the gaps of otherwise useful feminist critiques of globalization, as in the following:

> Policy shifts can affect which kinds of work fall into the productive and reproductive spheres, who does the work and how much time each individual within a household allocates to each. For example, consider the arrival of a cheap imported foodstuff. Previously, women made it in the home for the household's own consumption because it was too expensive or not available in the market. Now the family can afford to purchase it in the market. Consequently, the making of this foodstuff could shift from unpaid reproductive work to paid productive work. Might this free up some women's time previously spent on domestic chores? Might there be a disagreement between men in the family who

want the food to be made in the "traditional way" at home and females
who prefer the labor-saving market option?[12]

From the perspective of housewifization/informalization, one would also
have to ask, might the latter gender and class-based disagreement be resolved
through the informal/domestic-sector transfer of women's unpaid to paid
labor in the commodified form of home-based work? This and other similar transfers, which are neither transfers of place nor of time, but transfers,
as we shall see, of value and control, rapidly (cf. "invisibly") transpose the
critical terms of discussion about globalization from the political economy
of the international system and nation-state to the political economy of the
home and patriarchy. This is not to say that either "globalization" or the
home is the same everywhere all the time, nor that patriarchy is sufficiently
specified a term to apply equally just anywhere. Global and domestic geographies, broken out of the Cold War freeze-frame but attuned to global/
local realpolitik, help to specify the twinning of structural and home-based
adjustment in place and time, a necessary step towards organizing (of many
kinds), as we shall see in the following chapters.[13]

## THE DISCIPLINES AND DIVISIONS OF HOME-BASED WORK

In the United States, home-based work never left the labor scene, even if
it largely dropped out of labor organizing and research for a period of
about fifty years following the economic depression of the 1930s. Once
principally, or purportedly, the domain of seamstresses, knitters, manufacturing workers, and self-employed artisans and professionals, homework
is now positioned across the spectrum of job categories and occupations.
From low-wage manufacturing and service sector homework to relatively
high-wage professional "at-home" work, including telecommunications,
administration and financial management, home-based work of all kinds is
gaining increased exposure. Evidence points both to a generalized increase
of home-based work in recent decades as well as the erosion of the roughly
two hundred year-old, *ideological* opposition between home and work, a
powerful fiction that was long premised on the certainty of an *increase* of
both paid and unpaid female labor within the home. However, today, wom-
en's increased rates of participation in paid labor both outside and inside
the home, especially of married women with children (roughly double what
it was at the end of the 1950s), has not significantly altered the division of
labor inside the home, as one knows from both social science and everyday observation (Christensen 1988). As sociologist Arlie Hochschild (1989,
1997) has argued, with the advent of women's increased full-time labor

force participation and flex-time, women continue to perform a far greater amount of labor at home, even as work and home shift place often and unexpectedly in their material and emotional lives, particularly (although by no means exclusively) for women with children, aging parents, and others whom they must care for.

Since the early 1980s, with an overall loss of manufacturing jobs, plus increases in information technology work and telecommuting capabilities, it is estimated that 30–40% of home-based work in the United States is low-wage service sector and manufacturing work of one type or another (Silver 1989). As in the wider economy, there is a trend towards increasing wage polarization, with both relatively high-paid and very low-paid home-work (Christensen 1988). However, in nearly all cases, wages, salaries or piece rates for home-based workers are *below* the lowest average wage for comparable "on-premises" work. Not only is there more than one price for working at home, and more than one value, there is more than one sense of "worth."

There is no definitive number of homeworkers globally, although there is a growing sense of the scale and magnitude of home-based work. Estimates of the number of homeworkers worldwide have now reached as high as 300 million.[14] Definitive counts, even at the local level, are difficult to generate, as most homework remains relegated by both social science practice and neoliberal government accounting to the uncounted informal sector and incalculable household economy, a curious empirical cul-de-sac for the past two decades that shows little sign of being displaced (Smith, Wallerstein, and Evers 1984; Mitter 1986). Surveys from country to country, however, have found that from 30% to 95% of home-based work is low or very low wage (Felstead and Jewson 1999; Rowbotham 1993); and tellingly, it is estimated that as many as 90% of *these* homeworkers worldwide—based in manufacturing, clerical, child-care and personal service homework—are women (Boris and Daniel 1989). And female homeworkers are frequently rural to urban and international migrants, as well as, in some or many cases, numerical ethnic minorities in the countries, cities, towns, or communities where they work.

In relation, and addition, to these sexual and ethnic divisions, which quantitative social science unaccountably continues to treat as "unexplainable wage gaps," one encounters in home-based work tremendous cost savings to employers (including the state) as a result of the absence, elimination or reduction of health, pension and vacation benefits, job training, as well as other not so incalculable infrastructure costs such as plant, electricity, water and quite often, supplies and basic machinery. Put all this together and there exist vast labor forces and productive space—female workers at home—located squarely in the midst of super-exploitative international and racial divisions of labor where, as Mies (1986), pointed out, they are most often seen not as workers, but as racially-distinct "housewives" who by official definition and practice are located "formally" outside the labor force, and thus ineligible for established labor protections, including old-age insurance and unionization.[15]

The sexually and racially inflected politics of work at home have a tremendous impact at the macro-levels of social and political organization, of course, since capitalist employers and their state allies benefit directly from the exploitation of labor forces at home, forged by "housewifization" and the extensive chains of global commodity production. As Ela Bhatt, a noted advocate of home-based worker organizations, has noted:

> Home-based producers form a dispensable pool of workers for the employer. He employs them whenever and as frequently as he needs them and dismisses them when he no longer requires their services. Employment is irregular and uncertain for the workers. They may have to work sixteen hours a day during a peak season and sit idle for three months during the lean season. Work is given according to the needs of the business, with no consideration for the workers' needs. (Bhatt 1987, 33)

Given the common conditions of homework around the world, as well as the history and social characteristics of homework in capitalist industry, low-wage industrial and service-sector homework has been regarded as both a leading edge and illustrative example of the ongoing international sexual division of labor (Boris and Prügl 1996; Mitter 1986). The implications of this for understanding both post-1973 political economic restructuring and the "place" of homework in it are significant. As Swasti Mitter has indicated in her analysis of the links between early globalization and the then "new international division of labor,"

> The growth of the unregulated or hidden economy becomes an important feature of the current industrial restructuring in the West, as capital increasingly comes home. Homeworking in the hidden economy, in this context, cannot be viewed as an isolated phenomenon: it is the ultimate form of flexible employment that management demands. [ . . . ]

> The role of homeworking in the global economy, therefore, can be understood only with reference to a chain of subcontracting that links home-based female workers to the business strategies of the global corporations. (Mitter 1986, 125–26)

More recent studies have suggested that the link in the chain of global commodity-production is also a link in the chain of global political-economic restructuring, that women's home-based work is an incalculable site of economic, political and cultural "value production" in the context of global financialization and struggles for hegemonic control (Hardt and Negri 2000; Prügl 2000). Why "incalculable"? As I discuss at greater length in the next chapter, labor confined to the home takes on the appearance and characteristics of traditional, that is to say modern, "women's work": literally "worth less" and moreover bound to housework and familial care responsibilities which together comprise the literally and morally "invaluable" labors of love, duty, and personal sacrifice to be found at home (as well as at the office, as Hochschild [1989] and Hardt and Negri [2000], argue in very different registers). The contradiction of "own account" and self-employed, as well as exchanged and subcontracted labor which resists being monetized, from multiple sides and for multiple reasons, presents capital in particular, and the state in more nuanced ways, with a uniquely exploitable, and specially governed, supply of surplus labor.

A number of place-based studies have documented how low-wage homework conditions and conjunctures shape the domestic and political economies of regions, countries, cities and localities throughout the world.[16] Benería and Roldán's (1987) study of industrial homeworkers in Mexico City was a landmark essay in laying out the class and gender dynamics of the expansion of homework and homeworking strategies in an internationally subordinate, industrializing, mega-urban economy. They accomplished this by examining the generational, household and internal migration dynamics integral to the urban composition of class and gender. They documented as well the uneven and unequal entry of women, and men, into global and local capitalist industry. In this context, women's industrial homework was a linchpin in a class, sex and race-divided historical process of subsumption, whose difference from classical political economic and so-called "development" paradigms, and whose specific dynamics of the age, place, and mobility of labor, revealed an important movement of the global/local substructure, the "substrate," of capitalist hegemony. "What is important to stress here is that the making of the subproletariat in industrial homework is not separated from but rather subordinately linked to other processes of female and male proletarianization," they wrote (Benería and Roldán 1987, 102). "Subproletarianization," or what these and other writers have also referred to as "quasi-proletarianization," epitomized for them the gendered class composition of internationally divided labor.

> The historical conformation of Mexico City's proletariat is . . . a production not only of migratory waves from the hinterlands, but also of gender and generational "waves" of female proletarianization and subproletarianization of wives, heads of household, and daughters who facilitate the proletarianization of spouses, sons, or fathers. It can be argued, therefore, that a kind of "functionality" of gender subordination exists for capital, not only through cheap reproduction of labor power by means of the housewife's non-remunerated domestic work, but also through the subproletarianization of the wives in countries such as Mexico (and one can assume in other peripheral societies) where no family salary exists that would permit the reproduction of the worker and his family. (Benería and Roldán 1987, 103)

The difference of the wage that "would permit the reproduction of the worker and *his* family" is in many ways still the difference of organizing in the field of homework, as Eileen Boris noted about the political struggle over the ongoing existence of industrial homework and the drive for a "family wage" in the United States around the turn of the twentieth century. " . . . [T]rade unionists and women's reform groups from the 1880s had juxtaposed organization and abolition as oppositions, choosing the end of homework over the empowerment of homeworkers, accepting the goal of the family wage over a cross-class alliance of women working at home and in the factories." Interestingly, Boris goes on to write, "The only time that the ILGWU (International Ladies Garment Workers Union) attempted to organize homeworkers along with inside workers was in 1937 during a strike among Mexicans in the San Antonio dress industry where a shared ethnic community facilitated their effort" (Boris 1994, 250). I examine some of the implications of the racial division of homeworker organizing in chapter three; for now, it bears asserting that as in homes in Mexico City in the early 1980s, homeworking housewives (a profound term, to be sure) in San Antonio had struggled, fifty years earlier, under the premise that homework was organized to supplement the difference between the *female* factory wage and the family's reproduction. The U.S. male factory wage at that point, and then again after 1973 as we shall see, was insufficient on its own for the reproduction of the *working-class* family, by which we should understand, as Benería and Roldán made clear, both proletariat and sub-proletariat gender and ethno-racial formations. Moreover, as they documented and analyzed at some length, homework neither shortened women's collective household labor time, nor did it lead in most cases to greater financial autonomy or control of collective household income.[17]

Similar studies have not been confined to the so-called peripheral, or newly industrializing, countries and regions of the "global South." In *Common Fate, Common Bond*, Swasti Mitter provided extensive analysis of the subcontracting chains of transnational corporations (TNCs) in the electronic manufacturing and assembly, garment manufacturing, clerical and service sectors situated in the United Kingdom and Europe. The "new international division of labor" heralded by free trade agreements, structural adjustment programs, and export processing zone creation beginning in the late 1960s was, like the TNCs themselves, never intended to be geographically limited. Through subcontracting, the TNCs exploited the sexually and racially divided, and quite often transnational, workers who comprised the "out-sourced," "offshore," and home-based labor supply in the globalizing North. "Trapped between the racism of the host community and the sexism of their own, women of the ethnic minorities offer the advantage of Third World labour in the middle of the First," Mitter wrote (1986, 123). Following Mitter, other studies of home-based labor in the United Kingdom appeared, confirming and deepening Mitter's and others' findings that homework was expanding and intensifying in the cities and countryside of post-imperialist Britain (e.g. Allen and Wolkowitz 1987; Phizacklea and Wolkowitz 1995).

In North America, home-based labor studies have focused, in roughly equal measure, on telework and low-wage industrial homework. The homeworking picture in the United States remains far from complete, however, as the small group of researchers of home-based work in the US have often noted (Boris 1994; Boris and Daniels 1989; Christensen 1988; Lozano 1988). As a major focus of public and corporate investment in the ongoing pursuit of "flexibility," telework has had great appeal in terms of business organization, technology and labor management. It also has had the merit of slotting into the contemporaneous drive for the mass electronic networking of the house and home. In this context, Alvin Toffler's prediction in 1980 of the rapid rise of "the electronic cottage" in the United States and industrialized North wasn't entirely unwarranted. However, as I explore in the next chapter, telework in the networked home is represented today as *the* revolutionary wave of the electronic future. Or as Toffler envisaged, "The leap to a new production system in both manufacturing and the white-collar sector, and the possible breakthrough to the electronic cottage, promise to change all the existing terms of debate, making obsolete most of the issues over which men and women today argue, struggle and sometimes die" (Toffler 1980, 223). As we know from more recent studies of telework, neither have men's and women's "issues," nor old production systems (nor domestic violence, if

I understand correctly) entirely receded in these new and revolutionary times (Felstead and Jewson 1999; Huws 2003).

More important, there is nothing new about homework *per se.* To reiterate, centralization of industrial production was always premised on a readily available out-source of labor, on the one hand, and the daily reproduction of (stereotypically male) labor at home and in the streets. Telework, taking home unfinished work, running a home-based business—all of these represent significant trends, and mark the most discussed and officially sanctioned forms of homework; the promises of "flexibility" in the post-industrial home conceal, once again, what the home has always been expected to offer.

Foremost among these expectations is access to unregulated female, immigrant and Black labor—a fact which U.S.-based homework studies is less adept in documenting. Giles and Preston's noted study of Chinese and Portuguese immigrant female homeworkers in Canada, taking off on the theme of global economic restructuring and trade liberalization, turns to home-based labor that is subject to both "informalization" and "domestication"; that is to say, to home-based flexibility which avoids labor protections and workplace regulations and relies on existing social hierarchies and divisions of labor to devalue work which is done in the home. As with Phizacklea and Wolkowitz's (1995) study of Black and Asian immigrant homeworkers in the United Kingdom, Giles and Preston are careful to articulate the link between ethno-race and the informalization and domestication of work. "The relative invisibility of homework in the garment industry," they write, "is attributed as much to the marginal positions of the women who do the sewing as to its location in the home" (Giles and Preston 1996, 155).

Such a formulation has the merit of highlighting how the perceived invisibility of homework is more than, or not only, a problem of valuation; even if they were relatively well paid, which they are not, ethno-racial minority women working at home would be only somewhat less invisible than their low-wage factory-based peers, that is to say neither visible nor invisible. Moreover, as Giles and Preston, note, "the diversity of women's experiences of homework . . . underscores how involvement in paid work is defined by and through their ethnicity." That is to say, not all female homeworkers' experiences are the same; and not all low-wage, female *immigrant* homeworkers' experiences are the same. In addition to these differences, they go on to write, we should also consider "patriarchal relations within the family, limited access to state services, class position, the racism that ethnic minorities experience in Canada, and the working conditions characteristic of homework" (Giles and Preston, 174).

There are relatively few contemporary studies of low-wage homework in the United States. Most to date have focused on white, working-class, rural, female homeworkers in the manufacturing sector (see, e.g., Boris and Daniels 1989). Betty Beach's (1989) study of home-based shoemakers in Maine looked at the trade-offs between lower wages and increased control of the work process for white, working-class, female workers. Jamie Faricellia Dangler's study of predominantly white, home-based electronic assembly workers in upstate New York (1994) analyzes their positioning in the global economy as well as in the context of historic social and sexual divisions of labor. Christina Gringeri (1994) documented the case of state-sponsored economic development strategies in the Midwest, which brought hundreds of agrarian white women into low-wage, home-based auto parts assembly work. Edwards and Field-Hendrey's (1996) study of home-based workers, which is based on microdata samples of the 1990 census, in many ways mistakenly justifies the focus on rural white women homeworkers, while pointing correctly to a significant increase in service sector self-employment among the same sectors of female homeworkers. On the other hand, Edwards and Field-Hendrey's assumption that the self-employed status of the majority of known home-based workers in the United States negates the possibility of labor exploitation is highly problematic. Knowledge of how the use of "self-employed" status operates as a strategy to separate firms from responsibility for more or less exclusively contracted or subcontracted home-based, "self-employed" workers, has been available for some time (Christensen 1988; Mitter 1986). Moreover, as was the case in homeworker surveys in the United Kingdom, there is an undoubted undercounting of the lowest-wage homeworkers, who are also likely to be women as well as ethno-racial numerical minorities.[18] For instance, in Edwards and Field-Hendrey's study of 1989 census data, there were a total of 334,658 women counted in home-based personal and professional service occupations. Just ten years later, the census counted 478,000 self-employed, home-based child-care service providers alone, a figure which doesn't include home-based child-care center employees.[19]

It seems quite clear that not only was there a significant growth in home-based child-care in the 1990s, but there was also a significant under-counting of home-based child-care and other services ten years before. Moreover, as the Bureau of Labor Studies itself points out about child-care in general, "Employment estimates understate the total number of people working in this industry *because family child-care homes run by relatives often are not counted*, and because many other family child-care providers operate illegally without a license to avoid the expense of licensing and tax-ation."[20] Even official labor statistics emphasize the deficit of information related to low-wage urban and rural homework in the United States where, as researchers point out, one also "expects" to find non-white, migrant and undocumented female workers (Dangler 1994). Mary Tuominen's (1994a; 1994b; 1998) studies of African American and immigrant home-based child-care providers are extremely important efforts, in more ways than one, to highlight not only the historically significant home-based work of African American women (see Boris 1989), but the vast sector of home-based child-care work, where studies typically have focused on nannies and domestic workers to the (clearly unintended) exclusion of "own-account" home-based workers.[21]

As the ground of economic restructuring has shifted over the past three decades, and as homework and female labor have become such vital local forces in the era of internationally mandated structural adjustment policies, organized political and social responses to the extremely vulnerable situations of home-based workers have proliferated (Boris and Prügl 1996). Policy studies have pointed to the need for concerted local and international political action to improve the conditions of homeworkers worldwide (Boris and Prügl 1996; European Commission 1995; ILO 1990; Mitter 1994; Prügl 1999; Rowbotham 1993). Yet, home-based worker organizing is certainly as old as home-based work. The fact that there is relatively little social scientific, historical or cultural analysis of the politics of homework should not mislead us in this important respect (Boris 1994). Nor should the fact that the contemporary impetus for home-based labor organizing (as well as for studies of home-based organizing) has been, in many respects, the political response of home-based workers, advocates, and academics in the global South to local political and economic divisions as much as, if not more than, the local onslaught of globalization and structural adjustment (Balakrishnan 2001; Boris and Prügl 1996).

## THE CATEGORY CONFUSIONS IN WOMEN'S (HOME-BASED) WORK

What, to repeat the question somewhat differently, is "work at home" for women? Most historical and contemporary studies of home-based work agree that it is volatile work, closely connected to local and global capitalist divisions as well as the historic, male-centered definition of labor. In the era of political-economic globalization and structural adjustment, I am suggesting that one look at the home, and work at home, somewhat more emphatically than many homework studies have to date. I am suggesting that researchers begin to look more at the home as an expansive place of women's work, where invisible threads of value and control are weaving new kinds of material for political and economic organization on multiple sides of the international exploitation line.

As one sign of the growing turbulence of women's work which homework studies indicates, women are working more, and in more places, than ever before. The official rate of women's labor force participation continues a broken but steady rise, with notably few exceptions throughout the world. Women's so-called informal labor, occurring outside or alongside historically recognized and officially counted forms of labor (including some home-based labor), is growing rapidly throughout sub-Saharan Africa, Latin America, and Central and South Asia. That is to say, homework is growing in most, and in the most populated, areas of the world. Add to this surge in informal (and formal) sector work, women's subsistence agricultural production. And then add to informal and formal sector work and subsistence agricultural production, so-called traditional "women's work," including housework, domestic work, homemaking, cooking, shopping, taking care of children and the elderly, nursing the sick, community work, volunteering, budgeting, planning, educating, advocating, community and neighborhood organizing, etc. I offer this "laundry list" of domestic activities to draw attention to the facts that virtually all of the latter activities are done predominantly (if not exclusively) by women, and virtually all of them are done without remuneration. Thus, stepping aside from the divisions of home-based work for a moment, one might stop and briefly consider the more general economic structure which invests most, if not all, laboring activity—most expense of human energy—with sex and moral coding of one sort or another. From the perspective of the turbulent field of women's work today, the home remains a super-expansive site, a non-place, if you will, of and for the perspective of globalization, structural adjustment, and internationally and sexually-divided labor organizing, as the homework studies cited have so clearly shown. However, it also remains a site for the continued elaboration of sex and gender, especially in relationship to the rapidly fluctuating, sexually divided relationship of paid to unpaid work, of homework to housework, and of productive to reproductive labor, areas where homework studies have noted considerable connections, but made relatively few interventions.

What is "work at home"? Who does it? When? Why? What is it worth? Who owns it? Who controls it? Who needs it? Who wants it? The answers to these questions increasingly inform the global and local histories of sex, gender, and race, in which the neat distinctions of public and private, formal and informal, and productive and reproductive tend to distort (or make one forget) the actual struggles and conditions of home-based work and life in today's era of global and local structural adjustments. As one major indication of the power of that distortion: women provide two-thirds of the labor that is both economically essential yet literally "worthless" in the world. Only slavery and bonded labor may be considered worth less than "women's work", as the former are for the most part illegal (UNDP 1995).[22] Labor that is historically cited as a civic institution and cultural contribution, a "natural force" of social life, "women's work" is generally excluded in the annals of social policy, the law, economics and political science, to name just a few of the more power-oriented academic fields (Folbre 2001). Some, maybe most, of it is "valued" in one way or another, but what little is actually paid is generally paid very little. Most of it—an estimated $16 *trillion* worldwide in 1995—isn't paid at all. By way of this undoubtedly underestimated figure, we are asked to forget that sex has a value, too.[23]

At the general economic level of all laboring activity in the home, analysis can be as unclear and turbulent as the transitions between paid and unpaid activities for home-based workers, as spontaneously and imperceptibly as these often occur.[24] For now, let us take the commonly made or presumed distinction between home-based production, on the one hand, and housework, on the other. (Shortly, I will return to show how, in fact, each holds the other in place.) By itself, home-based work (including work as diverse as manufacturing, telework, child-care, and, in an extended way, "domestic work") is organized, structured and classified in diverse and contradictory ways. There is considerable effort being made today to classify those who work for pay principally at home, but little agreement on how to accomplish this. Is one a "homeworker," "outworker," "self-employed entrepreneur," "petty commodity producer," "informal" or "underground" worker, "subsistence" worker, or a combination of these, at any given moment? The home-based workers I turn to in chapter four, home-based child-care providers, often referred to as "family day care providers," fit into most of these (as well as other) categories of home-based work. Turbulence, it appears, resides not only in the home and work, but in systematic classification as well. How to sort and make sense of the categories becomes a struggle at once over how to organize the space and the worker(s), but also how to divide the time and the labors; how the flows of money and time and value will be arranged and coded; and how the (female) labor and its value will be controlled, and by whom. The analysis of home-based work, thus, draws one more or less immediately into the heart of much more common, and much more divided, forms of social labor, political organization and sexual reproduction.

There are pitfalls and strategies in the use of any name. The ruse of homework is its established affinity to housework. When I use, for the most part, the terms home-based work or homework to refer explicitly to the wide variety of work done primarily in the home for monetary payment of one kind of another, I refer implicitly to the multiplicity of forms of social organization and reproduction bound up in the domestic economy. Here it should be evident that I am making a very partial choice. In such a conflation, "homework" tends to unify the common characteristics and classifications of the diverse forms of home-based work, including how these forms share theoretically and practically with "housework," "homemaking," and "household survival" (which are rarely the same strategy or experience), as well as how housework, homemaking and household survival are stereotypically sexually divided labors. For in the theory and practice of homework, the rhetorical, and perhaps more often the empirical, question is almost always posed: how many home-based income-earners self-identify as homemakers, mothers, or housewives, rather than homeworkers? The classic confusion in the question should be quickly put to rest: many, maybe most, do. And many, and in some places most, do not.

The consequences of these differences are incalculable in a way that labor organizers perhaps have yet to realize (that is, in the way that both large and petty capitalist subcontractors of homework have): production, including the production of value, in the home is infinite. Home-based industrial producers (e.g. in assembly, sewing, manufacturing) work on and off, throughout the day and night, throughout the week, month and year, and decade, interweaving homework with housework, child-care, shopping, agricultural work, community work, and the rest. There are seasonal changes, speed-ups, and periods of inactivity. Apparently, for many teleworkers and home-based child-care providers, the new service-sector homeworkers par excellence, the same conditions apply. And some do not. Indeed, many set specific blocks of time aside to focus, successfully or not, on their (or their spouse's) homework, leaving the housework aside. The "trade-offs" and "imbalances" are continuous, around the clock, and assume more or less importance depending on the day, the week, the season, the year.

Thus, making a distinction between homework and housework doesn't necessarily simplify things. One has to keep this in mind, even while refusing to watch the clock and mind the turbulence. Sociologists Alan Felstead and Nick Jewson (1999), in an effort to develop the kind of typology of home-based work I am arguing is theoretically impossible (and yet still "empirically" necessary), identified and described strategies which home-based workers—principally in the United Kingdom, although they draw on international data as well—employ to negotiate the difficulties and advantages of home and work when home is work and work is home. Useful as such a typology may be for the experts, even the authors admit that there are far more in-between, crossover, and hybrid strategies than one could possibly identify. And it is important to note how such typologies, in attempting positively to clarify the field, can end up creating false distinctions and missing important connections.[25]

Analysts of home-based work have attempted to show that the multiplicity of situations, strategies, and scenarios of homework is in part related to the absence of explicit rules, theoretical, legal or otherwise, governing home-based work. Indeed, much as there is virtually no law governing "housework," there is very little regulation for home-based labor, such as labor protections for homeworkers or organizational frameworks for managing, disciplining, unionizing or otherwise organizing homeworkers (European Commission 1995; Prügl 2000). In the United States, homework was regulated in a number of industries, in particular garment manufacturing, where unlicensed homework was illegal, at least on the books, for decades. In practice, there was little enforcement from local, state or federal labor inspectors, especially in the past few decades, as restrictions on the employment of homeworkers were gradually removed (Boris 1994). The social exposure of large-scale scenes of illicit homework, such as the case of the thousands of immigrant, home-based garment workers tracked down across New Jersey in the 1980s, illustrate both the weaknesses and complicities in the enforcement system, as well as the widespread, underground nature of officially outlawed home-based work (New Jersey State Department of Labor 1982). Internationally, the first-ever International Labor Organization convention on homework was passed in 1996, largely as a result of the organization of home-based workers and the lobbying of home-worker advocates (Prügl 2000). I discuss these efforts in greater detail in the next chapter. Since passage of the homework convention, only four countries have ratified it, indicating the difficulties in forcing the issue onto national agendas, but also heightening the prospect of long-term national and international organizing and lobbying around specific issues of home-based work (ILO 1990; Tate 1996).

Absent formal regulations, home-based workers find themselves in situations where they may often be able to control their time or work process (although this generalization strains against itself as well: "may often . . . be able . . . to control . . . their time"), but rarely how much they will get paid, or *if* they will get paid, another frequent problem among low-wage home-based workers; or whether the supply of work will last more than a week, month or season. On the other hand, where better-positioned home-based workers have more leverage on wages and supply of work, they may have less or no control over time or quality. Or, at any given time, they may have both. Or neither. In short, control over time and the value of labor are turbulent areas for those interested and invested in home-based work. That is, there is always something else happening in work at home which impedes and resists empirical classification and measurement; positivist specifications—or more theoretical framing such as I am proposing—are useful only to the extent that one is willing to exclude those populations of home-based workers, and those kinds of work, which are not counted or classified or known. Thus, I am arguing that with the tight relationship to women's unpaid labor in the home, "homework" or "home-based production" (or whatever one wishes to call it) cannot be "properly" classified, counted, or rationalized. This doesn't mean that powerful forces have not tried, or will not continue to do so—dangerously and erroneously, I would add. However, the obverse is also true: that if anything could be said to characterize the world of home-based work, it is uncertainty and confusion. And over time, uncertainty and confusion have a way of looking a lot like volatility and turbulence—where change is not only likely; it is planned, organized and expected. As one moves from wealthier to poorer sites and regions within a country, and between world regions, this "turbulence" grounded on change tends to rise and fall, as it does, in different ways, when homeworkers organize themselves and each other to expose and change the conditions of their work. The dynamics of home-based work, thus, are positioned within the conflux of the powerful home-based forces of production and consumption, sex and reproduction, work and leisure, and the lived, "at home" experience of class and culture. The "energies" of home, in short, fuel a different kind of political economy than has been imagined thus far.

## DECONSTRUCTING HOME-BASED LABOR

Political economy has long relied on analysis grounded in multiple dichotomies, such as public and private, formal and informal, production and reproduction, which have been seen theorized as more or less autonomous foundations of capitalist historicity. As with binary oppositions in philosophy, in social practice (as well as hegemonic conceptualizations), typically one term of the dichotomous pairs was given preference over the other. Both classical and Marxist political economy focused on the public and formal economic sectors, on production, and on the interactions between and among these areas. Political economy's failures or inabilities to address the sublated term of each opposition—in this case, the private, the informal, the reproductive (as well as non-productive)—have been criticized, and remedied in certain ways, in recent decades, by some Marxists, feminists, and others critical of the "productivist" and male-centered orientation of dominant political economic approaches.[26] The mutual determinations *within* the dichotomies have also received critical attention, offering a resource to begin thinking differently about social and economic activities that are constantly and simultaneously public and private, formal and informal, productive and reproductive (Redclift and Mingione 1985).

It remains important and challenging to deconstruct those binary oppositions, as one simultaneously develops theory and analysis appropriate to the crossing and movement between and among the oppositions. As we find, for instance, home-based work shot through with public and private pressures and interests, so much so that it is unclear exactly what either of these terms actually signifies, we can question whether "public" and "private," together or separately, are still appropriate concepts for understanding the dynamics, trajectories, or force of home-based work either within specific locales or across geographies. When we theorize homework at the intersection of formal and informal economic processes, or formal at one point in time, informal at another, we begin to question what the convenience of the distinction between formal and informal sectors is designed to accomplish. In vast regions of the globe, the majority of monetized economic activity is being classified, or reclassified, as "informal sector" work, with street vending and homework being two of the largest categories of so-called "informal work" (ILO 2002). Within the informal sector, we note the absolute heterogeneity of activities, so diverse, and so interspersed with "formal" economic activities (the difference often a matter of statistics, not to mention on-the-ground relations of power) that "informal sector" as it is increasingly being used, ceases to connote anything really useful for a counter-hegemonic politics (Redclift and Mingione 1985). On the other hand, early researchers of informal work such as Phil Mattera suggested retaining the distinction between formal and informal because of the possibilities of progressive social and political struggle, arguing that "capital uses the new arrangements [of "off the books" and decentralized economic activity] to increase the degree of exploitation." "But," he went on to write, "insofar as people are able to turn the new forms of income-generating activity to their advantage, the structure is less of a *market* and more of a terrain in the struggle for some measure of social autonomy" (Mattera 1985, 26).

I return to elements of these themes in later chapters. What is important to recall for the discussion of home-based labor, as Mattera wrote about the geographic and political economic shifts towards decentralized (including home-based) production in the globalizing North in the 1970s and early 1980s, is how "the increasing dependence of regular enterprises on marginal and underground labor suggests that the dividing line between the formal and informal sectors is far from clear" (Mattera 1985, 38). The distinction between formal and informal, useful as it was in discovering forgotten (but to whom?) elements of social and economic organization (Benton 1990; Portes, Castells, and Benton. 1989), continues to be made at the risk of forgetting the sexual, racial and geographic divisions which underscore the dialectics of liberal political economy, as well as the continuous and complex interactions between different modes and spheres of social and economic action which mark such time, body and place-specific analysis. Thus, the not-so archetypal case of a female worker who, having recently given birth or forced to take care of an ailing relative or child, shifts from formal industrial or service-sector work to paid home-based, "informal sector" work: she now ends up working far more at home on the unpaid domestic labor that she previously had less time for, but ultimately remained responsible for. Unnoticed in this (ethnoracially and geographically unspecific) account of formal and informal laboring is the unaccounted for transfer of domestic labor-time and, in many cases still, the paid home-based labor, which analysis of both the informal sector and the formal sector respectively still largely conceal. And even this is only a partial acknowledgement of the cost of replacing her labor from outside, of greater household "reproductive" and "care" needs, and of the continuous need for monetary income, the absence of which remains the ultimate determinant of economic status and, given social and geographic conditions, partially or wholly determines physical survival.

Thus, what may be forgotten in this brief description, which crisscrosses the formal and informal, productive and reproductive (as well as, implicitly, the public and private) divisions, is the specifically sexual division of domestic labor, which in this account vies with money as a last-instance structural determinant, in the language of the Marxist philosopher Louis Althusser. Both sex and money are aspects of the economic, but so thoroughly interwoven with other social and cultural texts that they demand another kind of analysis, one that at least acknowledges, as Althusser didn't, that the economic, in the first or last instance, is not an undivided geopolitical or sexual political perspective. The description of the formal-to-informal home-based female worker I offered above also obscures precisely how sexual determination operates: through internalized gendering, racial and national formation, desire and violence; such that homework is engineered as the failure or impossibility of convincing husbands (or homeworkers themselves) of the social (i.e. national, global/local, and cultural) desirability of wives' earning outside (and "not-earning" inside) the home (Benería and Roldán 1985; Boris 1994; Singh and Kelles-Viitanen 1987). In classical Marxian political economy, this *structurally* violent patriarchal control of women's labor and bodies should constitute a barrier for capital to overcome; but far from slowing things down, home-based work, in lowering "the costs" (and increasing the controls) of production and reproduction, in fact speeds the systematic circulation of value.

The key dichotomies exposed by home-based labor studies are between homework and housework (with child-care appearing ever more frequently to stand in for "housework" in the globalizing North) and, to a lesser extent, paid and unpaid labor. (One might also add, on a more challenging and unattended level, "visible" and "invisible.") Given the public record of industrial homework around the world, it appears that any contemporary analysis of homework requires a concurrent account of the ways in which women's domestic labor (e.g. cleaning, cooking, shopping, caregiving, etc.) is undergoing major transformations as women worldwide simultaneously work more and more outside, and more and more inside, the home. Homework studies, in this context, have certainly contributed to breaking down many of the false distinctions between public and private, and to a lesser extent, homework and housework, which underlay United States labor history (Boris and Daniels 1989; Boris 1994)—although, as Dangler (1994) notes, the implications of this breakdown still remain important to theorize.

Part of the way that homework studies have succeeded in closing the theoretical gap between homework and housework is by starkly posing the problem of the sexual division and definition of labor as such. As Eileen Boris illustrated so well in *Home to Work*, the twentieth-century landmark history of homework in the United States, virtually all of the twentieth century social and political debates over the continued existence of homework in the United States centered on homeworkers' position as mothers, caregivers, and "homemakers," far more than on their super-exploited status as out-of-factory workers. Similarly, Jeanne Boydston's (1990) discussion of eighteenth- and nineteenth-century home-based labor demonstrated how thoroughly the "gender division of labor" at the turn of the eighteenth century became a "gender definition of labor." As Boydston notes:

> Although women have been involved in cash-based labor throughout the history of the United States, much of that work has been comparatively unorganized and erratic, interwoven with their unpaid labor. Consequently, the history of paid work, especially when "paid work"

is analyzed as an experience separable from other aspects of social life, is most visibly a history of men's experiences. The result is a construction of industrialization as a largely genderless process—genderless both because men are treated as un-gendered creatures, and becomes the transformation is assumed to have raised gender issues only peripherally. (Boydston 1990, 122)

With "labor" as a denotation for men's paid work, or work which women might do occasionally or under special circumstances, vast ranges of women's experience—which men often shared—became defined and organized variously as homemaking, household management, home economics, domestic science, childrearing, leisure activity, etc.: not "work." As Boydston and others have shown, such definitions have always been contested by individual women as well as women's organizations, privately and publicly, in both writing and in collective action. Yet, the power to transform them has remained elusive. Legal scholar Reva Siegel (1998), for instance, discusses the efforts of the white, middle-class women's movement of the mid-nineteenth century to put a price on women's domestic labor in order to make a case for women's property rights. As she and others note, courts have refused valuing housework, including child-care, to this day (see also Crittenden 2001; Folbre 2001). Nor has the economic necessity of women's home-based earning challenged the hard "empirical" distinctions of housework and homework. Homework researchers regularly and critically report that women's earnings from home-based labor are stereotypically viewed by both official and unofficial observers as "pin-money," "supplemental income," "extra earnings," etc., even when, as in the majority of cases, they are used for basic household expenses; or alternatively, as is increasingly the case in the global South and globalizing North, they constitute the largest source of income in the household (Benería and Roldan 1987).[27]

The supplemental dichotomy to housework and homework, is paid and unpaid labor, and what tends to drop out in treatments of home-based labor is the unpaid labor of housework and child-care. This remains, in many ways, the underlying problematic which this work seeks to examine. Income-distribution strategies, time-use strategies, conditions of paid work, international subcontracting links, employment status, social protections of wage and piece-rate workers—all of these tend to dominate the analysis of and research response to homework, and rightly so. What I will argue in subsequent chapters is that in losing sight of, that is not theorizing, the conditions that govern *unpaid* "home-based labor," including the productive work of housewives and caregivers, well-intentioned researchers and advocates risk forgetting that the invisibility of home-based labor is itself productive of other important, and highly valuable, disappearances.

Thus, waged and other home-based labor is not the "final link in the chain of production," as a growing number of homework researchers are claiming. In their own way, the petty capitalist and labor contractors of home-based production (to whom homeworkers are not invisible in the same ways they are to researchers and advocates) know that the logic of "work at home" isn't only, or even ultimately, decentralization, lower-costs, or flexibility. They know the logic is about—and desperately want it to be about—women's "traditional," that is to say "modern," work and "place," a geographic, sexual and racial control of labor power that undergirds the social division of labor as well as the flows of value that the home circulates in abundance.

In the context of hegemonic relations of force, the difference between housework and homework—the tenuous distinction still remains important—is not which work is paid and which is unpaid. There is ample and growing research that documents how, particularly in the class context of low-paid homework, virtually all house/homework is economically "vital" and "valuable." Most of the time, monetary income is "obviously" most important, as is often noted. Yet the substitution of unpaid for previously or potentially contracted-out work (such as child-care, cooking, or cleaning) may be equally, if not more, important at times, according to at least some schools of economic sociology (Redclift and Mingione 1985). Paid and unpaid, many women do certain work or jobs at home because they need or experience a demand for monetary income, and for a variety of reasons do not or cannot or will not do similar (and typically better paid) work *outside* the home. The "reasons" are as varied as the material and immaterial, manual and emotional, educational and sexual labors brought together under the rubric of "housework." What the latter has come to represent is not only the taken-for-granted baseline reproduction of capital and the *socius*;[28] it is also the major repository of the planet's sexually, racially and nationally divided surplus labor (Mies 1986). For in the lingering patriarchal logic of neoliberal capitalism, if you don't work, you are either unemployed or a housewife. And as has been noted literally all over the world, if you are a homeworker, you are (still) a housewife.[29] By the same token, housewives are generally never unemployed. Except in times of war, housewives have generally been considered out of the workforce and/or unavailable for work. Until recently, that is. Since the 1950s, the percentage of married and unmarried women, with and without children participating in the paid labor force outside the home, has risen, "dramatically" in common journalistic parlance, in almost all countries of the world.

To this point, I have sought to draw out the distinctions between housework and homework, indeed to more or less collapse them, in order to begin theorizing the dynamics which both link and underlie them. The "relationship" of housework and homework, I am arguing, is one of *différance*, to borrow Jacques Derrida's philosophical term: a relationship of one to the other which is different in space and deferred in time, but which remains in the economy of the same. Different in space and form, and deferred in time and memory, the forgotten labors of home, are also, researchers of home-based work commonly remind us, "hidden" and "invisible." Hidden and invisible because capitalist employers (which also include and involve husbands and fathers and other male heads) want (to keep) it that way. Hidden and invisible because concerned researchers and advocates have difficulty measuring and calculating it, and because they are few and it is vast. Hidden and invisible because governments, with few exceptions, wish to generally encourage it or ignore it (often the same thing); or where they wish to do something about it, lack the means, will or force. Forgotten because its invisibility hides other secrets grounded in the sexual and racial divisions of labor—in violence as well as in desire—which everyone is complicit with at any given moment. I turn now to the crisscrossing of these themes, especially the crossing of homework with housework, in the capitalist workplace which remains arguably the most under-theorized in the sociology of labor today: the "non-place" of home.

# Chapter Two

# 'No Place Like Home':
# Marxist and Feminist Topographies
# of House and Homework

What the Nation must realize is that the home, when both parents
work, is non-existent. (Agnes E. Meyer)[1]

## THE HOME/WORK REVOLUTION OR, "IF YOU LIVED
## HERE, YOU'D BE AT WORK NOW"?

By the 1990s, the home was being heralded in the United States as a new
utopia. Not for the first time, of course. It appeared that Alvin Toffler's
prediction a decade before of the "mass electronic cottage" was being realized on an altogether new scale. A trade magazine devoted entirely to the
home-based e-business "explosion," *House of Business*, was launched at
the turn of the century. A lead editorial in an early 2001 issue of the magazine, entitled "The Bandwidth Revolution," proclaimed:

> It's a new year, and a new vision is sweeping the land—the vision of
> total connectivity at home. All the injustices of the old order are dis-
> solving in the path of this new marvel: Gone are death by dial-up, meg-
> starvation, and imprisonment and slow torture in graybar land. In their
> place is the shimmering new world of electronic proximity, networked
> homes, and universal work anywhere-anytime connectivity.[2]

While noting some of the "bugs" in the home connectivity social program,
the editorial had the requisite spirit of the networking day, up-beat and
down-to-earth at the same time. History, not to mention anachronism, is a
thing of the past! The editorial continued:

> . . . [R]ead about the art gallery owners who have an artist in residence
> in their stunning gallery/office/home. That's a place with 'no dividing line
> between home and work,' says one of the owners. In antediluvian times
> you would have assumed she was complaining. But then she adds, 'But
> we like it this way. Open space makes for a nice flow.'

This description of the free-flowing, electronically networked house is unusu-
ally similar to that of the pre-industrial town house—with workers and others
circulating in and out day and night, and work and leisure running paral-
lel and often simultaneous courses. Only the family and privacy had not yet
acquired their objective status and significant connection to each other (Rybczynski 1986). Thus, the difference of today's home "revolution" is precisely
the family, as the editor of *House of Business* notes in the closing lines of the
editorial:

> . . . [L]est all this seem too future-oriented for you, it's good old-fash-
> ioned love of family that our subjects cite over and over as their reason for
> working in a house of business.
>     "I have three kids for whom it is just so much better to live here," says
> [Andy] Stewart [Martha Stewart's ex-husband, living/working in Ver-
> mont, out of New York offices].
>     Yes you can live anywhere. With the revolution, all distances are cre-
> ated equal. [3]

The propaganda of networked home e-business is fomented through an
appeal to the privatized family, on the one hand, and social (that is to say,
socio-spatial) equality on the other. Located somewhere between the desirable
and necessary reproduction of the family and the democratic space of social
equality, I am arguing, is the contemporary (hidden, invisible) homeworker.
Neither free from familial responsibility, nor with immediate access to democ-
ratized space, the homeworker finds herself in the very place where she is purported to be most safe, most free, and most respected: at home. Only she's not
really there, or not yet, or not enough. The Enlightenment discourse of social
equality serves here not only to obfuscate the realities of home-based work;
it also reinforces the value of the disappearance of the antediluvian industrial
economy and its social woes. On the other hand, in the ghostly re-imagining
of the broadband home, the pre-capitalist town house meets the modernist
family in an open space, flowing with people and work, and effectively erasing the nineteenth century's ideological and material separations of home and
work, private and public, production and reproduction—if not also the sexes
and races.

I cite this editorial of the "new economy" for several reasons. First, to recall (once again) that not all homework is the same, despite the class-inflected exposure of "work at home" as a socio-economic utopia in the early twenty-first century. To illustrate in part how home-based work in the U.S. is being treated more or less hegemonically, I would turn to the U.S. Occupational Safety and Health Administration's (hereafter OSHA) first directive on home-based work, which was released in 2000, not all that late considering that OSHA itself was forced on a reluctant government by labor unions only a few decades before. Under the terms of the directive, home-based worksites in general, while falling under the rules and regulations of the agency, would nevertheless *not* be inspected by OSHA field agents for health and safety conditions. The directive cites the privacy of the home as the general rule guiding the decision to not inspect. Home-based *offices* are explicitly named in this context: they are not to be inspected under any circumstances. Home-based industrial worksites, involving certain kinds of machinery, electronic equipment, and so on, may be inspected, but *only if a complaint is made.* [4] Low-paying and industrial homework, though acknowledged to be different from home-based office work in terms of health and safety risk, is nevertheless subordinated to telework and other forms of white-collar or, in the parlance of the day, "entrepreneurial" home-based work in the regulatory context of health and safety. All home-based work begins to look the same through such exposure, and the apparent virtue of home-based work goes more or less unexamined. Indeed, the health risks of routine office work such as data processing—i.e. risks addressed by ergonomics, among other specializations—are out of the question in the publicly sanctioned privacy of the home.

Second, in the "new economy" literature, home-based work is rationalized or normalized across class lines by an appeal to reproduction of the family. Family, of course, has many meanings, some obvious and mundane, others rooted out by social scientists, psychoanalysts and therapists. The theme I will be pursuing in later chapters is that in home-based work one continually sees the displacement of the value of labor onto the affective value of family and child-care, which has the circuitous effect of devaluing the work (both paid and unpaid) itself. In the most stripped-down sense, homework "informs" an economy of familial emotional attention, where the absence of the "dividing line between home and work" appears as the presence of the (becoming-productive) life of children: take care, get dressed, go to school, take tests, make the grade, and of course, do your homework (Fraad et al. 2000). It is no coincidence, as French political scientist Jacques Donzelot noted in *Policing the Family*, that mandatory education began in the midst of very broad and divisive political debate on whether and how much children should work, whether in the factory, at home, or in the orphanage.

The extension of mandatory public education a little over a century later is the form of combined and expanded public-private education which homework continues to subtend.

By this I am not suggesting that homeworking mothers (as well as some fathers or "househusbands") have so much more time available to work and play with their children than other mothers. Studies suggest that home-based workers have less or, at best, the same amount of time available for unpaid work than when they work outside the home (Silver and Goldscheider 1994; Smith 2002). What I wish to suggest is that homeworking positions parents, mothers in particular, in an "affective economy," well beyond the reproduction, in Marxist terms, of one's own and other household members' labor power (Negri 1999). The investments and expenditures (of time, money, energy, emotions) one makes in work at home are overdetermined by the socially mediated impulses to love and oversee one's children, elderly parents, or spouse. Such an impulse, I would argue, is "economic," not in necessarily calculated or rational ways (although these must be acknowledged) but rather in the pro-active and reactive drives to be present to children, for example, to protect, supervise and discipline them. In the "new economy," as in the old economy, this invisible, "immaterial" labor of mothers and "care providers" is written not as labor, but as predication of the (future) laboring subject—and therefore, as a form of social and political antagonism (Fortunati 1995; Fraad 2000; Negri 1999).

Third, I would also note the continuing extension by the "new economy" text of one version or another of sovereignty to the family/working home. Undoubtedly, one could trace this far back in the volatile history of the home, but for the purposes of this study, I would suggest we turn, as other researchers of modern homeworking have, to the rise of the bourgeois distinction and separation between public and private spaces, as well as gendered definitions and divisions of labor as such, in the latter part of the eighteenth century. The twofold effect of these emergences were to valorize (and monetize) the growing number of market-based exchanges, including labor (of men, primarily, with women and children as lower-valued reserve laborers), and to forge a new kind of household space, rooted in the unpaid labor of women, and materially configured in the new arts (and, later, sciences) of domesticity. The bourgeois European-American home emerged in the nineteenth century as the ideological shrine of bedrock values of civilized, white republicanism: property rights, accumulation of wealth, male sexual supremacy, and humanistic education. Given the excesses of the age, and ensuing class struggles, the reproduction of the bourgeois home in working-class society became not only a moral and political necessity for the ruling classes in the late nineteenth and early twentieth centuries, but increasingly an enticement for multi-national working-class men, in search of their own ideological and material homes.

This by now familiar history is complicated, like the national cultural and political history of the United States, by the sheer racism of its account (Saxton 1990). In terms of work, "home" in African American historical accounting is inflected by the experience of slavery, sharecropping, forced labor, industrial and union exclusivism, and paid and unpaid service of and in white homes (Davis 1981). The reproduction of the African American working-class home was continuously undermined by extreme prejudice, exclusion, and exploitation. Given the numbers of African American women involved in domestic service from slavery to the turn of the twentieth century, it makes less sense to see the white "cult of domesticity" as a re-articulation of the sexual division of labor in home and work, or the ideology of separate private and public spheres, than as a re-articulation of a specifically racial and sexual division of labor and populations in public and private life. The ideologically, if not practically, enforced domesticity of white middle-class women between the mid-nineteenth and mid-twentieth centuries, was materially premised on the labor time of African American women in paid and unpaid domestic work of all kinds, housecleaning and child-care in particular—a historical phenomenon Wong (1994) has referred to as "diverted mothering" in the contemporary ethno-racial context of child-care provision in the United States. This, along with the physical and economic degradation of African American men and women under slavery and Jim Crow, had profound repercussions for the organization and reproduction of the specifically African American family and domestic economy, which took different historic form from white and immigrant working-class families in any case (Mullings 1997).

In comparative U.S. social history, African American women's and men's differing resistances to, and exclusions from, the white, bourgeois "cult of domesticity" and Fordist social relations thus rise to the top, as do collectivized notions of home and community (hooks 1990; Collins 1990). One result of this difference is that African American homeworking and houseworking wives at the turn of the century, and later for that matter, were perforce thrown into the volatility of a fast-changing political economy, where home-based work was sought as a refuge from the sexual and economic punishment of the worst industrial jobs or service in white homes (Boris 1989). African American women's paid and unpaid work at home, in this respect, partially reversed the charge of the white women's cult of domesticity—while launching African American house and homeworking women's own pioneering political, civic and community leadership roles

(Landry 2000). As we will see in chapter four on African American and immigrant home-based child-care worker organizing at the turn of the twenty-first century, taking the historical separation of home and work, or public and private, as foundational for study and management of the *sexual* division of labor in U.S. society effectively conceals the ongoing violence against racially subordinated female workers, families, and populations, inside and outside the otherwise divided perspective of home/work.

## IDEOLOGICAL HOMES

Researchers across political and disciplinary divisions have noted major shifts in the relations—social, economic, political, geographic, architectural—between work and home over the past two decades. Shifting time and space boundaries are influencing definitions of work and leisure time, as well as the practical understanding of the social organization of labor (Harvey 1990; Massey 1996). In *The Time Bind*, for instance, Arlie Hochschild describes how both female and male corporate workers with children often find themselves going to the *office* for moments of privacy and relaxation, away from the time-intensive and emotional demands of *home*; the flip side of this coin is the grim reality behind corporate capital's much-hyped "family-friendly," "flex-time," and in-house child-care policies and programs, as Hochschild discusses at length: if you don't work overtime (at the office, at home, during your commute), you may be out of a job—or soon seeking work at home.

While much of this and similar research is concerned with shifting perceptions of home and work, restructuring of family life, and new distributions of "free time," "leisure," and "care," few sociological studies have focused on the co-location of life and work, of consumption and production, in the home. Studies of home-based labor have implicated sociologists and political economists for ignoring the significance of work at home, or of obscuring the divisions and forces at play in home-based work (Allen 1983; Allen and Wolkowitz 1986, 1987; Mitter 1986), much as studies of housework and domestic labor did in the decade before (Oakley 1974; Hartmann 1976). A broader critique would suggest that sociologists and political economists have largely ignored the home as such, that is the home as a unique subject and object of social, political and economic interaction, focusing largely instead on marriage, family and gender (Chapman and Hockey 1999; Huws 2003). The failure to take the home itself as a social subject has been addressed little as well by the recent entry of urban studies and geography, which with few exceptions (e.g. Boyer 2003; Pratt 2004) have treated the home less as a singular space or site of intervention and more as a placeholder for class-inflected discourses and practices of economic development, race-based politics, and the shift from local to regionalist approaches in urban political economy. It would appear that architects have had more to say about the home as such than social scientists (Hayden 1984). I return to this observation a bit later in this chapter.

Home-based labor studies, along with domestic labor studies, have better understood the home as a complex place for the interaction of divergent social forces than any other social science sub-discipline. Hsiung's (1996) study of homework in Taiwan, *Living Rooms as Factories*, disclosed the powerful political, economic and social forces, including state economic development policy, economic globalization and patriarchy, which resulted in a large-scale, distributed urban network of home-based workshops and female house/homeworkers, managed largely by petty capitalist middlemen, as well as husbands, brothers and fathers. Benería and Roldán (1987) and Miraftab (1994) also examined home-based labor in the context of economic globalization, specifically home-based work and economic development strategies in Mexico City and Ciudad Juarez, Mexico. In these studies, not only was the home a significant site of political and economic development on both sides of the local/global divide; the home was also a significant site of gendered division of labor, contestation of patriarchal and class power, and rearrangement of domestic social space.

Felstead and Jewson's (1999) study of homeworking offers a meta-description of changes wrought by the home/work transformation, as well as strategies adopted or adapted by homeworkers to make homework "work" for them, their families, and their employers. Building on existing research on home-based work as well as their own surveys of at-home workers, Felstead and Jewson develop a typological approach to understanding how home-based workers situate themselves in relation to their work, outside contractors and employers, and other household members. They argue that home is "a paradigm case of the compression of time-space and the disembedding of economic relations from place." Home "thus reflects contradictory processes with respect to space and place in late modernity" (Felstead and Jewson 1999, 177–78). They cite, among other processes, struggles over the control and management of labor, the reconciliation of domestic and home-based labor, and, borrowing from the French social historian and theorist Michel Foucault, "technologies of the self."

> It is our contention that the distinctive features of home-located production arise from the way in which relations of production become embedded within differing household contexts. This is what justifies

regarding home-located production as a suitable subject for sociological
investigation and as a clearly delineated field of enquiry. Home-located
production comprises a distinctive social configuration, characterized
by the spatial and temporal juxtaposition of relations of household and
economy (Felstead and Jewston 1999, 151).

Felstead and Jewson's approach to how work at home affects households and how this, in turn, relates to broader spatio-temporal shifts in
late modernity, falters, I would argue, in understanding the crossing of
homework with housework. They employ the notion of "household understandings" to explain the power-laden social relations of the home. Their
point is to suggest that the regulation and control of home-based labor is
achieved not merely by the external constraints noted by researchers of
home-based wage labor. Indeed, Felstead and Jewson go to some length in
*In Work, At Home* to argue that while these constraints are important, they
have obscured the ways that regulation and control of work at home are
achieved: through internalized discipline, self-management techniques and
"technologies of self." I will argue in chapter five that Foucault's notion of
technologies of self is an analysis of a strategy implemented but not devised
by worker-subjects themselves. The self-exploitation "managed" by home-
based workers is a common, but not inevitable outcome of the overarching race, class, and gender strategy of the neoliberal state and its business
epigones. Moreover, as feminist respondents to Foucault have suggested,
if researchers and scholars are to employ technologies of self as a key to
understanding or explaining women's subordinate or constrained status (as
in the case of home-based wage work), then they must do so with a view
not merely to how power is experienced (or "practiced") subjectively and
locally—but how "power" as such is subject to change.[5]
    "Household understandings," a concept derived from Pierre
Bourdieu's notion of *habitus*, is an analytical euphemism—in this case a
misleading one—for sex and power relations that circulate through the
economy and home. Most treatments of home-based labor, while varying
in terms of theoretical approach, in one way or another acknowledge the
combined historical forces of sexual oppression and capitalism which have
situated low-paid or unpaid work at home, and thus situated the home as a
place to embody and engender materially (which is to say, also conceptually
or ideologically) unequal social relations, *especially* relations of social
and sexual reproduction.[6] In redirecting analysis of the dynamic forces
of sex and work to *habitus*, Felstead and Jewson dangerously circumvent
the political economy of sex, value and money which theorists of home-
based labor have treated as not mere historical context, but as material

foundation for situating paid and unpaid work at home—as well as for rethinking the place of home in post-1973 modernity.[7] For now, it should be noted that a substantial tradition of sociology of housework, and even the most mundane observations, have found that the household division of labor proceeds far from equilibrium, even in the critical realist sense one finds in Bourdieu's approach, where household "understandings" must always be read as *méconnaisances*, or "misunderstandings."[8] Taking far-from-equilibrium household dynamics as a starting point, rather than a conclusion, should clarify, rather than obscure, the place of home in the cultural embodiment and launching of sexual, race, class and local/global struggles over power and sovereignty in the early twenty-first century.

Earlier studies of homework, which Felstead and Jewson unaccountably fault for failing to examine the subjective, self-exploitative dimensions of home-based work, were careful to clarify the implications of homework for women's sexually and racially divided labors. Sheila Allen and Carol Wolkowitz's path-breaking studies of racially and ethnically diverse homeworkers in northern England made clear some of these implications.

> Indeed in many respects homeworking is more onerous than going out to work. This is partly because there is no spatial separation between paid and unpaid work. Homeworking is 'always on your mind, always there.' As homeworkers recognize, 'You do not come home from work and leave it behind you.' Moreover, while those going out to work are at least allocated tea breaks, the homeworker's day is so dominated by simultaneous demands on her labour that a break in one kind of work is used to get on with another. The use of domestic space means that this way of organizing work is not even convenient. Few homeworkers have a separate place to work, and they are therefore unable to leave their work set up. (Allen and Wolkowitz 1986, 255)

With Allen and Wolkowitz, we learn that homework and housework generally take place together, if not simultaneously, and that this knowledge transforms social understanding and uses of the home as a unified place away from work into home as a divided live/work place. In practice, homework studies such as those of Allen and Wolkowitz, as well as time-use studies of home-based workers, show how this utopian co-location of housework and homework becomes extension of the female workday in the subterranean economy of capitalist modernity. Allen and Wolkowitz are emphatic about the constraints homeworking imposes—and about deconstructing the myth of home-based work autonomy for low-wage, piece-rate and other low-paid homeworkers. They equally stress how *homework re-positions housework* as the defining structure of women's work and status: in the situation "in which the wife is perceived as *already* doing a full-time job (i.e. a housewife), then the homework becomes invisible as work and as a source of income. When homeworkers collude in this definition, homework becomes the wife's 'choice' in the use of her free time rather than an extension of the working day" (Allen and Wolkowitz 1986, 259).[9] The implications of this recognition are enormous: whereas a great number of homework studies, including Felstead and Jewson's, acknowledge the force of "housework," such as child-care, in (partially or largely) determining women's entry into homework—that is, how housework positions homework—Allen and Wolkowitz make clear that the effect of the sexual definition and division of labor is the reinstantiation of unpaid "women's work" via the circuit of home-based work and productivity: i.e. how homework positions housework.

Homework and housework studies, then, constitute an ideological home in and of themselves. Allen and Wolkowitz take to task those researchers and advocates who fail to lift the veil concealing unpaid labor in the home, as well as those who fail to account for the ethno-racial diversity of the home-based labor force. They and other Marxist and feminist sociologists, geographers and political economists analyzed shifts between home and work in the context of the gradual reduction in social, temporal and spatial differences between "productive" and "reproductive" labor (e.g. Allen 1981; Collins and Gimenez 1990; Massey 1996). For a time in the 1970s and early 1980s, there was a substantial theoretical and ideological debate among Marxist-feminists over the value and productivity of housework.[10] Much of the highly politicized theoretical debate centered on the question of whether housework was productive of surplus value for capital (or not), as well as the political ("revolutionary" or not) implications of responses to this question. Key proponents of the housework-creates-value camp were affiliated with the nascent Wages for Housework Campaign in Europe and, later, in the United States. Advocates of "wages for housework" argued that women's struggles for justice under capitalist patriarchy were bound up not only with sexual and political oppression; they were equally bound up with women's servile positions as unpaid household laborers (Dalla Costa and James 1973). As the unique unpaid labor of women at home was resisted and rejected, they theorized, capital and patriarchy would be forced to surrender, and the bonds of domestic slavery would be thrown off.

The provocative thesis of the Wages for Housework Campaign, which continues in theory, and some minor practice, today, did not meet with universal feminist approval. The liberal (and in some cases, radical) feminist rejoinder to "wages for housework" was that demanding payment for their lowly household labor would guarantee women lifetimes of (at best, low paid) domestic drudgery. Better to struggle out from under the grip of housework and the internalized oppression of patriarchy, get a higher education degree, and pursue a career (or so the un-caricatured liberal feminist argument went). Wages for Housework theorists returned fire: liberal feminists missed the revolutionary point of "wages for housework." The point is not simply to get paid for drudgery, or wages for housework, but to demand social and economic change from capital and the state, as well as husbands and families, i.e. wages . . . for housework!

> If we start from this analysis we can see the revolutionary implications of the demand for wages for housework. *It is the demand by which our nature ends and our struggle begins because just to want wages for housework means to refuse that work as the expression of our nature*, and therefore to refuse precisely the female role that capital has invented for us. (Federici 1980, 257; emphasis in original)

The political struggle over the definition of value in domestic labor has been taken up in diverse ways over the past two decades, from the organized refusal of housework, to re-organization of the domestic work industry, to the socialization and commodification of various kinds of household labor (see, e.g. Davis 1981; Glazer 1993; Romero 1992). In many ways, the theoretical impasse of Marxist feminism in the 1970s, and the debate around wages for housework, have given way, as theory must, to these on-the-ground, in-the-home changes. However, the commodification or valorization of housework, child-care and sexual reproduction is not a unilinear movement. For as we have been seeing for some time now, capitalist society demands (formerly domesticated) "service" not only with a smile but with increasing degrees of care and attention both to the consumer as well as the "third party payer" in many instances, all modulated by continuous customer service, vocational, and professional development training—and all subject to more or less traditional routes of trade union organizing and workplace resistances (Macdonald and Sirianni 1996). The "expanded textuality of value" (Spivak 1997b) which I follow is rapidly appearing as the struggle for a limit to capital's exploitation of house/home work, that is the struggle for counter-domesticity and counter-servitude, energized by internationally divided female home-based/domestic workers (Parrenas 2001; Sassen 2000).

For contemporary critical political economy, the information, service, and affect industries are the engines priming the capitalist pump of world market growth (Witheford 1994). In earlier times, non-wage work such as housework had to appear as a natural force of social labor so that it could produce, or lower the cost of producing, value. More important, it had to be provided for free in order for the home to operate as the essential site of the consumption, distribution, production and circulation of value in society. This was the premise of the twentieth century Fordist political-economic arrangement. The question was how the "domestic mode of production" was articulated with the "capitalist mode of production"; and at stake was the violent social and political balance that had been built on the backs of predominantly male factory workers and predominantly female houseworkers. The homeostatic/social-balance premise of the Fordist arrangement was ruptured by the 1960s and increasingly became a less important goal for macro-political-economic managers. This was partly because of the increasing presence of "multinational" women in the workforce and partly because of the increasing ideological and material rejection by women of unpaid housework as the "expression of . . . their nature."[11] As a result, Marxist-feminist concerns with analyzing the exploitation of women's domestic labor gave way, at least in part, to attention to the valorization of caring labor, on the one hand, as well as to the gendered allocation of time and money, and the flows of value, *inside* the household (Gibson-Graham, Resnick, and Wolff 2000). Thus, the female proletariat, locally and globally, might be thought of as providing more monetary value to household expenses under post-Fordist (or non-Fordist) conditions (and more than appears), but controlling less and less of that wage and the labor which they now exchange for it (Benería and Roldán 1987; Pearson 2000). Wages for housework, it seems, are no less important today than in 1973.

## THE PLACE OF HOME IN SOCIAL THEORY

The home—against all bourgeois ideology and mystification—is neither politically, socially, nor geographically isolated (Markusen 1980; McDowell 1998). At the beginning of the twenty-first century, the home, and housing more broadly, remain the spatial focus of social policy and practices centered on the reproductive family, work, local development, public education, land use, and public health, as well as capital investment. Jacques Donzelot's (1979) history of the family shows how social policy in nineteenth century France took the form of the *policing* of families, and how for the next 150 years, the point of family, housing, child welfare and educational policies would be to transform the patriarchal/nuclear family for the sake of several key constituencies and sectors: a restless class of proletarian men; fast-growing social welfare, public health and psychiatry industries; a virtuous class of wealthy philanthropists; and the new capitalist masters of industry.

Much of this strategy rested on the creation and reformation of the stereotypical family home that we know today—with the health, preservation and education of children being the ultimate point of evaluation. Where working-class men and women lived in a libertine manner, marriage and co-location were prescribed. Where children of different ages and sexes slept together and with parents, separate rooms were to be provided. And where dwellings typically housed multiple unrelated individuals dormitory-style, or provided private escape rather than public visibility (as with hovels), a new kind of "social" housing was provided. The latter strategy in particular, Donzelot reports:

> . . . rested on the woman, therefore, and added tools and allies for her to use: primary education, instruction in domestic hygiene, the establishment of workers' garden plots, and Sunday holidays (a family holiday, in contrast to the Monday holiday, which was traditionally taken up with drinking sessions) . . . In practice, the woman was brought out of the convent so that she would bring the man out of the cabaret; for this she was given a weapon—housing—and told how to use it: keep strangers out so as to bring the husband and especially the children in. (Donzelot 1979, 40)

Thus, the creation of what we might call the modern working-class home operated in France and elsewhere as what political economist and geographer David Harvey (1990) termed a "spatio-temporal fix" for capitalist sociality. The home concentrated the effects and targeted efforts of the state, philanthropists, and social elites to structure and fashion order among the laboring classes. The order would be provided by a space regulated not only by bourgeois morality but by capitalist "time-discipline"—and the instrument of this regulation would be the home-based female worker. Donzelot emphasizes quite rightly, the political nature of this effort, as opposed to the economic. "The worker's adherence to public order was ensured by his desire to keep his lodging; and if he was lacking in this regard, his wife would take charge of the matter, as Reybaud remarked with reference to the workers of the Cunin-Gridaine factory at Sedan, where it had become the custom for the wife to 'come and ask forgiveness for the failings of her husband'" (Donzelot 1979, 42). Here, "public order" was understood not merely to mean sobriety and right-living, but obedience to the law and above all, counter-insurgency. Thus, "public" order was very much a problem of "domestic" and indeed, patriarchal, order. Bringing the supposedly private and personal struggles of laboring men, women and children, of "working-class families," into public and political discourse was a necessary strategy for capitalist state control and, as Donzelot also revealed, the state's philanthropic representatives and cultural allies.

Given this history, one might argue that the home remains, two centuries later, a highly *privatized* social space of struggle over reproductive labor, including housework and sex, in large part due to the discursive and regulatory practice of the state (and its sociological epigones) to police the working-class family into "public" (i.e. bourgeois) standards on the one hand, and to privatize and de-politicize *the* (bourgeois, middle-class) family—monolithic and undifferentiated—on the other (Coontz 1997).

Returning to the theme of domestic labor, feminist economists and activists have documented, among other crucial examples of state power, the practice of concealing the materiality of home life and labor through national accounting statistics that exclude unpaid labor in the home (Folbre 2001; Waring 1988). Depending on how housework is valued, at average wage levels or at (considerably lower) prevailing market rates for specific occupations (child-care workers, cleaners, cooks, etc.), the value of the "household economy" in the United Kingdom in 1997, for instance, was anywhere from half to over 100% of the United Kingdom's official gross domestic product (McDowell 1999). Moreover, women's increased work outside (and inside) the home, and increased monetary contributions to family and household incomes in recent decades, have led neither to a reduced share of domestic labor by women, nor to great changes in men's and women's perceptions of the sexual division of labor (Hochschild 1989; Silver and Goldscheider 1994). It has also led to women's greater fiscal responsibility for family survival and reproduction, with little gain in terms of social control or political power: women's increased "micro-earnings" flow into men's accounts, a global phenomenon which undercuts many of the stated intentions of women in development programs, including micro-credit and home-based labor strategies.[12]

So despite the fact that in the post-industrial and industrializing nations of the world, women are working more and earning more outside the home, work inside the home remains relatively unvalued and women's earnings, wherever they derive from, highly expropriated. Homework, coupled with an ideology of domesticity and material practices of separating women from their own property and wages, reshapes the materiality of the home for female workers worldwide. In a similar vein to Felstead and Jewson's analysis of homework, Sherry Boland Ahrentzen (1992) broadens research perspectives on homework not only by examining the real variations in women's experiences of co-located homework and housework. She also points to examples of the ways in which homework shifts boundaries

inside and outside the home for specific groups of home-based female workers.

> Historically, being at home means doing domestic work. Because
> women's contribution of domestic work in the home has been roundly
> devalued in this century . . . , it is understandable why homeworkers are
> upset with the association of their occupational role and status with the
> domesticated home. The advent of women in the paid labor force out-
> side the home may have further denigrated work done in the home by
> making housework—and the home workplace—more socially isolated
> and culturally marginal. (Ahrentzen 1992, 131–32)

The question researchers such as Ahrentzen and homeworker advocates and organizers pose, as a result, is what is the relationship between the
home as a traditional, if not patriarchal, kind of anthropological or sociological place of family, marriage, identity, socialization, etc., and the home
as a volatile workplace made modern by the inscription and incorporation
of domesticity, servitude, and the invisibility of its racially marked female
labor force? Insofar as the histories, relationships and identities of the home/
work place remain in many ways subjugated, forgotten, and untheorized,
the homeworker and researchers alike are confronted with the dilemma, as
Ahrenzten has put it, of replacing "an ideology of the home as haven with
one of the home as work place" (Ahrentzen 1992, 133).

One may infer from postmodern anthropologists such as Marc Augé
that it is in fact such a dilemma that informs broader social categories of
place and space in theory, as well. Augé (1995) argues that the traditional
experience of "place" that one encountered in communities and homes
(in the "territorial" rather than household sense) was strongly associated
with anthropological identifiers such as place names, fictive and territorial nations, and extended kinship. In the burgeoning sites of what Augé
terms "supermodernity," where many of these identifiers lose significance
or actively disappear, he argues, the palpably marked places that previously
contained people's identities now contain only movement, flows, and end-
less circulation of bodies. Citing "super-modern" airports as a principal
example, Augé suggests that such spaces function as "non-places" owing to
their smoothed-out, yet hyper-differentiated environments and boundaries:
multinational, generic, volatile, and in continuous motion.

"Non-place" may be the wrong name (rather than a bad translation)
for what Augé is describing, I would suggest. For, as I explain below, airports are indeed places, although admittedly not in the traditional anthropological sense of ethnically named, claimed, and identified spaces, as Augé

describes. It is clear to me that with the notion of "non-place," Augé does not intend a nihilistic erasure of "place." Rather, by non-place, he wishes to call attention to the gap in social theory about how places are being radically altered or modulated in conditions of postmodernity, where far from being places of formal destination ("homes," as it were), they are or are becoming sites of informal and incessant transit, spaces produced, as Henri Lefèbvre famously framed it, out of the crisis of specifically capitalist social reproduction. *Mutatis mutandis*, one would be tempted to make a similar argument for the home, as I have been describing it here: homes, no longer "homes" in the traditional sense, but refashioned home/work places. Yet these homes, as we know from home-based work studies, are also volatile and in constant motion, and therefore more and more non-places in the "supermodern" sense: non-places like home.

And yet, such an argument would be wrong, for precisely the reasons that the sexually and racially divided histories of homework tell us it would be. I want to return to one of the quotations I begin this chapter with. In times of war, with women working both outside and inside the home—that is to say, under conditions where "women's work" is remunerated—the home as such was no longer thought to exist. Yet the home had always been defined, in transient terms and "invisible threads," by the absence or presence of gendered and ethno-racially marked workers. The ideological home of bourgeois reproduction concealed not only the unpaid and "invisible" labor of housewives. It also concealed other homes, homeworkers' homes, which themselves concealed homeworkers and home-based laborers, and so on. Likewise, the supermodern airport has more than multinational, transnational and stateless travelers in it. It also has (quite often, multinational) workers, who labor all day, every day of the year in it. Where the anthropological understanding of place breaks down, I would argue, is in theorizing not what, but who (in the old, embodied, fleshy sense) actually makes or creates a place, a view which is understandably partially at odds with the Western, androcentric anthropological tradition (Trinh 1989).

Writing on classical and critical empiricist philosophies of space and place, Edward Casey argues that what locates or situates place in the intellectual history of space is neither territory nor surface, but the body. The binary oppositions in Western philosophy between mind and matter, spirit and body, space and place, have typically resulted in a hierarchical suppression of one term in each oppositional pair. Thus, matter, body and place have occupied a suppressed or subordinated place in the history of Western thought—resurging in recent times only through the concerted efforts of postmodern, critical, feminist and deconstructive theorists. "The only trace of place remaining after it had been incorporated into space," Casey argues, "occurred in the form of site, which in Leibniz's deft hands became the dominant spatial module of the modern age, affecting and infecting every aspect of modern life: architecture and medicine, schools and prisons, not to mention philosophical thought itself" (Casey 1997, 334). The subsequent rethinking of place which Casey outlines draws on hybrid discourses of the body and space to break place free of the philosophical shackles of pure space. "The new bases of any putative primacy of place," he writes "are themselves multiple: bodily certainly, but also psychical, nomadological, architectural, institutional and sexual."[13] From where I sit, the home/work place may be archetypal in terms of the complex integration of these bases. Like the racially and sexually divided labor that creates and re-creates them, houses and homes are profoundly taken-for-granted places in the literature of social sciences. They are everywhere, yet one rarely sees the relationships, especially the political-economic relationships, inside them. Huge amounts of work take place there, and yet little of it is counted, one way or another. But what makes them homes ultimately, and what make the home a place (even if a "misunderstood" or paradoxical place) and not a non-place, are the socially engineered bodies, relations, and labors the home is supposed to contain, if not conceal.

The philosophical tradition of space that Casey traces is rooted most powerfully in the differentiation of interior and exterior, which in the context of the house and home marks the clear distinction between them and other places. Writing on the relationship between architecture and philosophical deconstruction, architectural theorist Mark Wigley observes:

> The house is always first understood as the most primitive drawing of a line that produces an inside opposed to an outside, a line that acts as a mechanism of domestication. It is as the paradigm [literally, the architectural model] of interiority that the house is indispensable to philosophy, establishing . . . the distinction between the interiority of presence and the exteriority of representation on which the discourse depends. (Wigley 1993, 104)

House as home, that is space as place, literally domesticates its occupants from the inside. The interior space of the home, which Wigley has traced to the fourteenth and fifteenth century architectural design of the studio—literally a closet, and the only space of privacy in the house—was always a "sexed" place. The studio was intended as, and historically served as, a man's private place of study, reflection, accounting, concealing, and withdrawing (Wigley 1992). Man's habitation of the home might also be thought, in this respect, as his habitation of thought, knowledge and language, Wigley observes. One communicates from inside a system of signs which one inhabits. Echoing the French philosopher Jacques Derrida, Wigley argues that the spatial metaphor in Western philosophy extends itself to the house because of the precise correspondence of the interiority (privacy, dwelling, security) which house-space is thought to contain, and the interiority of voice, rationality and identity which consciousness is thought to contain.

> The edifice of metaphysics is necessarily a house. Within every explicit appeal to the necessity of stable construction is an implicit appeal to the necessity of a secure house. The philosophical economy is always a domestic economy, the economy of the domestic, the family house, the familiar enclosure. Deconstructive discourse must therefore be first and foremost an occupation of the idea of the house that displaces it from within. (Wigley 1993, 106)

The domestic economy of presence and place—of being "at home"—promises "ontological" stability, if not security. In expert traditions of space and place, it has also promised and delivered identity, meaning, kinship, and normative socialization, as Augé shows. However, we know through examination that what underwrites the twenty-first century domestic economy of presence and place at home is, among other things, a shifting, unstable sexual and racial division of labor, and fast-changing technologies, such as time-altering machines, *pouvoir-savoir* (to use Foucault's term), and "affective technologies" such as attention, care, and love. More troubling for the home = security paradigm is, once again, the sexed body: worldwide, women and girls are far more likely to be violently treated in their homes by men they know, for example, than outside the home by men they do not know (Goldsack 1999; Heise, Pitanguy, and Germaine 1994). For the bodies of homeworkers, home is not necessarily, or even often, a place of security or stability. Stability at home is always, at best, relative to the instability of forces inside and outside the home, that is to say, inside and outside of everyday practice, or *habitus* (Bourdieu 1977). Calculating the health, safety, security and value of home-based labor remains, philosophically speaking, impossible, which doesn't mean of course that such calculations are not necessary or, indeed, desirable.

In the context of home-located production, Felstead and Jewson have rightly contrasted what I am calling domestic-economic instability with Anthony Giddens' notion of "ontological security": "a sense of continuity and order in events, including those not directly within the perceptual environment of the individual" (Giddens 1991, 243). In tandem with a "defensive protection which filters out potential dangers impinging upon

the external world and which is founded psychologically upon basic trust,"
ontological security, for Giddens, constitutes the root form of mundane
trust, psychic freedom, and self-identity which characterizes the individual
in modernity (Giddens 1991, 244 and *passim*). In the hands of sociologists,
the home becomes the quintessential site of such a notion of ontological
security in late modernity, i.e. the *locus classicus* Wigley (1993) critically
suggested the home would have to be.[14] In the contest between expert systems of knowledge and home-based worker-centered research, the home
thus becomes a *site*, once again, of ideological and material struggle, this
time over the safety, security, and stability of the twenty-first century home
as divided live/work *place*.

## MOTHERHOOD AND WORK AT HOME

Shifting conditions and divisions of social labor continue to place racially
divided women where the work is unpaid or low-paid—and to situate
unpaid and low-paid work at home, where women are expected to be (but
not be seen). The structuralist logic of locating work at home conceals the
home as a site of work and labor contestation for the most part outside
the scope of law—literally "outlaw." It also conceals the agents who are
continually re-building and maneuvering around the shaky structure of
home-based work: employers, contractors, policymakers, trade unionists,
homeworkers, organizers, etc. In her extensive archival research on homework in the United States, Eileen Boris (1994a, 1994b) has clarified both
the contradictory discourses of women's home-based work, as well as how
the politics of home-based worker regulation and organization were consistently overdetermined by changing discourses and practices of an always
racialized motherhood. Her analysis of the twentieth-century politics of
homework in the United States implicitly questions a traditional U.S. working-class history that uncritically configures the male worker as *the* class
and laboring subject, the male-centered factory and workplace as *the* site of
labor organizing and class struggle, and itself as the story of how Fordism,
driven on by these subjects in these places, defined the twentieth century
regulation and organization of labor and capital.

Most important for the purposes of understanding the politics of
home-based worker organization today, Boris draws the contradictory lines
of argument around the existence and regulation of home-based industrial,
clerical and service work to their common point of connection, or nodal
point, in the circuit of homework organizing: "motherhood." Understanding the historical and political economic implications of "motherhood"
holds tremendous significance, on the one hand, for future homeworker

organizing and, on the other, for the ethics and politics of child labor and the education and socialization of children, to name two major turning points in the reproduction of labor under capitalism, which I will return to later in this work. Writing in the early 1990s on an episode of the politics of homeworker organizing involving predominantly white and immigrant clerical homeworkers in post-World War II New York, Boris concludes that the result of identifying these homeworkers as mothers was that women's home-based productive and reproductive labors were *both* denied. Flowing from that denial, two other extremely important facts emerged: "neither side in the regulatory debate of forty years ago addressed the conditions of homeworking mothers," and black homeworkers/mothers were almost universally positioned by these and other debates as workers first and foremost, not as mothers.

> Women like Mrs. K. had to type envelopes to make ends meet without much guarantee that the work would be there for her tomorrow at the same rate. Without child-care or other employment options, mothers made the best out of what they had. Neither trade unionists nor most organized women's groups ever proposed alternatives for homeworkers; their concern ended with the stopping of an exploitative labor system rather than the organizing of homeworkers or the improving of their labor standards. Only the Congress of American Women recognized the need for an alliance between homeworking women and those who labored in shops and offices. It alone challenged the false division between mother and worker. Trade unionists, other women advocates, and employers reinforced this separation, albeit in a manner to buttress opposing positions. (Boris 1994b, 175)

Boris' rich historical and political analysis of early and mid-twentieth century homework in the United States, careful as it is to note the continuous racial divide in the organization of homework around motherhood, is a valuable resource for homeworker organizing today. Her analysis points to the failure of trade unionists in particular to overcome their historic compromise with the state and capital on the place of women's work. The cult of domesticity, in the twentieth century context of male-centered industrial production, capital accumulation, and family-based consumerism was not merely a framework for the reproduction of working men's material, sexual and emotional lives. It was also not simply a framework for reproduction of the family as the ethical and political resolution of a far-from-equilibrium political-economic system. It was a concerted social and political response to the efforts of white and immigrant women to break out of the double bind of motherhood, a position that at once demanded women's work and labor to reproduce husbands, children and families, and denied the labor value of this work. And it was a silent and complicated response to the efforts of black women to challenge racist violence and break out of the cult of servitude, which involved not only domestic work in white homes but, on a smaller scale, home-based work in black homes (Nakano Glenn 1992).

Domesticity defined the home as a place of non-work and found in a diverse, but by no means all-inclusive population of "unemployed" mothers and wives, supple agents of seemingly infinite moral and emotional support, family nurturance and care, and manual household labor. Yet this unpaid, seemingly invisible labor was a force of its own. The variety of prohibitions on women working outside the home, race- and class-specific as they were (and continue to be on a dwindling scale), forced, and allowed, certain sectors of women to seek and conduct paid work inside the home from the dawn of industrial capitalism, a situation that was increasingly preferable for employers, who saw in it a way to increase profits through the disorganization of the growing power of unionized labor. Homework also appealed, less profitably perhaps, to a white middle- and working-class patriarchalism that invested in the cult of domesticity, a wife and mother at home, as it faced up to the necessity of at least two earners to "get ahead" or "keep afloat." Despite the multiply unequal exchange of the increasingly mythical status of male breadwinner for a "non-working" (and/or "homeworking") wife and mother at home, the compromise worked for about one hundred and fifty years, with structural changes coming, for the most part, very slowly and on the margins.

Yet there were always several "resistances" built into this powerful machine. One was capital itself, which, paraphrasing one of Marx's most Hegelian phrases, always confronted its own limit in labor. In continually struggling to reduce industrial labor to the cost of its own reproduction, the formulation and practice of which relied on the "invisibly," or freely given and taken domestic labor of women and children, capital would inevitably drive some, and at some times many, sectors and populations of workers under the escalating costs of living. This, in turn, would force more women into industrial production of one kind or another, including home-based production and a whole range of what we still mistakenly call "informal" economic activities. This process continued in almost linear fashion throughout the twentieth century in most of the industrial and post-industrial countries of the global North, as an ever-increasing proportion of wives and mothers entered the "formal" workforce.

As one consequence of this, there was a slippage in the white, middle-class cultural restrictions on women's participation in employment (for as we have noted throughout, white and immigrant working-class women and black women faced restrictions in the other direction, i.e. a positive expectation of work and a negative one of motherhood). Alice Kessler-Harris and Karen Sacks (1987) termed this the "demise of domesticity." Women could, and did, claim more in the way of jobs, wages and status as workers of the world, a global process which took off at a rapid pace beginning in the 1960s, and which has accelerated decade by decade since then. Subsequent demands from female workers would inevitably extend to the home, since women had always been working at home (paid and unpaid), and since the 1960s-era breakdown in cultural and economic distinctions put wages for housework, and somewhat differently today, wages for child-care, on the social and political agenda.

In the wake of these changes, which are complexly related to grass-roots feminism's second and third waves, the intertwined discourses of work and motherhood—the latter with its now somewhat anachronistic sound—have taken on different tones, but lost little of their power or determination. They now circulate in the ever more dispersed discursive networks of "work-family balance," the "mommy track," and "child-care," which encompass much of the crisis in today's political economy of home and work, much as motherhood, in previous conjunctures, brokered a wide range of discourses and practices that would situate labor, gender, race, class, and nation in the formally de-politicized home. In short, the politics of home-based work today are being tracked through a new material crisis of "motherhood," one that still centers on who will bear and care for children, but now in the context of far more volatile and dispersed forces of social reproduction.

In the twentieth century era of mass industrialization, socialization, and education, the home, as we have described it up until now, was a functional and yet contested site for the attempted resolution of the unmet needs of whole classes of mostly male industrial laborers. This bland observation conceals both the magnitude and scale of industrialization, socialization and education in the home, as well as the continuing social and political struggles of household labor in relation to what Marx termed total social labor, which for him did not include the "natural" social labor of housewives and other domestic workers, unpaid or otherwise. Exploring the relationship of home-based laborers to their invisibility within dominant categories of political economy is not entirely new. Feminist and other historians, as well as social scientists, have for some time been excavating the subjugated histories of housewives and maids as well as the practices and discourses of housework, home economics, domestic work, etc.

The domestic labor debates of the 1970s and 1980s directly addressed the needs to theorize housewives as laborers, and domestic labor as socially productive and valorized work. Much of the domestic labor debate, it appears now, had little to say about the paid home-based labor of mothers as such. That is to say, there is little from the side of the previous generation of sociologies, histories, and critical political economies of housework to complement the more contemporary work of historians of home-based industrial, service sector, and clerical labor. And while today's generation of housework studies, focused either on paid domestic work or on the gendered distribution of labor time in the household, do shed light on the calculable trade-offs between paid and unpaid work, they almost resolutely fail to relate these trade-offs, which are massive in aggregate form, to a broader political economy. In other words, while homework studies have noted and analyzed the inter-connections among ideologies and practices of patriarchy and motherhood, the sexual division of labor, and homework, there is considerably less material in sociological studies of housework to begin to theorize the relationship of homework to housework in the context of specifically capitalist production and social reproduction. What the theorists of domestic labor and sociologies of housework failed to notice, and here I risk great overgeneralization to make the point, is that the unpaid labor of housewives and mothers was never exclusively unpaid. The presence of paid home-based labor in the industrial and post-industrial home complicates the focus on domestic labor, I shall argue, in politically important ways. What studies of paid homework tell students of unpaid housework is that housewives and mothers, through force and widely constrained choices, continually seek and find ways to valorize their work as wives, servants, cleaners, cooks, caregivers, educators, guardians, sexual partners, and so on. They seek "wages for housework," in other words, and it is here that one must leave aside questions of "class consciousness" in order to get first to questions of social organization and practice.

Three
# Homeworker Organizing: Child-Care Workers Under Welfare Reform in the United States

Yes, there was a guiding thread: the trouble lay with those hapless beings against whom the entire social and medical thought of the eighteenth century raised its voice: the house servants. (Jacques Donzelot, *The Policing of Families*)

The extended example that I begin to explore in this chapter, the organization of home-based child-care workers, underscores how changes in the social production and provision of child-care in the late twentieth century have led less to a "demise of domesticity" than a resurgence of home-based work by a new working class of predominantly women of color. In examining the organization of these workers, who include licensed and unlicensed child-care workers, or so-called "family daycare providers," who take care of their own and other people's children in their own homes, I link the contemporary shift of the home from a privatized space of social reproduction to a socialized and politicized home/work place to the transformation of unpaid domestic labor, in this case child-care, into low-paid homework.[1] As with the classification of homeworkers in general, the classification of home-based child-care workers can be confusing. Home-based child-care includes the paid and unpaid provision of care by parents, grand-parents, siblings, other relatives, neighbors, friends, nannies, maids, other domestic workers, as well as licensed and unlicensed family daycare providers. While much of the focus of this chapter will be on the so-called family daycare provider, this is at best a tenuous distinction given that many such workers are unlicensed and officially uncounted. Moreover, many others provide paid care for children in their own home, as well as in children's own homes. Finally, a still greater number (mostly of parents and relatives) provide unpaid care at a variety of social and economic costs.

In discussing the rapid increase in home-based child-care work as a result of welfare reform in the United States, I will propose that the link between the transformation of the home/work place and the valorization of unpaid labor is in part the organized labor of child-care providers and their struggles over the control of work and value. In so doing, I argue that the transformation of the home/work place, linked to the socialization and politicization of traditional "women's work" and domestic labor, continues to be a major impetus to the rise of the "service sector" and "affect economy," which are uniquely grounded in women's waged labor outside and inside the home (Collins and Gimenez 1990; Glazer 1993; Hardt and Negri 2000).

This reading of the transformation of home via the organization and valorization of child-care suggests that the relative spatial isolation of the home/work place does not necessarily signify social or political isolation, and that child-care and child-care workers are thoroughly linked to changes in social policy, economy, culture, and power. Among other things, a significant proportion of home-based child-care workers, like many, perhaps most, industrial homeworkers, typically work under contract with the same employer(s) in a given geographic area. In the United Kingdom and the United States, for example, the vast majority of licensed home child-care workers are under contract with local government authorities, particularly in the wake of welfare state structural adjustments. Moreover, home-based child-care workers, similar to other sectors of "care workers," are women (by sex as well as gender definition) who are typically more active than other women and most men in a range of social institutions, including civic associations, schools, community and grassroots organizations, religious congregations, and of course, their own and other families (Ahrentzen 1993; Naples 2002). These and other characteristics which I will explore suggest that home-based workers in general, and care workers in particular, are at the cusp of social and political movement-building which directly links the reproduction of society to their status as labor. I take up implications of these themes in the second half of the book, as I explore how the organization and valorization of this "reproductive labor" proceeds in a biopolitical realm of control that at once affects and surpasses the material calculation of value—the traditional starting point for Marxist critique of political economy.

## UPSETTING THE STRUCTURE OF HOME-WORK: GLOBAL HOME-BASED WORKER ORGANIZING

In cultural-political discourses of home, as Karen Hansen (1992) discusses in *African Encounters with Domesticity*, one must look beyond the balanced, dualist models (production-reproduction, structure-agency, base-superstructure) of domesticity on which feminists, Marxists and others have attempted to ground shaky theoretical and political interventions. Emphasis on the structural economic constraints of an always already existing sexual and racial division of labor, on the one hand, and cultural or ideological expressions of some form or other of subjective determination (i.e. patriarchy, racism, heterosexism, etc.), on the other, have served only to reinstate the problem of domesticity in a gesture not unlike the one on which Derrida bases his deconstruction of Heidegger's metaphorical return (to) "home" (see Wigley 1993). Somewhere beyond such dichotomous thinking, one may begin to resurface into what Gayatri Chakravorty Spivak (1999) terms the "vanishing history of the present," or as Hansen describes it in the African postcolonial historical context:

> . . . how domesticity gets reinvented or changed in the process of local and foreign development planning, and how project implementation affects the attempts of women and men of different backgrounds to bridge or widen the gulf between their personal lives and public activities. How variously constituted feminisms in Africa react to and incorporate ideological elements of domesticity is a question of critical concern for social movements aimed at transforming gender, race, and class inequalities in many societies. (Hansen 1992, 26–27)

Home, as Linda McDowell (1999, 93) writes, "is one of the most strongly gendered spatial locations." Yet it is important not to take this, too, for granted, as McDowell also notes. In deconstructive terms, home, like domesticity, does not exist *as such*. Home is, however, as Spivak (1990) occasionally remarked about the persistent critique implied by deconstruction, the structure that one cannot not inhabit. The forced displacement of the homeless and urban slum dwellers in cities across the world in the 1980s and 1990s is an example at the opposite end of the spectrum of home/domesticity, where street-level codes and simulacra of home were fiercely policed and destroyed (Desai 2002), and the "homeless" themselves were "de-housed," often into mass shelters or prisons (Feldman 2001). The material and ideological structures of houses and homes can and do change, but that is not the point. Top-down views, which privilege neo-liberal, racist and patriarchal structural forces, do not aid in seeing how social and political resistances and grassroots-level changes implicitly, if not complicitly, challenge both those forces and the expert knowledges that theoretically underwrite them.[2]

Elizabeth Prügl (1999) takes up this theme in her studies of global homeworker organizing. In her account of the post 1973-era of "globalization," Prügl discusses how "bottom-up" homeworker organizing began to challenge both the hegemonic globalization of gendered home-based labor, as well as the developmentalist discourses and practices that invisibly thread work into the sexually divided home. Under neoliberal hegemony, economic development in geographically and economically diverse countries has been premised on the promotion and expansion of work-at-home, understood as the combined value of "culture production" with traditional "women's work." The rule-driven practices of development which she frames, suggest that homeworkers must find ways to engage counter-hegemonic rule-forming development institutions, such as the International Labor Organization (ILO) and national labor legislation, in order to contest their highly exploited and politically subordinate positioning in global, national and local schemes of highly culturalized economic development.

In home-based work, Prügl notes, one can trace capital's move to sites of production located largely outside the Fordist regulatory regime of labor and capital. Traditional labor organizing had long seen home-based work both as a threat to unionized labor, as well as a desecration of the working-class family and traditional motherhood. The traditional struggle over a "family wage," premised on the myth of the *male* breadwinner, left the rising numbers of homeworkers worldwide not only outside the principal framework of labor-capital struggle, but in an organizational and political vacuum. Absent institutional force, homeworkers sought forms of self-organization, allying themselves with grassroots and community-based organizations, as well as trade unions which, in the face of the post-Fordist decomposition of labor, were finally forced to recognize that homeworkers, part-time and contingent workers, and laborers of the informal sector, were, in various manufacturing industries, the primary workforce of many or most of the new "glocalities" (Portes, Castells, and Benton 1989). The factory workforce and factory work had, more perceptibly than in previous decades, "gone home." Late as they were to the seismic changes in work, labor unions found themselves confronting two new roles: one, as organizers who had to walk into the dispersed geography of home-based factories in order to communicate to workers; and two, as power brokers who had to operate between and among capital, the state, and the newly self-forming organizations and networks of homeworkers.

Prügl describes the case of Homenet, an international network of homeworker organizations, informal sector labor associations, trade union representatives, and homeworker cooperatives, which succeeded in putting the labor rights and social protection of homeworkers onto the ILO's agenda in the early-1990s, and later in lobbying for the ILO to pass a convention and recommendation on homework. The ILO's conventions on work are few and notable—including conventions on child labor, discrimination and forced labor, and workers' rights to unionize and freely associate—and in this respect constitute foundational standards and discourses of international labor practice. Homenet's success merely in having a convention proposed and discussed, let alone approved, by the ILO, was significant then. Despite the 1996 Homework Convention being only nominally effective once individual countries approve and ratify the treaty (and only four countries—Finland, Ireland, Albania and the Netherlands—did so in the first decade after its approval), it bears analyzing the nature of Homenet's organizing/lobbying success, and the nature of organizing in the homework field itself.

First, Homenet was a network, not a non-governmental organization (NGO), and its member organizations, likewise, were for the most part not NGOs.[3] It was comprised of homeworkers' and informal sector workers' associations, unions and grassroots organizations such as the Self-Employed Women's Association (SEWA) in India, the Self-Employed Women's Union in South Africa, and the National Homeworking Group in the United Kingdom, which are member-based and for the most part member-led grassroots organizations. As such, these organizations typically represent and struggle in the interests of their own members and leaders, as well as in the interests, indirectly and obliquely, of similarly situated workers, social sectors, and communities elsewhere. Their complicity with global and local capital or with globalizing institutions, and thus their accountability to workers and members as such, are considerably different from the nongovernmental organizations following the international human rights and grant money trails, with the required camouflage of "grassroots presence" and "native information" (Cheah 1997; Elyachar 2002; Spivak 1999). This difference, which I am loosely characterizing as "bottom-up" versus "top-down" grassroots organizing, can be traced, in great part, to what drives the demands for action, justice, or political change. In the case of the ILO Convention on Homework, the impetus was not from the trade union, employer or government representatives who comprise the ILO's tri-partite decision-making structure, and, in a broader historical context, the key players in the Fordist and Keynesian regimes that dominated through both class struggle and class compromise twentieth century political economic arrangements. Although, as Prügl notes, the trade union representatives on the ILO governing body played an instrumental role in influencing state representatives to pass the convention over the objections of employers, the impetus for change, and pressure on the unions, came from the new post-Fordist organizations of home-based workers.

What one sees in the case of Homenet, and in particular of SEWA, Homenet's founding member, is an NGO-like actor, with the scripting coming from its variously differentiated grassroots "bases" as well as the particular, formative histories which surround its development. Formally, or legally speaking, SEWA is a women's trade union based in Ahmedabad, India. For SEWA, their grassroots base includes several hundred thousand individual members, mostly very low-wage, lower-caste female workers, who are participants and leaders in more than a dozen component trade associations, federations and cooperatives, as well as a large number of on-going local organizing campaigns, service and building projects, and community and leadership development activities. As a uniquely structured trade union of sectorally diverse female workers, SEWA operates both like a traditional union, organizing for increased worker power and higher wages, as well as a "self-help" organization, mobilizing diverse social sectors into and around a range of globally and locally configured social and economic needs, such as health care, child-care, financial credit, housing, clean air and water, food and agricultural production, and insurance.

Its combined organizing objectives and practices challenge the notion of the home, especially the home work/place, as a site of structural oppression, unconscious subject-positioning, and entry into sexual and racial subordination. Indeed, as Prügl remarks, "SEWA recognized that the houses of women in the informal sector often were workplaces, so that investing in housing was productive investment . . .housing loans were the most common type of loan the SEWA Bank extended to home-based workers" (Prügl 1999, 126). As a place outside the law, and outside official control, in various ways, the home work/place has thus been a site of legal prohibition as well as of immanent struggle for auto-valorization (in the language of autonomist Marxism) and "empowerment" (in the language of grassroots political organization and economic development) against patriarchy, exploitation and psychic subordination. Forms of communal sharing of resources, rearrangement of housework relations, collective home/work/ place organizing, mark the history of home-based labor struggles, which also include, of course, the refusal of housework (and sex). Homeworkers have repeatedly found themselves objecting that there is nothing morally or politically wrong with working at home—except everything wrapped up in home and homework themselves: sexual and racial divisions and definitions of labor, the relative volatility and instability of paid work, devaluation of labor, and the ongoing modulations of home-based work, including changes in home design, state or capitalist-led "counter-planning" and counter-organizing, and technological change.

What many of these "post-structural" shifts suggest is that the home work/place is primed for an uncertain and potentially turbulent social and political transformation. In capitalist modernity, the factory/office workplace and civil society were perceived and fashioned as places and spaces for the exercise of political and social speech, labor's countervailing power, and democratic contestation, with varying and accompanying levels of repression, policing, and reprisals (Aronowitz 2003). One of the key questions being broached by home-based workers of all kinds is whether and how the home will become such a place/space. "From below," one might argue, home-based labor appears now to be "jumping scale," to borrow geographer Neil Smith's felicitous phrase, as homeworkers shift the borders between home and work in response to global and local forces which, as we have seen, see the home as a new kind of "spatio-temporal fix" for the problem of an increasingly highly valorized "total social labor force" (Harvey 1990; Negri 1991; Smith 1993). "Seizing place" through a reconnection of collective work to collective homes, home-based workers worldwide are "doing their homework" in wholly new ways: organizing, networking, protesting, cooperativizing, lobbying, and transforming relations inside, around, and throughout the home/work world (Boris and Prügl 1996). The difference between this and the "entrepreneurial" mode of self-organization detected by Felstead and Jewson in their study is considerable.

In spatial terms, Sherry Ahrentzen (1992) has noted how in this new and uncertain context, ethno-racial, kin, gender, geographic and labor-centered neighborhoods, networks and "communities" might be the models for home-based worker organizing, posing new definitions and attributes for class and class composition. Moving from the top-down model of the home—the solitary, isolated, self-contained household space—and the socialist feminist models of collective home/workplaces whose critical history Dolores Hayden (1981, 1984) has traced so well, one can begin to see in the expanding organizing programs of home-based workers, circuits of socialized space that are constructed through the self-valorization and control of its highly cooperative, creative, and politicized workers. A major example of this is to be seen, I argue, in the organization of predominantly African American and Latina immigrant home-based child-care workers in the United States. The self-organization of *these* workers informs a political re-shaping of the boundaries not only of home and work. As Leith Mullings, among others, has noted:

> In doing transformative work, then, women seek to construct a space in which they can ensure continuity for themselves, their children, and their communities . . .But what is perhaps unique about the experience of African American women is the dramatic way in which their experience has linked the domains of household, community, and the larger society. For women of color, working-class women, and increasingly for middle-strata women, protection of their children, which

mobilizes their activism, requires the protection and transformation of
their households, their communities, and the larger society. (Mullings
1997, 100)

And while the professionalized versions of these workers, including telecom-
muters and middle-class child-care providers, are certainly "top models"
for the post-Fordist re-arrangement of home and work, capital is already
confronting the limits of these workers and is forced now to deal with the
dynamic contestation of home-based work on a much larger scale. Prügl,
for example, describes how in attempting to define home-based workers
as non-employees, and thus outside the protection of the ILO convention,
employer representatives on the ILO convention committee unintentionally
acknowledged that in post-Fordism, arguments for "true self-employment
had become impossible as well" in the home-based work field (Prügl 1999,
134). Thus, it would appear that homeworkers across the board, from the
high-paid home-based management and design consultant to the home-
based assembly worker at the (spatial) end of the global chain of commodity production, are dependent upon, and employed by, the circulation of
capital. Their labor is encountered by capital and the capitalist state not
as an alien force with its own mode of organization but as a racially and
sexually divided class that is immanent to the formation of capital—a phenomenon that Marx referred to as the "real subsumption" of labor.[4] The
version of "scale-jumping" in the organization of homeworkers which
I referred to above, then, is a kind of "dialectical utopianism" forced to
acknowledge the slippages in what is meant not only by "dialectical" but
by "organizing," "class," and "self-valorization" in what appear as circuits
and cycles, and not dualist forces, of simultaneously global and home-based
class struggles.[5]

As is commonly the case, the slippages become most evident in the
examples. In the case of Homenet's organizing victory at the ILO, Prügl
concludes that "bottom-up" organizing, or what she calls "emancipatory
politics" at the level of international regulatory organizations such as the
ILO, must not be conflated with homeworker organizing at varying "local"
geographic scales, on the one hand; and that the ILO convention on homework, intended to regulate home-based workers into formal equality with
the mass workers of the Fordist regime, must not be confused with the misleading universality which pervades human rights discourses and practices,
on the other. Organizing at the global level is, for her, organizing in another
space of the social, a space which profoundly shapes and informs the various scales of "the local" which, she critically notes, have been treated by
feminist and others critics of human rights discourses as the preferred space

of counter-hegemonic politics. That Prügl feels she has to defend her focus on organizing at this scale underscores how the new global rules of homework she analyzes constitute, as Pheng Cheah (1997) has critically said of international human rights, a "violent gift" to "local" homeworkers. For as the rules reductively work their way, as Prügl suggests they will, through vast social institutions, networks and codes, homeworkers should expect, indeed they will increasingly be forced, to organize.[6] In a similar vein, Julia Elyachar has noted how World Bank-led microlending in Egypt has resulted not only in the forced creation of dubious "grassroots organizations" which now are representing the interests of the disorganized peasantry. It has also re-arranged the field of global development, the place where Prügl begins her analysis of global homework:

> What might have been previously seen as informal economy—that which is external to the state, that which is not the real economy—is now being assimilated into prevailing notions of *the* economy. And microlending looks like what we think *the* economy really is. Money is exchanged, interest is collected, enterprises are established, and unemployed women become, at least on paper, entrepreneurs. (Elyachar 2002, 507–08)

I do not intend this as criticism of Prügl's excellent analysis and work. That emancipatory politics and bottom-up organizing may be changing things so radically—so much that the changes they seek are preemptively re-appropriated at the "top"—points obliquely back to the political limit of the location of "individual home-based workers," as Prügl herself notes, workers who are becoming, "at least on paper," something different than they were a few years, or even a few months, ago (Prügl 1999, 148). The problem with global labor regulations and human rights, in the context of competitive organizing at and of the "grassroots," is that those invested in "emancipatory politics" and "bottom-up" organizing still believe in the *idée fixe* of the power of rules and rights *for others*—even as "our" constituencies are getting organized with these rights in mind by someone else (e.g. the World Bank, the "anti-welfare/pro-warfare" state, the local social service agency, the petty capitalist employer of home-based workers, and more often than not, a combination of these forces working together or alongside each other)—and for someone else's profit. Paraphrasing Marx, capital is the most aggressive "organizer" the world has ever known! Jumping the scale of home thus requires supplementing the new global and local rules of homework with recognition of a re-routing of the specifically sexual and racial divisions of labor through capital.[7]

With these aporias in mind, I turn next to "organizing" of home-based work on a variety of scales in the United States, conscious both of the fact that the United States has ratified only two of the ILO's eight fundamental conventions in its history, and that the movements of labor in the United States have for a variety of reasons either not felt compelled to force ratification or not succeeded at forcing ratification of the conventions; that is to say, conscious not so much of the "exceptionalist" social and political history of the United States, as its ongoing political, economic and cultural imperialism.

## THE CRISIS OF SOCIAL REPRODUCTION IN THE UNITED STATES

Home is where, it might be said, work begins. The growing focus on various kinds of home-based work, from industrial production and assembly, to telework, to professional work, to so-called "care work," must be mindful of the sexual and ethno-racial divisions of labor that situate these various kinds of work in class and race-differentiated homes. Staking homework on women's continued marking for family and sexual reproduction responsibilities—including women's own powerful investments in this marking—has been the hallmark of political-economic, regulatory, institutional and grassroots debates around homework for over one hundred fifty years. What is becoming more obvious today are the situations that straddle the paid/unpaid, productive/reproductive, and housework/homework divides: domestic work, care work, counseling and therapy, education, and so on. As vast as these laboring sectors are, they do not occupy an exalted place in labor studies, political economic theory, or sociologies of work and gender. Rather, they remain a challenge to conventional thinking about who does work, which workers are expected to be organized, and how the broad sets of social and political constraints and possibilities which these emerging sectors mobilize differ powerfully from traditionally dominant sectors.

Child-care labor is a case in point. The child-care market in the United States has grown tremendously since the mid-point of the twentieth century. Certainly, a great part of this increase has been driven by demand—although, we will see, the supply of child-care labor has been of particular interest to policymakers and observers over the past decade. Staying with the demand side for the moment, the Bureau of Labor Statistics indicates that nearly 60 percent of all women with children younger than six were participating in the general work force in 1996, up from 12 percent fifty years before, and 30 percent in 1972 (see NCJW 1999). The proportional increase in the number of single parents over the same period has also led to an increased demand for child-care. Of the total of 19.6 million children under five years of age in 1997, 63 percent were in some form of child-care arrangement other than a parent at home, and of these 56 percent were cared for by someone other than a parent, grandparent or relative. 86 percent of children of partly or fully employed women were in some form of child-care arrangement other than a parent at home (Smith 2002). Nearly seven million children were cared for by non-relatives in 1997, including home-based providers (the largest sector of child-care providers at 36 percent), day care centers (33 percent), nursery or preschools (16 percent), nannies and others in children's own homes (12 percent), schools (8 percent), and the federal Head Start program (2 percent).[8]

The Personal Responsibility and Work Opportunity Reconciliation Act of 1996 (PRWORA or the euphemistic "welfare reform") mandated work requirements for single parents with young children who receive (newly renamed) Temporary Assistance for Needy Families (TANF) payments from the state, also contributing to increased child-care demand—and a growing crisis. In 1997, 812,000 children under fifteen years old received some form of government-subsidized child-care (Smith 2002, 18). The following year, this number increased significantly to nearly 1.25 million children served by programs funded through federal and state child-care and TANF block grants.[9] However, these numbers belied the increasing crisis in child-care. Nationwide, at the time, it was estimated that between ten million and fifteen million children of all ages were eligible for child-care subsidy under state and federal income guidelines (NCJW 1999).

The apparent crisis of child-care in the United States has several dimensions. One, the sheer expansion of demand due to the increasing number of mothers (and more or less steady number of fathers) employed outside the home, has affected the availability, affordability, and quality of child-care (Uttal 2002). Two, the cost of child-care is very high for most families in the U.S., and prohibitive for others, averaging around $75 a week, or $3,800 per year in the 1990s.[10] This represented approximately 25 percent or more of the average household income of the 6.8 million families (including 23.2 million parents and children) under the U.S. federal poverty line in 2001,[11] and 7 percent of the average 2002 family income of approximately $51,000. The Urban Institute estimates that of the 48 percent of families with children in the United States who paid for some form of child-care for at least one of their children in 1997, the total cost represented 9 percent of average income (Giannarelli and Barsimantov 2000). The Children's Defense Fund and others reported that close to the end of the twentieth century, the average annual cost of child-care for a four-year-old was greater than the average annual cost of public college tuition in all fifty states, and that child-care expenditures represent a typical family's second-highest expense category after housing.[12]

The reverse side of the crisis (what is actually making it a crisis?) is the problem of supplying sufficient levels of child-care labor. Volatility among both employed and "self-employed" child-care workers (who have a job turnover rate estimated to be around 30 percent annually) and rapid turnover in clientele, contribute to an unstable and uncertain supply of child-care labor. Overshadowing, and partially determining this volatility, is the virtual absence of employment benefits and above poverty level wages for most child-care work (Salmon 1999; Uttal 2002; Whitebook and Phillips 1999). The overall poor conditions that pervade the industry, which apply differently but equally to determinations of the quality of child-care, are felt keenly by parents and children (at all income levels), it is true (Uttal 2002). Yet the pivotal agents in the crisis are not the parents, or the children, or policymakers, for that matter (who, it will be shown, have enormous power, mostly unused, to act), but the paid child-care providers, 98 percent of whom are women, on whom the state, public and private agencies, parents and children ultimately rely.

The Administration for Children and Families, the federal agency in charge of a variety of state funding programs for children, including child welfare, child support, Head Start, and child-care, provided a profile of the United States paid child-care work force near the turn of the century:

- Approximately three million child-care teachers, assistants, and family child-care providers in the U.S. cared for ten million children each day.

- 97 percent were female, 41 percent had children, and 10 percent were single parents.

- Child-care teaching staff earned an average of $6.89 per hour or $12,058 per year (based on 35 hours per week and 50 weeks per year, salary data in 1993 dollars).

- Only 18 percent of child-care centers offered fully paid health coverage to teaching staff. Although they earn lower wages, child-care teachers were better educated than the general population.

- One-third of all child-care teachers left their centers each year.

- Family child-care providers who cared for and educated young children in their homes also had very low earnings. These workers earned $9,528 annually after expenses.

- Unregulated providers, who care for fewer children and are offered fewer supports, earned just $5,132 after expenses.[13]

What this profile fails to convey is how vital a part of political-economic changes—driven by structural adjustment of the welfare system in the United States—the provision of child-care became in the 1990s. As two leading researcher-advocates in the field argued in a 1999 briefing paper on child-care employment:

> [C]urrent policy decision and research efforts are largely focused on how to build the U.S. child-care supply, but unfortunately, they typically pay scant attention to child-care employment itself as a precarious, low-wage job sector . . .Child-care is one of the fastest growing occupations in the country, and one of the largest employers of low-income women; it is being increasingly identified as a job opportunity for women coming off welfare . . .(Whitebook and Phillips 1999, 1)

The structural changes signaled by welfare state reform in the United States in the 1990s were built on a pre-existing structure of sexually and racially-divided child-care labor which had followed a more or less traditional pattern of home and market-based industrialization in the preceding decades, including state de-regulation and other policies. These policies had created the conditions both for formal exploitation of a growing and informalized labor force as well as the large-scale quasi-privatization of the workforce that occurred in the late 1990s.

Political scientist Mary Tuominen has analyzed this phenomenon extensively and discussed its implications for home-based child-care workers and similarly situated labor sectors. In her political economic and feminist ethnography of ethno-racially diverse home-based child-care workers in the United States, Tuominen sought to critically de-center the "ideology of motherhood" from the study of home-based child-care, in order to expose the material determinations of child-care labor, much in the same way that researchers such as Boris have done in the field of homework studies. The difficulty in the task of analyzing child-care work in this way is that motherhood *is* the moral and political economy, so to speak, through which child-care labor operates, one way or another. Tuominen differentiates her own work from those such as Nelson (1990), who focused on the ideological and practical commitments to "full-time motherhood" of Vermont home-based family day care providers:

> Clearly, researchers of home-based child-care, while not seeking to identify the factors that draw women into the work of family day care, identify motherhood as a primary factor organizing home-based child-care work. The very choice to describe providers in relation to their status as mothers and, explicitly, to use various stages of motherhood (early motherhood care-giver, later motherhood care-giver) as a means of characterizing diversity among care-givers makes clear the centrality of motherhood to the formation of a pool of labor for the work of paid, home-based child-care. (Tuominen 1994a, 88)

Citing Mary Romero (1992) and other studies of domestic work (e.g. Wrigley 1995), Tuominen further acknowledges the ways in which employers appropriate the ideology of motherhood as they exploit women of color as household workers, nannies and child-care providers. Noting that the "interaction between paid labor and the ideology and practice of motherhood is both reflected and recreated in the choices of women," she seeks to discover other factors and forces—economic, cultural, political—which affect these choices.[14] Primary factors such as ethno-racial identity, language, geography, and immigration status powerfully shift the material structure of motherhood as the latter significantly influences women's needs and choices to work, to seek child-care, and to seek child-care work (Tuominen 1998). In her ethnographic studies of predominantly African American and Mexican immigrant home-based child-care workers in the state of Washington, Tuominen notes that while these workers cited the "responsibilities of motherhood" in the choice of their home-based child-care work, "responsibility" here extends primarily to income earning in the context of community-based and national crises of inadequate child-care supply. Women in Tuominen's studies frequently entered child-care work because they were approached by neighbors, relatives and friends looking for care from someone they knew and trusted. Among African American providers, Tuominen also notes what she refers to as an ethical and religious "call to service"—to fulfill the need for child-care in historically oppressed and impoverished communities and neighborhoods (Tuominen 1997, 1998).

In these instances, it is evident that what Tuominen terms the "practice of motherhood" has a tremendous effect on its ideology and socio-normative value. While there is as well a reciprocal effect—ideology certainly mobilizes individual and social forces, as Nelson's (1990) studies of predominantly rural, white child-care providers finds—the ideology of motherhood is meaningless absent the practical effect of so much unpaid labor time that must be valorized in order for mothers to provide for themselves, their children, and the children of others whom they value in one way or another. The myth of the male breadwinner is the obverse image of the distorted ideology of motherhood. Were it simply a question of ideology, motherhood should or would become more like fatherhood in time, which of course wouldn't be unaffected by a dramatic change in the practice of motherhood. The fact that fathers are among the fastest growing group of (unpaid) home-based child-care providers is one indication, among others, that ideological arguments are less persuasive in the political economic context of women's historic paid and unpaid labor participation.[15]

One key point which underscores Tuominen's argument is that the sexual division of labor is itself always already differentiated, by race and ethnicity, by class, by education, and by "community" or culture. In this sense, the contrast she draws between family day care providers and domestic workers or nannies is instructive. Noting how the bulk of research on domestic work concerns middle and upper-class women hiring working-class reproductive labor (to both ideological and practical ends), Tuominen emphasizes the class, cultural, and geographic specificity of home-based child-care providers and the families of the children they care for.

> Clearly family day care work, like domestic work, is paid, reproductive labor occurring in households and is also part of the "societal reproductive system." However, family day care work reproduces material and ideological structures in a manner somewhat different than paid domestic labor. By providing child-care in their own homes family day care workers, regardless of their racial/ethnic and economic backgrounds, recreate ideologies that identify women with home, family and nurturance. By providing care to families who share their own cultural backgrounds, racial/ethnic identity and employment histories, family day care workers foster and recreate class, cultural and racial/ethnic identities and norms. (Tuominen 1994a, 183)

The implied double-bind which Tuominen suggests researchers attend to is that the exposure of home-based work is always at risk of re-imposing gendered stereotypes and mythologies. Analysis of homework must be elaborated through other determinations, such as ethno-racial difference, immigration history, geographic location, and educational attainment. That is to say, one can't simply separate paid from unpaid labor. That is the "impossible" practice of motherhood.[16] One can, however, look to others, such as co-workers, parents, community leaders, and peers, to see how the engagement of mothers with home-based work, home-based child-care work in particular, extends the politics of homework, and the place of the home, well beyond the geographical imagination of sexual oppression and subordination. In home-based child-care, especially, one must look beyond the confines of the home to see where women's always constrained choices—and differently constrained political and social power—are being directed.

Tuominen (1997) takes this point up in her analysis of state policies affecting child-care, as well as, by practical extension, the sexual division of labor locally, nationally and globally (by way of immigration). She points in particular to a political struggle within the state that I would summarize, for lack of better references, as socialist versus neo-liberalist practices of the state. The neo-liberal dominance of the American state since the end of World War II resulted in an ongoing effort to shape and re-shape federal child-care and sexual policies in favor of a market-based, capitalist and patriarchal privatization of social welfare programs.[17] Since the ascendancy of the neo-conservative wing of the Republican Party in the federal government beginning around 1980, federal policy has been focused extensively on the curtailment of the welfare state, including state-sponsored child-care as a key matrix of state family and employment policies. Tuominen (1994a) cites five key initiatives of the Reagan Administration during the 1980s: 1) reducing direct federal support for child-care (cutting support for services to low-income families from $835 million in 1981 to $422 million in 1986, offset only partially by increased support during this period to the Head Start program); 2) use of federal tax credits for child-care as a substitute for direct support (expanding the tax credit by 350 percent in the same period, from $956 million to $3.4 billion); 3) creating corporate tax benefits for employer-sponsored child-care; 4) eliminating federal regulations in an effort to increase the supply of unlicensed providers; and 5) related to the elimination of regulations, stressing the sufficiency of the supply of child-care by emphasizing the informal sector.

The 1980s were characterized by an internal struggle on the Right between southern and Sun Belt religious neo-conservatives who were attempting to take over the Republican Party via a grassroots appeal to "family values" and anti-abortion rhetoric, and mainstream conservatives bent on advancing the party through a broader appeal to "traditional" suburban values of motherhood, family and work. Coming out of this struggle for hegemony, a convergence was shaped between neo-conservative and neo-liberal approaches that would assert more or less nationwide political hegemony by the late 1990s: " . . . the Republican Party itself," Tuominen writes, became "an arena of struggle regarding the societal roles of women in general, and mothers, in particular" (Tuominen 1994a, 243).

The struggle for hegemony within the Republican Party was duplicated in the Democratic Party in the early 1990s, with the rise of Bill Clinton's "New Democrat" bloc, masterminded by the right-leaning Democratic Leadership Council (and paralleling the Republican Party's neo-conservative and neo-liberal convergence). The weak version of the Family Medical Leave Act agreed to by Clinton, as well as his signature "welfare reform" legislation—stricter than any proposed by Republicans in the previous two decades—were instances of a broad political attack based on privatization of the welfare state, including the privatization of child-care.[18] Clinton's welfare reform further advanced privatization by shifting responsibility for welfare and child-care to the states. A key result of welfare reform privatization was the expansion of a low-paid, home-based, child-care workforce:

> While mothers on public assistance move into paid employment, another group of women emerges to provide, for pay, the unwaged child-care previously provided by mothers. These child-care workers are also mothers. And the working conditions of these state-funded child-care workers consistently reflect the working condition of the low-income mothers of the children for whom they care . . . some of these child-care workers make so little money in providing full-time, state-funded child-care that they, themselves, are low-income workers who qualify for government-subsidized child-care (Tuominen 1994a, 254).

Two points are worth noting in this passage. One, although most family day-care providers in the United States do qualify for subsidized care, most states and local jurisdictions deny payment to child-care providers for taking care of their own children. The child of a child-care provider must go to another provider, or else the privatized logic of home-based child-care work would be upset on a structural level. So, with the ideology of home-based motherhood more or less in retreat, the objection to paying homeworkers for the care of their own children concerns the economic and political power of home-based female workers, the "practice of motherhood," against the state and capital. This goes to the heart of the argument I am proposing: class composition proceeding through struggle over the provision of auto-valorized child-care.

Two, structural adjustment by way of welfare reform has had the multiple effects of cutting state subsidies to low-income women and children, turning the same women onto the very low-wage market, including home-based child-care, and re-instantiating the power of the state to control women's work and wages. In the case of child-care workers, the state has done this more or less directly, rather than through male breadwinners as in the Fordist era. With the declining power of trade unions (again, a calculated political objective of the state in the era of structural adjustment), the possibility of configuring home-based child-care workers as public employees (whom trade unions had most successfully organized in the previous two decades), was hardly a question from the perspective of top-down organizing. Were the United States a signatory of the ILO homework convention, state and local governments would not be able to exploit the indeterminate category of home-based worker as they currently do. As Tuominen notes:

> I found no indication that any discussion has ever arisen among state or federal policy makers regarding alternatives to contracting-out child-care services (i.e., the option of the state's directly employing women to provide child-care). While the state is willing to purchase these services (in fact the purchase and provision of these services is essential to the employment goals of the current welfare state) the historical provision of child-care outside of the structures of the formal market economy and the gendered ideologies of motherhood and care-giving continue to shape the state's policies regarding child-care work. (Tuominen 1994a, 289)

The result is a growing, super-exploited home-based child-care workforce under direct contract to the state. And a workforce that has no formal labor rights and is barred technically by antitrust law from joining forces to increase the prices they charge as a result of their status as "self-employed" workers. On top of this, federal child-care legislation sets a limit to how much the state will pay a home-based child-care worker. The maximum the states which administer federal child-care subsidies can pay providers is the 75th percentile of local market rates: that is, higher than the prices charged by 75 percent of providers in a local area, but lower than those of the remaining 25 percent. Tuominen found that state-contracted family day care providers in the state of Washington, where she conducted research, earned half as much as state-employed child-care center workers, counting the value of employment benefits such as health care. By employing the majority of family day care providers in the country, and paying them at or, in most cases, below the 75th percentile of local market rates, state governments exert powerful pressure against any rapid increase in child-care wages. With poverty-level income, the majority of family day care providers can little afford to supply themselves with employment benefits, such as health insurance, the cost of which has risen rapidly since the 1990s, or pensions.

## TOP-DOWN VERSUS BOTTOM-UP ORGANIZING OF HOME-BASED CHILD-CARE PROVIDERS

Examining how diverse women are drawn to highly-exploited home-based child-care work both by the state as well as by parents seeking affordable care for their children, helps readers understand political-economic determination from the top better than it does from the bottom.[19] One has to look elsewhere, for example at early efforts to organize domestic workers in race-exclusive unions, to see the complicated experience of bottom-up organizing of the home-based work force in the United States (Van Raaphorst 1988). Eileen Boris (1994b) has argued that the twentieth century U.S. regulatory debate involving trade unions, employers and the state, reduced homeworkers to a more or less rhetorical figure in efforts to organize them either into or out of existence—from above. The successful efforts to gain the ILO's approval of a homework convention may be understood as a case of bottom-up organizing for top-down changes that should give rise to greater efforts by the state, employers, as well as grassroots organizations and trade unions to organize home-based workers, for their own diverse purposes. The complications that arise from regulatory changes are, no doubt, beginning to be felt in the few countries where the convention has been ratified. That is to say, "organizing" has its divisions as well. The state and employers, or in the case of home-based child-care in the United States, the state as national policymaker *and* largest national employer (or "purchaser of services" in the entrepreneurial jargon of the structural adjustment age), also seeks to organize homeworkers, and is better positioned to organize them than trade unions and community organizations in most instances. Better positioned, in this case, means they are in frequent contact with providers; they license and supervise them; in some instances they train and educate them; and for virtually all child-care workers, the state/employer determines what levels of training and education are required for providers to be licensed and/or subsidized. And this "better positioning" is precisely the arena of social and political struggle for home-based child-care workers in the United States in the twenty-first century. Given the social and political forces arrayed against them at the federal level, home-based child-care workers must (and in any case do) organize locally, where they can and do exert their own considerable political power against the more direct, and often more arbitrary, forms of discipline and policing meted out by local government agencies.

In the field of home-based child-care work, local governments act as local authorities often do, as if their mission were to rule "positively," to govern "morally," to act as the agents of morality and protectors of humanity (and of children most of all); in short, they act as the "police," in the quaint turn-of-the-nineteenth century French usage outlined by Donzelot (1997). Donzelot's account details how nineteenth-century social workers began to deal with those seeking or receiving welfare and other forms of economic and social support and assistance patronizingly, "educatively," intrusively, and ultimately, punitively (or, less commonly, with complete neglect). As a result of some of these functions, the new social workers were often "bad" organizers; as a result of others, particularly the educational and punitive functions, these agents of local authorities and service agencies wielded tremendous force in mobilizing the populations in their midst into various kinds of action: learning a trade, getting a job, marrying and having children, abstaining from law-breaking activities, etc.: in short, local authorities endeavored to police people into policing themselves, as well as their peers, family members, friends and neighbors, along productive and reproductive—what Michel Foucault (1978) termed "biopolitical"—lines, dictated in large part by educators, academics and philanthropists, and later by government officials, political parties and business interests.

As we will see in the next chapter, local government practice, in general, is little different in the child-care field today, where localities place greatest emphasis on the "professionalization" of the child-care workforce via financial and other incentives for educational certification—a professionalization which does not significantly increase providers' incomes, but does appear to reduce the massive turnover which plagues the industry. Indeed, the majority of state and local government initiatives to improve, ameliorate or otherwise affect the conditions of child-care work have had little impact on improving compensation.[20] While most offer some sort of financial incentive to child-care workers to participate in "professional development" and early childhood education learning of one sort or another, already well-educated child-care workers tend to benefit the most in terms of increased compensation and professional status. As two leading advocates, note, "the degree of emphasis on education and training in many initiatives is problematic for family child-care providers who typically have lower levels of formal education and child-related training and may have restricted access to relevant, affordable, and accessible training" (Whitebook and Eichberg 2002, 15). They offer a useful typology of the diversely pitched government efforts to re-tool child-care work, suggesting that given the top-down politics and weak funding behind most of these efforts, those interested in improving the child-care labor system should be evaluating improvements by the extent to which "various initiatives contribute to a movement to secure a better child-care system."

> Specifically, does the initiative contribute toward building the necessary will to support a greater public investment in comprehensive services for all young children? Is it well-publicized? Is there a growing awareness of the need for skilled workers in child-care, and how the initiative is taking steps to achieve this goal? We should ask whether an initiative contributes to an ever-expanding group of stakeholders who understand the components of child-care and are willing to advocate on its behalf. (Whitebook and Eichberg 2002, 20)

But, as these well-positioned writers—Whitebook was a founder and former director of the leading national advocacy organization for child-care workers, the Center for the Childcare Workforce—go on to note, "because most child-care workers are not represented by a collective bargaining agreement or are not members of a work-related or professional organization, they have not necessarily been represented or engaged in the development or implementation of policy initiatives intended to meet their needs" (Whitebook and Eichberg 2002, 20–21). Only a handful of community-based and union organizations do "represent and engage" child-care workers, home-based providers in particular, in "policy initiatives intended to meet their needs." Whitebook and Eichberg cite Coleman Advocates and Wu Yee Children's Services in the organization of child-care providers in California, the Home Daycare Justice Committee in gaining health insurance coverage for providers in Rhode Island, and union organizing efforts in Washington, Massachusetts, Pennsylvania, California and elsewhere to create systemic change via legislation as well as unionize child-care workers for collective bargaining.

However, in contrast, I will argue that the difference of these bottom-up efforts is not merely that they are more systemic in their approach to improving child-care working conditions, or that they contribute to broader movement-building—important and rare as these attributes are. Grassroots organizing that demands the leadership and action of child-care workers, especially, for a variety of reasons, the leadership and action of home-based providers, has the additional effects of reconfiguring the power-laden relationships between child-care workers and government authorities, challenging the racist and sexist configuration of child-care work, and positioning child-care workers at the leading edge of social and political struggles over the production and appropriation of value in an era of intensified social policing and control. In short, the kind of organizing that advocates cite as movement-building, and most worthy of top-down political support, is also the organizing that most challenges top-down control, that embodies counter-racist and counter-sexist hegemony, and exposes the violent costs of child-care work in the circuit of government authority.

Four

# Child-Care Workers In and Against the State

As a woman of color and working-class, I believe we child-care providers should be treated fairly; we should make a decent wage, and we should be respected. When we help other families to get out to work, we help make the economy work. (Sheryl Bell[1])

In this chapter, I discuss two related examples of home-based child-care worker organizing projects in the United States: the Home Daycare Justice Committee in Rhode Island and the Unity Campaign in Alexandria, Virginia. Each of these were relatively successful efforts led by African American and Latina immigrant home-based child-care providers working with established, community-organizing groups. The organizations which began the projects practice a form of "bottom-up" community organizing, involving a variety of techniques which distinguish this organizing from other kinds. Such techniques include participatory research, direct action, participatory planning and evaluation, and rank-and-file-led lobbying and advocacy. Such an approach corresponds generally to the "women-centered" (as opposed to Alinksky-style) organizing typology identified by researchers of community organizing (Martin 2002; Stall and Stoecker 1998). Allie B. Smith, a home-based child-care worker and participant in the Unity Campaign, commented that in this kind of "bottom-up" approach to organizing, organizers "teach you how to do for yourself . . . They're there to help you, but they're not there to tell you 'sit down and I'm going to do this for you.' You've got to do it on your own."[2]

The case of the Home Daycare Justice Committee (hereafter HDJC) in Rhode Island has proven to be a significant model for other "bottom-up" child-care worker organizing elsewhere, some of which I discuss below.[3] HDJC was a project of Direct Action for Rights and Equality (hereafter DARE), whose mission since the 1980s has been to organize low-income people of color to win social, economic and political justice. Between 1990 and 1996, before its spin-off into a cooperative of home-based child-care providers (the Daycare Justice Cooperative), the HDJC project successfully organized home-based providers in Providence to win state-subsidized health insurance, a policy that was eventually extended to cover center-based child-care workers elsewhere in the city and state in 1998. Today, most of Rhode Island's center-based and state-licensed home-based providers are eligible for health insurance coverage under the state's managed health care (Medicaid) program as a direct result of HDJC's six-year struggle—one of only two such state initiatives in the United States.[4]

HDJC's protracted campaign for health insurance for home-based child-care providers began in 1990 with word that the state's Department of Human Services was late again—three months in the case of some home-based providers—in reimbursing its contracted providers. Shannah Kurland (a DARE intern at the time, and later the HDJC organizer and DARE executive director) recalled that the experience of organizing home-based providers around late payments was an unexpected catalyst for the future campaign for wide-scale health care coverage.

> . . . I had run into an article somewhere about organizing home workers . . . it just wouldn't go totally out of my brain . . . I didn't realize at the time we were thinking about something immense. I thought we were talking about something on the scale of door-knocking on a street and getting neighbors involved around a playground . . . It didn't strike me how big it would be in terms of DARE . . . [that we would be] creating a new chapter of history in organizing low-wage women workers. (Abrams 1999, 7–8)

The intervention of home-based workers, and the response of community-based organizers to seek a collective solution, marked the HDJC campaign from the beginning. It foretold, as well, the struggle over the six-year period for home-based child-care providers to claim the organizing issues, including late payments, lack of health insurance, and political disrespect, in the face of government officials who refused to grant meetings, stonewalled, and used a variety of other delaying, dividing and diversionary tactics to force the providers off the campaign trail.[5] In pursuing health insurance coverage, the home-based providers had identified a need that the state otherwise didn't care about—and spent five years denying. As Kristy Abrams notes in her account of the HDJC's struggle for health benefits:

By the 90s, the state (at least the state of Rhode Island) had begrudgingly admitted that low-income families need help paying for child-care, since these families can't afford to keep a parent at home or to pay for child-care themselves. But the tradition of racism and sexism continued, metamorphosing from complete silence on the issue, to treating child-care workers deplorably. How else could the $2.38 per hour wage without benefits have come about, unless politicians and officials didn't consider providing child-care a real job—unless they consider it "women's work (and in particular, women of color's work)"? DARE's providers realized that the state was in the wrong, that providers perform an incredibly important service, and that they deserve to live a healthy life. (Abrams 1999, 9)

Indeed, DARE's providers named names, called those in control to account, and forced both cooperative and uncooperative government officials and policymakers to action. They put a name and face, phone number and address, on those who were in positions to control, and alter, the daily oppression of unaffordable or non-existent medical care which they were experiencing. In transforming individual and collective oppression into a campaign led by home-based workers for structural change with identified individual bureaucratic and institutional targets and allies, HDJC aggressively cut through the top-down model of negotiated and incremental "change" which pervades the child-care system.

HDJC also sought "to make it clear that the ideas behind [the health insurance] legislation came straight from the community it would affect, rather than from well-intentioned advocates who think they knew what the community needed. They wanted to make the reality of their lives and work concrete" (Abrams 1999, 17). The stakes of the HDJC campaign were real and concrete enough. Three years into the campaign, HDJC member and home-based provider Yolanda Gonzalez died of undiagnosed leukemia, which marked a turning point for campaign leaders. Still, it would take two more years of direct action, including office invasions, hearing take-overs, day-care sit-ins and negotiation cut-offs for HDJC to win subsidized health coverage from the state. Even then it took the promise of increased federal funding to the state as a result of the 1996 welfare reform legislation to move state legislators to allocate funding for the insurance which they had agreed, by then, was warranted.

There is much worth examining in this case. Indeed, DARE's Home Daycare Justice Committee campaign may be all the more important as a result of its effects outside of Rhode Island. Advocates and organizers seized on it as a landmark in the otherwise slow movement to improve the status of child-care workers. Yet as Whitebook and Eichberg's study of child-care compensation policy initiatives implied, such a radical result—a major employment benefit worth thousands of dollars a year to an individual worker and her children—particularly since it benefited (and was led and organized by) the most degraded and devalorized among the child-care workforce (home-based providers), was far from the norm of contemporary child-care "movement-building." The otherwise unexpected result of home-based providers organizing and winning employer health benefits, nevertheless, informed similar bottom-up campaigns and organizing efforts in other places in the United States.[6] In Illinois, for example, Service Employees International Union Local 880, together with the Association for Community Reform Now (ACORN), began organizing home-based child-care and home health care workers simultaneously in the mid-1990s, including a lengthy statewide legislative campaign for a so-called Living Wage law calling for both higher wages and health insurance provisions that would specifically cover these home-based workers. Through the direct action of home-based child-care workers from Local 880's base of 2,000 child-care worker-members, the union succeeded in 1999 in forcing the state to increase the daily reimbursement rate to home-based providers from approximately $13 per day to over $20 per day.[7]

Comparable in other ways to HDJC's home-based child-care provider organizing campaign was the Unity Campaign in Alexandria, Virginia. Like HDJC, the Unity Campaign was a home-based child-care provider organizing project of a democratic grassroots organization, the Tenants' and Workers' Support Committee (hereafter TWSC), whose organizing mission is to build the power of ethno-racially diverse tenants, workers, women, and youths in the Northern Virginia region to win social and economic justice, fight against racism and sexism, develop their own political leadership, and collectively control and own community resources such as housing and child-care. The parallels of the Unity Campaign's struggle for improved working conditions, "respect and dignity" to HDJC's efforts are not coincidental. TWSC organizers were familiar with DARE's child-care worker organizing of the 1990s and their success in gaining statewide health insurance coverage. Both organizations were formed in the mid-1980s, and their similar organizing approaches, including "base-building" and political leadership development directed towards pro-active policy and social change benefiting racially and economically oppressed groups, reflected the political sense that in the face of worsening social and economic conditions throughout the late 1970s and early 1980s, including massive gentrification and public and private disinvestments from low-income neighborhoods of majority people of color, new kinds of community organizing that could challenge racist and class-based oppression were necessary. The durability of both of these organizations, each of which has grown incrementally over nearly two decades, is an indicator of the success of each organization in developing and mobilizing its community membership and leadership bases, developing internal political skills and resources (such as public policy development, participatory planning and campaign implementation, and power analysis), and political perseverance in the face of top-down pressure, opposition, resistance, and refusal.

Aware of HDJC's six-year struggle and ultimate success, TWSC organizers realized in late 1998 that the difficulty Latina immigrant child-care providers were having in obtaining licensing from the City of Alexandria's Department of Human Services (hereafter DHS) was likely just a piece of a larger set of political problems. At the time, the TWSC had recently completed formation of a nearly 300-unit limited-equity housing cooperative, a milestone for the organization, which had begun in the mid-1980s as a multiracial community coalition of established, working-class and poor African American residents and newly-arrived Latino (predominantly Salvadoran and Honduran) immigrants, all of whom were facing planned evictions as a prelude to the gentrification of the neighborhood. With a strong foothold in the emerging majority Latino immigrant community, the TWSC continued in the late 1980s and early 1990s organizing tenants to prevent evictions, put pressure on local government to enforce housing codes and have dangerous building conditions fixed, and push for public support of limited-equity housing cooperatives as a solution to the local crisis of unaffordable housing.[8]

With preliminary formation of the housing cooperative beginning in 1993, the group began organizing many of the same tenants around the problems they experienced as low-wage workers. The TWSC began organizing hotel housekeepers in 1994, a project that resulted several years later in the first unionization of a hotel in the state of Virginia in nearly twenty years, a campaign jointly conducted with the Hotel Employees and Restaurant Employees union. Among the estimated 1,000 low-income Latino and African American owner-residents of the newly formed Arlandria-Chirilagua Housing Cooperative, a number of African American residents and a smaller number of Latina residents were licensed home-based child-care providers. As Tumoninen (1998) has documented, among the major impetuses to women entering home-based child-care work is parental demand, often of neighbors, friends, and relatives. Parents typically seek trusted, convenient, as well as culturally and linguistically appropriate care.

Among Latino parents of the housing cooperative and nearby apartment buildings, the demand for child-care became increasingly problematic as the prevailing informality of home-based care was transformed by a number of residents who sought, or were forced to seek, licenses for the opportunity to sub-contract with the Department of Human Services and offer subsidized care for the eligible children of low-income Latino parents. However, in early 1998, the DHS had cut off funding of bilingual certification classes, which had been provided under previous contract to the city by a neighborhood-based pre-school network. Members of the TWSC's Women's Leadership Group, which was involved at the time in developing both a community health access project and participatory research and action project to gain public investment in outdoor recreation facilities in the neighborhood, seized the initiative. They began by gathering signatures of home child-care providers, parents and others on a petition to DHS. In a letter to the director of the city's Office of Early Childhood Development, the office of DHS responsible for child-care provider licensing and oversight, the coordinator of the TWSC Women's Leadership Group wrote:

> The Arlandria / Chirilagua community wishes to relay our concern about the situation of *Home Child-care Providers* in our community, especially 5 women that, to date, Social Services has not approved to become city-licensed *Home Child-care Provider*s. These providers are appreciated for the important service they provide to our community. Not approving them affects both the women and most important the children who are denied access to quality Spanish-speaking child-care.[9]

With their experience organizing tenants into cooperative housing and low-wage workers into a union, the TWSC knew that the five Latina child-care providers who first approached them were part of a larger force of racially, economically and sexually oppressed women of color who, as history would have it, were for the most part contracted to the same entity: the city's Department of Human Services, which looked increasingly like the "employer of record" for what were (in 1998–1999) approximately two-hundred and fifty licensed, home-based child-care providers. With one small but significant step, a letter that linked linguistically-appropriate child-care to the training (as well as compensation) of home-based Latina child-care providers, an organizing project was born. The petition was successful. DHS began offering bilingual certification classes, and TWSC organizers met in late 1998 to discuss strategies for organizing the licensed home child-care providers in the city, who were about 90 percent African-American, along with a small but growing number of Latina as well as South Asian immigrant providers.

Throughout 1999, TWSC organizers began the process of communicating with the city's 250 licensed home-based providers, to recruit members, gain information about their work and experiences, and begin identifying organizing issues. They obtained the DHS list of licensed providers and began contacting individual providers in several neighborhoods. They invited providers to meetings to learn more and begin building a community base. It gradually surfaced, again not coincidentally, that providers in Alexandria were experiencing the same problems as providers in Rhode Island, and that the first and possibly easiest of the issues to tackle was the scheduling of payments by DHS to individual providers. Organizers and workers began a meticulous door-to-door campaign late in the year, building up to a meeting in April 2000 with the director of Alexandria's DHS, Meg O'Reagan. "About 50 angry Alexandria day-care providers are taking the city's human services director to task over their paychecks, many more than three weeks late and some not received at all," read the lead paragraph of one journalist's account of the meeting. The story continued:

> Sheryl Bell, a mother for 28 years and a child-care provider for 18, said she wants the city to take her protest seriously.
> "We are not babysitters," she said. "We are child-care professionals."
> She called caring for children one of the most important jobs there is. "What we do counts because we are raising America's future," she said.
> Other women told how they were behind on making credit card and rent payments, and their gas was turned off because they live paycheck to paycheck.
> "Ya'll have messed up my credit," said Tammy Ingram, with 6-month-old Antonio Goodman, one of her child-care charges, on her lap. "I can't buy a house. I can't get a car."[10]

I cite this necessarily partial account for several reasons. One, it reiterates one of the principal goals of the bottom-up organizing embodied both by the HDJC and Unity: having local government authorities hear the collective workplace demands of organized home-based child-care providers. The appearance of organization among presumably isolated home-based workers, in this context, is powerful. Two, it suggests that the valorization of home-based child-care operates through both a political appeal to professionalism and a discursive appeal to the production of an "imagined" ethno-racial community. Three, it acknowledges the violent, power-laden conditions of home-based work that surround and invade the economic, physical and psychical (the "ontological") security of home-based workers. And as with DARE, and with home-based worker organizing around the world, the violence surges from racism, and the ongoing technological evolution of racialized policing and management of subordinated populations.

> [DHS Director] O'Reagan said she had "tremendous respect" for the child-care providers, but in responding to their questions she twice referred to them as "you people."
>
> She said no offense was intended, the mostly-black crowd was clearly upset by the remark, with several saying that they were being addressed "like we're ignorant."
>
> In a Dec. 3 letter, the city's 213 city-paid child-care providers, each care [sic] for five or fewer children in their homes, were told to "please budget wisely" while the agency changes the way it processes invoices.[11]

It would take DHS six additional months to change the way it processed invoices, changes that O'Reagan claimed at the April 2000 meeting would have cost up to $250,000 in software rewriting, but that were eventually made at no apparent cost to the agency. However, it did take six months of continuous organizing, pressure, petitioning, letter-writing, and several follow-up meetings, including one in October 2000 with a representative of the city manager, the top appointed official in the city, to gain the change demanded by providers since early in the year.

The victory for timely paychecks, which as in the DARE experience was a symbolic victory in terms of political respect and power, led Unity leaders, who by now had become fully energized by the campaign, onto the next, and much broader, organizing issues: employment compensation and benefits. They continued meeting monthly, continuing the door-to-door strategy with organizers to inform providers of the paycheck victory and recruit members to the campaign. In Spring 2001, Unity leader (and later campaign president) Sheryl Bell testified before the Alexandria City Council about the need to increase the reimbursement rate of the city's home-based providers, to keep up with the rates in a neighboring jurisdiction. The Council approved $150,000 in June 2001, bringing the city's rate into parity with its neighbor, and signaling the growing power of Unity to make change through direct action and collective organization.

Around the same time, Unity members began focusing on employment benefits, and a campaign for city-subsidized health insurance began in earnest in mid-2001. A community forum on the issue scheduled for mid-September 2001 turned into a widely attended memorial in the wake of the Al-Quaida attacks on the Pentagon and World Trade Center days before— and a passionate demand for health insurance for home-based child-care providers. A hundred and fifty labor and religious leaders, elected officials, bureaucrats, Unity members, organizers, parents, children, community supporters and others heard testimonials from the home-based providers, received assurances from child-care and legal experts that the city had every right and reason to subsidize health care for the child-care providers it contracted, and were encouraged by the parents and children to whom the workers provided care to bring justice and stability into a system of care, education and support which they depended on heavily.

The four members of the seven-person Alexandria City Council who were present at the September forum indicated their tentative support for Unity's health insurance proposal. However, over the next six months, intensification of the conflictive relationship between DHS and Unity—spurred in part by the exposure of several unrelated "child protection" fiascos in DHS—resulted in the revocation of 10% of the licenses of the home-based providers in the city. This, in turn, led to temporary divisions among Unity members over how to respond to the mounting aggression of DHS to Unity's "campaign for dignity and respect" as well as to individual Unity leaders and members. DHS officials were under increasing pressure as a result of the department's perceived mishandling of the case of a child who died in the custody of her mother following a brutal beating by the mother's boyfriend. The three-year old child had spent the majority of her life in the custody of foster parents, and the Alexandria DHS, which had visited the child's mother's home on repeated occasions, failed to notice the emerging signs of abuse that culminated in the child's death within three months of being returned to her mother from foster care.[12]

As director of the agency in charge of overseeing child abuse cases, O'Reagan was under increasing pressure from her own bosses to account for her office's failings throughout the next eighteen months, a period during which Unity was gaining momentum around compensation and health care issues. Pressure on DHS was coming thus from a number of sides. One of the results was a clampdown by DHS on the licensing of home-based child-care providers. Providers, including approximately a dozen members of Unity, had their licenses revoked beginning in late 2001 and continuing into the spring of 2002. As Unity leaders began to learn the details of the revocations, startling news began to emerge about the arbitrary and apparently retaliatory nature of license reviews and decision-making at DHS.

With a number of Unity leaders facing the loss of their licenses, campaign members were confronted with how to respond. For a short period of time, debate about the relative merits of one provider's appeal over another began to divide Unity members across ethno-racial lines. However, Unity's leadership prevailed over the possibility of a breakdown in multi-racial unity.

Leaders united around a shared interest in pursuing the underlying problem of the cases: the complete lack of any due process in DHS's handling of license restrictions or revocations. Unity organizers began documenting the cases of the providers whose licenses had been revoked or suspended in the previous six months. More than half of the revocations appeared to be the result of controls newly imposed by the Virginia state legislature that outlawed local licensing of providers in whose home resided *anyone*—spouse, domestic partner, family member, etc.—who had been convicted of two categories of *misdemeanor* offenses at any prior point. (Providers themselves were already subject to stringent criminal background checks, with a broad range of convictions constituting so-called "barrier offenses" to licensing.)

The new controls, which augmented the existing regulations on *felony* offenders residing in the home of state- or city-licensed child-care providers, went beyond the regulatory requirements of most other states, which typically have a statute of limitations on misdemeanors as "barrier offenses" in determining a child-care provider's licensing eligibility. At a 2002 public hearing of the Alexandria Human Rights Commission attended by Unity, one white commission member noted the virtual impossibility of being an African American man in the late-to-desegregate state of Virginia of the 1960s and 1970s and *not* being convicted on one or more misdemeanor offenses. In mandating home-based controls that lifted the statute of limitations on counting misdemeanors as barrier crimes, the conservative-dominated Virginia legislature was effectively rolling back the clock to Jim Crow and inaugurating a new tactic in the emerging international "culture of control" (Garland 2001; Wacquant 2001).

The remaining instances of license revocation, while all quite different in case and point, nevertheless shared the common characteristic of an almost complete absence of due process in which workers could appeal their license review by DHS.[13] This was confirmed at a Workers' Rights Board hearing convened by Unity in August 2002, when DHS Director O'Reagan, pushed on whether providers had been given a fair opportunity to appeal the loss of their licenses, replied that providers were free to appeal their cases directly to her, and that in the cases of the providers who testified at the August hearing, the decision to revoke the licenses was hers alone to make. In other words, providers could appeal to the very official who had already arbitrarily decided the disposition of their cases. In extended and emotional testimony to the Alexandria Human Rights Commission two weeks later, Unity members who had had their licenses revoked—and, as they argued, their fundamental rights to due process negated—spoke to the loss of income, housing, community status and health which resulted from the revocation of their licenses, as well as the foot-dragging, punitive and accusatory manner in which DHS followed-up, or refused to follow-up, on requests to review their individual cases.

The testimony to the city Human Rights Commission was auspicious in more than one way. It came on the day that DHS Director O'Reagan was reassigned to another city agency and an interim DHS director appointed. Although it is difficult to assess the impact on her reassignment by city managers, Unity's two-year struggle with the DHS director likely contributed something to the decision to remove her from DHS. The increasingly explicit evocation of a pattern of paternalistic, racist and punitive treatment of child-care providers by DHS social workers and administrators was not what city managers wanted to see in the headlines. Unity's testimony to the Human Rights Commission exposed vindictive and unquestionably arbitrary treatment of providers by O'Reagan in particular, as well as by the head of the DHS Office of Early Childhood Development, Carol Farrell.

At the same human rights hearing, Unity leaders presented the commission with a proposal for the creation of an independent appeals board, comprised of child-care providers, labor, community and religious representatives, that would step in where O'Reagan had more or less usurped administrative-judicial power. Weeks later, four Unity members had their licenses restored, in an immediate response to the legal and political challenges Unity posed. Four more providers came forward later in 2002 to present their cases to Unity organizers. Around the same time, it was reported by Unity members that, in fact, not only had DHS administrators taken final judgment and oversight of the city's providers upon themselves, but social workers in the DHS had intentionally targeted Unity members for increased pressure and policing, including the probable loss of referrals for child-care placement. In the most telling instance, a Bangladeshi provider who had been participating in Unity meetings and actions for the previous year reported in the fall of 2002 to the interim DHS director that during the previous summer, her assigned social worker had told her and her husband that Unity would not get them health insurance and that they should quit Unity. For some time thereafter, she had not received any child-care placements (during a period when she was suffering from an illness that required medication costing $500 per month, as she noted to DHS at the time). Although it is possible that the particular social worker was not retaliating directly by withholding child-care placements to the Bangladeshi Unity member—other South Asian and African immigrant providers in the same zone of the city were also not receiving placements during the same period, although they were not Unity members—certainly the implication to quit Unity and the insistence to the seriously ill provider that Unity's campaign for health insurance was not the answer to her health problems, were callous and antagonistic responses.

Equally important to the development of the organization, in the fall of 2002 Unity's recently elected president, Sheryl Bell, a longstanding leader and child advocate in the city's African American community, was hospitalized with a life-threatening illness. As a founding member of Unity and key figure in the ongoing campaign for health insurance, Bell's illness put into stark relief for the campaign's leaders and supporters the traumatic conditions of home-based child-care work which they were addressing in the campaign. Indeed, the relatively older African American women who constitute the majority of home-based child-care providers in the city (which is typical for most U.S. cities), are at much greater health risk than the general population—and at even greater health and economic risk because of their medically uninsured status (Mullings 1997).

Moved by the events of the previous months and the illness of a key leader, by the end of 2002, the Unity Campaign was in full throttle: continuing the pursuit of city-subsidized health insurance, winning preliminary approval of a new due process policy and a community appeals board, calling for a complete review of the DHS's policies and practices affecting child-care workers; and drafting a legislative proposal to alter the new state controls which effectively re-criminalized the spouses and family members of home-based providers. Members readied a variety of direct action props—including a mock coffin symbolizing the death awaiting child-care providers without access to medical care—and planned strategies and tactics for the upcoming City Council budget session. However, while they began making their demands formally to city councilors in early 2003, the campaign encountered several challenges. One, a gap in leadership developed between the core membership of Unity and the paid organizer of the TWSC. The organizer, a white woman and former union organizer, had been brought on as a replacement organizer the year before. In contrast to previous TWSC organizers of child-care providers, the new organizer emphasized less a "bottom-up," rank-and-file activism and more an advocacy-oriented approach in which the organizer herself spent considerable time seeking administrative solutions to the problems of individual providers, such as the licensing revocations. The shift from bottom-up organizing to casework and organizer-centered advocacy had the unintended and undesirable effect (from the standpoint of some Unity leaders) of shifting the campaign's public leadership from, in this case, the African American and Latina immigrant home-based child-care provider-members of Unity, to a well-intentioned white organizer who had increasingly less accountability to Unity members as the campaign progressed.

In public budget hearings in the spring of 2003, where Unity's proposal for subsidized health insurance was presented and discussed, a stark ideological gap opened up between the campaign and the Alexandria city council. While indicating support for the campaign's claim that home-based child-care providers were an essential community service and deserved improved pay and benefits, no city councilor was willing to budge (or budget) from the position that if the city council were to provide an employment benefit such as health insurance to home-based providers (something which was reasonable enough to discuss), they would be acting as the "employer of record" of the technically self-employed providers. Even the most politically supportive city councilors could not overcome the ideology that separated home-based child-care workers (private, self-employed, informal, "providers") from center-based workers (public, employee, formal, "professionals"). Equally, if not more important, was the pervasive, normalized acceptance of work in the service sector as inherently contingent (Huws 2003; MacDonald and Sirianni 1996). And whereas in Rhode Island, when confronted with a similar illogic from lawmakers, HDJC responded by increasing their demands for health insurance for both home- and center-based providers, many Unity members fell into the ideological trap of seeing themselves not as contingent city-employed workers fighting privatization, which in a determinate way they were, but as self-employed day care providers fighting for dignity and respect for their life-long labors.

In June 2003, Unity won $250,000 in increased reimbursements for the city's home-based providers, but not health insurance. According to TWSC Executive Director Jon Liss, who monitored the campaign from its inception, "the deal Unity got was the best they could get. The city wouldn't yield on the ideological point of being employers. To win, Unity would have had to win the ideological battle, and have a higher level of mass power among the workers." Commenting on the latter point, Liss noted that Unity "had a fairly singular inability to move more than providers"—parents, churches, unions, other key allies—in support of the campaign. The campaign suffered from being unable to win the activist support of either white women (e.g. in labor or feminist organizations), who might have identified in gender terms with campaign demands, or African American men, particularly church leaders, who might have identified with the race and class dimensions of the providers' struggle. Just as problematic, the organizers failed to gain active support from labor unions, although the TWSC had had a recent history of decisive trade union involvement in a number of its organizing efforts, notably a successful Living Wage campaign and several local workplace-based organizing and unionization campaigns. According to Liss, the providers "didn't have such a strong workerist position. They still didn't entirely see themselves as *workers*, who should seek alliances with other labor sectors, even the center-based providers."[14]

In the years that followed the unsuccessful fight for health insurance, the Unity Campaign returned full circle to where it began. In 2004, Unity leaders began discussing a proposal to organize and conduct linguistically appropriate child-care worker education and training classes required for licensing approval and renewal—signaling the importance of these powerful areas of control for sustained leadership development, political education, and systemic transformation. And like the HDJC in Providence, which after its successful campaign for health insurance was transformed into a (short-lived) child-care cooperative, Unity members also began exploring the potential of a home-based cooperative to re-build the power of the predominantly African American and Latina immigrant home-based providers in Alexandria. As a cooperative business, members could conceivably negotiate with the city's DHS for a specified number of child-care providing contracts, including the cost of providing health insurance in the contract—thus circumventing the strong resistance of the city's elected officials to go on record as employers of the home-based workers. And as a cooperative, they could circumvent the looming threat that the undocumented immigrant childcare workers among them would be ineligible to contract for services with the city as a result of impending anti-immigrant state regulations on childcare provision.

The TWSC Unity Campaign began with the goal of uniting a local area's ethno-racially, linguistically and culturally diverse home-based child-care providers for what they termed "respect and dignity" and continued with a series of demands and proposals to gain improved compensation, benefits, and working conditions and to end the paternalistic, racist, arbitrary and punitive management and control which they had suffered as home-based child-care providers for more than two decades in some cases. There are obvious parallels in Unity's history to DARE's Home Daycare Justice Campaign of the early 1990s. Many of the goals and objectives, the approaches to community organizing, and the language and day-to-day experience of organizing home-based child-care workers are comparable, if not identical. With the action around licensing and due process, however, Unity members and organizers exposed a range of formal and informal, as well as institutional and individual, mechanisms of control and policing that exceeded, and in many ways, underscored, the better-known issues of compensation and "stabilization" of the child-care system. Although unsuccessful in their struggle for publicly subsidized health insurance, Unity Campaign leaders and members nevertheless exposed and transformed the paternalistic supervision and "outlaw" system of licensing review which positioned them as suspect, subordinate and subjugated home-based workers. While such a history may not emerge wherever home-based workers organize, it certainly transfigures what is known about the arduousness of the struggle for home-based justice, which may still be too little.

Indeed, the material contingencies of HDJC'S and Unity's organizing—the needs for sustained political leadership, skilled organizers, funding, support from larger organizations, internal unity, mass membership, and above all, organizational perseverance—are played down in my account, as in too many other accounts of home-based worker organizing I would argue. Yet these factors are undoubtedly just as important as the needs to form demands, educate and pressure elected officials, and gain media coverage. Analysis of the contingencies of organizing goes directly to the issue of "bottom-up" versus "top-down" organizing noted earlier, and textually links the organizations and social struggles of home-based, Black and immigrant workers in the United States with others around the world (Sudbury 1998).

## ORGANIZING HOME-BASED LABOR: BIOPOLITICS AND THE STATE

Analysis of the top-down and bottom-up politics of home-based child-care organization (alongside other kinds of home-based work, "caring work" and service sector work), gives one a sense of the global and local structures that unite paid and unpaid work, public and private spheres, production and reproduction, and homework and housework. Indeed, these structures appear more prevalent in today's "structurally adjusted" and "reformed" welfare societies, two hundred years after the birth of what Michel Foucault termed "biopolitics," that is the turn within liberalism to systematic government through the rigorous life-management and policing of specifically defined and distributed populations, and the extension of this systematization to all areas of life.[15] If the socio-economic policies of international financial institutions charged with managing societies in a globalizing economy are rooted in the global development of a specifically American liberalism, then Foucault's analysis of biopolitics, which is increasingly being taken up in the neo-Marxist critique of global capitalism, appears ripe for further consideration (Witheford 1999; Hardt and Negri 2000). According to Foucault,

> . . . American neoliberalism was a movement completely contrary to what is found in the social economy of the market in Germany: where the latter considers regulation of prices by the market—the only basis

for a rational economy—to be in itself so fragile that it must be supported, managed, and "ordered" by a vigilant internal policy of social interventions (involving assistance to the unemployed, health care coverage, a housing policy, and so on), American neoliberalism seeks rather to extend the rationality of the market, the schemes of analysis it proposes, and the decision making criteria it suggests to areas that are not exclusively or not primarily economic. For example, the family and birth policy, or delinquency and penal policy. (Foucault 1997, 78–79).

Read alongside analysis of the political economies of home-based child-care, analysis of American neoliberal biopolitics indicates a shifting reliance by the state on the top-down organization of the inter-looped circuits of women's productive-reproductive labor. Whereas academic feminism and sociologies of gender and work largely continue to treat the rise of the broadly configured service society in the dualistic terms of segmented labor markets and shadow or informal work, home-based child-care work and domestic work studies such as those of Tuominen (1994a) and Parreñas (2001) suggest more unified global/local approaches to the state-configured and controlled "services" of racially subordinated home-based female workers. The difference in approach is comparable to the way that earlier studies of homework countered the official and exclusivist labor studies that viewed homework as simply another kind of poorly compensated industrial work. "Operating within the norms of liberal individualism and the formal market economy," Tuominen writes, "dualistic notions of work emerged: waged labor equals work, unwaged labor does not. These dualistic definitions of work shaped dualistic notions of citizenship and, subsequently, the role of the welfare state including the formation of child-care policies and practices" (Tuominen 1997, 64).

Noting the wavering ideological force of the racialized reproductive norm of full-time motherhood, Tuominen focuses on the considerable power of the state, policymakers, and advocates in the ongoing "stimulation" and exploitative organization of home-based child-care work. Yet in seeking to understand how and why home-based child-care remains so highly exploited, she unaccountably argues that unwaged housework and child-care go unrecognized as work in liberalism. Because of the liberal focus on the normative value of independence, individualism, and autonomy, women's caring work remains undervalued: "the work of care-giving, work historically performed as unwaged work, by women, outside of the formal market economy, remains ignored in the theory and practice of liberal individualism," Tuominen explains. Drawing on feminist critiques of the welfare state, Tuominen ties the liberal devaluation of home-based work to specifically gendered divisions and definitions of work and criticizes both classical and Marxist political economy for failing to undo this devaluation as well as focusing exclusively on the production and productivity of waged labor. Following feminist critics of the welfare state such as Carol Pateman and Anne Showstack Sassoon, she suggests that home-based child-care and other caring work emerges contradictorily in liberalism, ignored in theory yet exploited in practice.

Foucault's description of the emergence of biopolitics in liberalism suggests that the apparent "ignored in theory/exploited in practice" dualism is neither a dualism nor a contradiction. Liberalism, for Foucault, is built through practices of biopolitical management, policing and control as a *critique* (and here may be the only place in Foucault's formulation where ideology may be thought to enter) of the excesses of government. In this sense, it makes more sense to say, as Gayatri Chakravorty Spivak does in relation to Foucault and Derrida, that "practice norms theory," and that in acknowledgement of the power of liberalism one must always "learn to learn from below" to see "the terminals of resistance inscribed *under* the level of the tactics, sometimes explicit, with which [ . . . ] women fill their lives":

> One must not stop here, of course. The homely tactics of everyday *pouvoir/savoir*, the stuff of women's lives, lead, not only to the governmentality of dress codes and work habits, guilt feelings and guilt trips, but also to the delineation of the great aggregative apparatuses of power/knowledge which deploy the family as a repressive issue, day care as an alibi, and reproductive rights as a moral melodrama in national elections and policy. (Spivak 1993, 35)

Indeed, at the turn of the twenty-first century, the American state (more so than others) is not exploiting women's home-based child caring nearly as much as it could, or likely will. With this in mind, it bears repeating that homework literally confuses the categories. While the critique of the dualism inherent in liberal and Marxist political economy is necessary, to argue that ideological norms embedded in liberalism discount women's home-based caring work in particular (ignoring it in theory but relying on it in practice) forecloses possible openings to other configurations of, and bottom-up struggles within, American neoliberalism: for instance debt structures of various kinds and the broad spectrum of race and sex-allied reproductive struggles within marriage, family and other biopolitical domains of state-supervised capitalism. Focusing on the question of why women would enter into the exploitative conditions of home-based work, as many studies do, obscures the active presence of women's organized resistance—and enforced compliance—from below, that is to say, the counter-revolution in the top-down configuration of ethical liberalism. An example of the complications of "organizing" can be seen in the fact that from roughly 2000 on, during the peak of Unity's community organizing efforts, the Alexandria Department of Human Services was attempting to organize, albeit ineffectually, its own association of family day care providers, along the lines of a company union. In the old Gramscian sense, such an association was to be responsible for the moral and political education of its organic intellectual members. It would be a mistake to say that this was a case of liberal misrecognition of the value of women's home-based work. Or to give one more critical example, Tuominen's position on the "call to service" as a powerful motivating factor in African American women's entry into home-based child-care, and a more broadly configured "caring Black community" ignores, ironically, the underlying conditions of the affective (and politically violent) control of Black women's laboring bodies in state-controlled child-care. In order to see from below where normative change from the top may be headed, the "call to service," which is indeed a powerful motivating force observed among African American child-care providers across the United States, must be heard alongside the historic "call to servitude."[16] The biopolitics of contemporary state-administered, home-based child-care resound with the machinery of plantation slavery, the degradation of Jim Crow-era domestic service, and the liberal racism and paternalism of post-1960s welfare administration.

A prison researcher and professor of ethnic studies, Julia Sudbury, documents similar dynamics in her exposition of black women's working-class and other organizations in the United Kingdom during the last three decades of the twentieth century. She notes how child-care referred in the 1970s and 1980s not only to the organized struggles of "black wages for housework" in the United Kingdom, but to the specific desires and perceived political needs for political education of black British children along anti-racist and cross-cultural lines (Sudbury 1998, 57–58; 165–66). The academic and cultural configurations of the "race-class-gender" debates of the 1980s in particular took distinct forms in autonomous black women's organizations in the United Kingdom, whose "other kinds of dreams" of class power were virtually always directly tied to the state through social service organizing issues on the one hand (in particular access to and delivery of child-care and education), and the combined policy and funding power of state and local authorities, on the other.

Foucault's naming of biopolitics in the formation and extension of liberalism from the nineteenth century onwards is thus an important corrective to the narrow, rights-based versions of liberal political theory that academic policy analysts, including many feminists, seem to consistently misread as normative before the fact. For in understanding liberalism as an ongoing *critique* of government through the active and tightly-woven life-management and control of racially, sexually, and otherwise marked populations, Foucault's analysis of biopolitics does not mistakenly displace onto the field of liberal political *theory*, women's historic struggles over value, sex, and power within capitalism.[17] One of the ways American neoliberalism has reformed the welfare state, at least in the local versions I have looked at in Providence, Rhode Island and Alexandria, Virginia, is to extend policing and penal policy to the management and control of the home-based child-care workforce as part of the ongoing rationalization through marketization of women's work, including child-care. While some advocates might choose to view this as an unfortunate and unfair limitation on black women's participation in child-care work, or a misguided policy from the point of view of child safety, it would be a mistake not to see in it an effort at weakening the child-care workforce politically by "racially" dividing it. There may be little more fearful to the predominantly white male lawmakers of a neoliberal southern state such as Virginia than African American (and Latina and Asian immigrant) women (and men) "rising up"—not only as workers, but as the rightful teachers, protectors, and guardians of the children who are "America's future," to return to the words of the Unity Campaign leader. This is one possible reading, at least.

Another, more literal reading would have to suggest that it is not through the narrowness of normative individualism or the sexism of normative autonomy and independence that liberalism succeeds in relegating unpaid and underpaid labor to racially divided women, mothers, nurses, child-care workers, and so on. American neoliberalism, in the home-based work context, succeeds less through ideology and discourse and more through pre-emptive struggle over the ever-expanding mechanisms of control, technologies of policing, and material forms of organization and contestation—e.g. home-based human service work/worker organizing—which are both cause and effect of sexually and racially (and we have to say today, internationally) divided labor. The top-down organization of home-based child-care today is just such an attempted response to a kind of "irresistible change" taking place as homeworkers challenge their assumed (non-)place as black women providing care to others' children and families. Thus, when Tuominen argues that "classical liberal political theory provides the basis for the emergence of the welfare state within the United States," 'emergence' here can be connected to what could only be called "history" by someone such as Hegel.[18] Foucault's understanding of liberalism as a strategic, rationalizing method and set of practices—not as theory or, even less, ideology—supplements the reproductive struggles structured in power which Marx, it is true, for the most part "handed over" to European and American *men* of various classes. Marx was certainly no feminist, but he wasn't exactly a liberal, either.

Taking off from this thought, I turn now to the struggle over what might best be called home-based "governmentality," a loosely Foucauldian framework for learning to learn from bottom-up kinds of home-based worker organizing.

**Fig. 1** Unity holds accountability session with Alexandria DHS officials in April 2000.

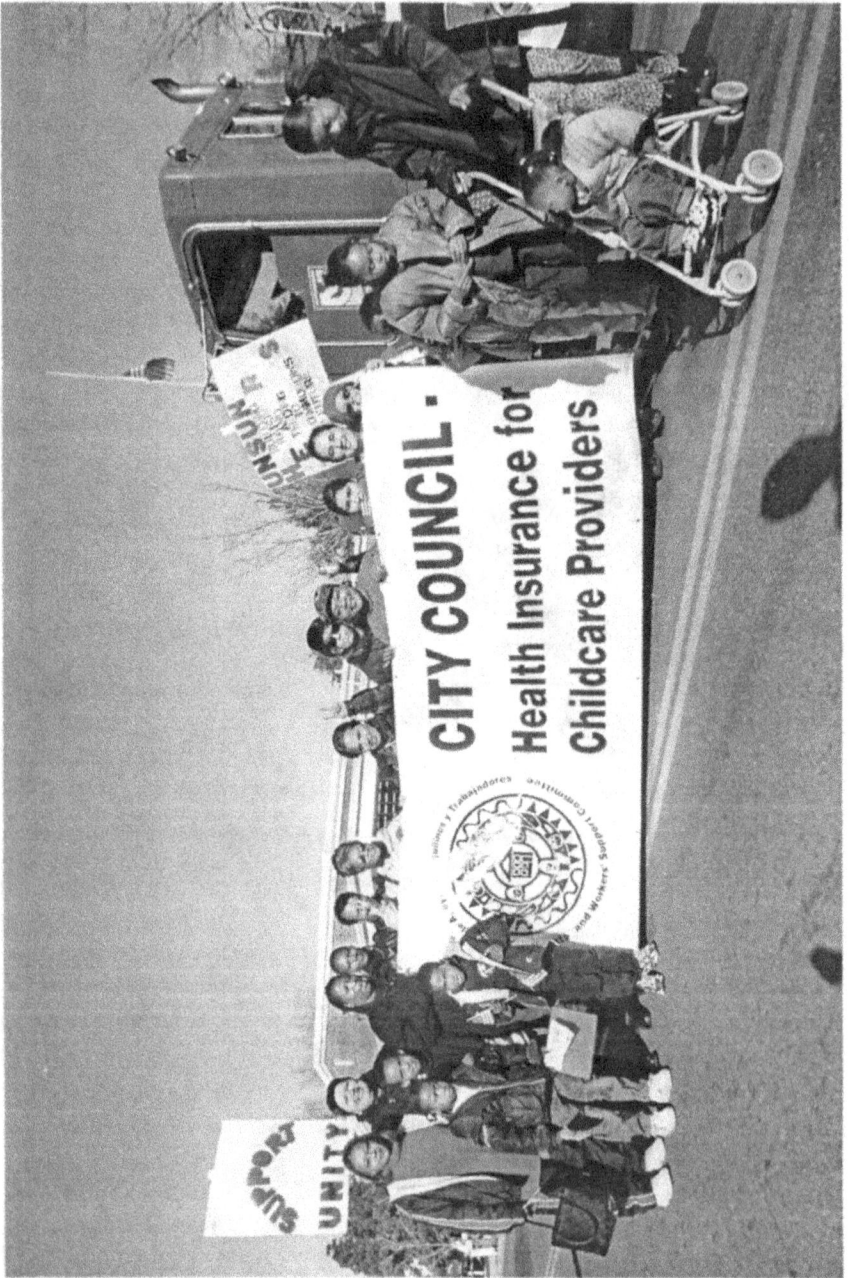

**Fig. 2** Unity members and supporters gather for February 2002 march to demand health insurance for child-care providers.

Chapter Five

# The Biopolitics of Homework

> Any policy aimed at eliminating the wage gap between men and women
> is likely to have limited results if a continuous restructuring of the labor
> process creates new labor hierarchies and places women at the lower
> end. (Lourdes Benería and Marta Roldán, *The Crossroads of Class &*
> *Gender*)

What careful observers of home-based child-care name the "call to service"
of African American child-care providers, crossed with the historic "call
to servitude" of African American women, is not simply another iteration
of the master-slave dialectic, or the powerful, re-composed class response
to patriarchal devalorization. Home-based child-care worker organizing,
where the stakes are "biopolitical" control, appears to bear this out. The
radicalism embodied in homeworker organizing thus is not met by academic human rights talk or even human rights activism, either in the United
States, where economic human rights have been rejected by liberal democracy, or elsewhere, where rights, when they are upheld, are vitiated by a
non-existent global economic democracy. The historic struggle of female
workers at home is lodged elsewhere, in the midst of an intensifying sexual,
racial and international division of labor and local/global state apparatuses
that render their labors paradigmatic for capitalist reproduction.

With this in mind, I am suggesting that strategies of home-based labor
organizing are or will be located increasingly in the circuit of what Foucault called governmentality, that is between what Antonio Negri (1999)
terms the auto-valorization of "affective" labor power and the technologies
of knowledge production, domination, and subjectivity (which are more
"familiar" than we realize). In this circuit, what we find, beyond the global/
local effects of structural adjustment, are the chains of subcontracted production to which organizations like HomeNet and the Unity Campaign

draw our attention. "Subcontracted" precisely. Beneath, and to an ever-greater extent, inside the structural relations of the capitalist contract on and of labor, there are few if any protections, laws, or regulation. This absence has emboldened theorists such as Michael Hardt and Negri (1994) to argue that not the state, but "civil society has withered away." Yet to focus only on civil society on the one hand, and cosmopolitan norms and labor or human rights, on the other, would be misguided, however benevolent (Cheah 1997). Civil society stops at the border between factory and home, between the "social factory" and biopolitical reproduction. There are few regulations governing homework, although this may be slowly changing (or changing back again). There are even fewer governing housework.[1] The number of these workers isn't known, officially or unofficially. Family child-care, domestic work, and other forms of homework are only in the last decade undergoing what might be called a "positive" reformation (in Foucault's sense of positive disciplinization), i.e. one in which homework is regarded as both desirable and able to be regulated by homeworkers themselves (Prügl 1999). The shape of this to come, which one can see in the growing practice of "time-use studies" by policymakers and censuses by home-based labor advocates in the global South, has much to do with how "domestic labor" will be used by the practitioners and politicians seeking one form or another of "progressive" social engineering.[2] So far, however, such change remains mostly off the state/civil society agendas, and much about the domestic economy remains, literally speaking, "uncivil."[3]

I am arguing, in a necessarily roundabout way, that the space of the "uncivil," routed through "the home," touches virtually all other domains of what many continue to misperceive as (only) state and civil society. For theorists such as Hardt and Negri, the response to the "withering away of civil society" is a recomposition of proletarian subjectivities that, as a constitutive force of society as such (what they termed "constituent bio-power"), expands and re-appropriates the political not so much to reform social and political institutions, as re-shape and modulate time and place ontologies (Witheford 1994). In the most advanced sites of capitalist sociality, this takes the form of the "multitudinous" auto-valorization of affect-value, that is the reappropriation of the social across the board by highly diverse, cooperative, communicative, and socialized labor forces (Hardt and Negri 2000). My own response would be that much that isn't inside, or an immediate effect of, the state, continues to draw the state towards it, in a reversal or transversal of directions of power and cause/effect. We were used to thinking with Gramsci, for instance, of the state as the source of norms, on the one hand, and dominating power on the other (or to put it slightly differently, the state as the source of law and order). Today, we must ask, what (hegemonic and socialist) strategy was that the thinking of? What we have instead today is a civil society-state struggle far from "war of maneuver" or "war of position," the result of a breakdown in the absolute necessity of normativity and disciplinization (the "war of position" having been won) and the consequent intensification and extensification of policing, surveillance and control of the gradually increasing (and widening) turbulence of multiply divided, global class society.[4]

As political (e.g. "community organized") subjectivities begin to form around homework and other subcontracted work—in spite, and because of, their "underground" and "uncivil" status—new narratives gain ground. If I am reading the diversely situated studies of home-based work correctly, what binds the structure of (forced) reproductive labor displaced in domestic labor/homework—what makes political subjectivities in this space flow—are the highly controlled technologies of "sex" and "race" both in and outside the state. At certain points, I have referred to Spivak's remark in the introduction to Mahasweta Devi's writings that "Internalized gendering perceived as ethical choice is the hardest roadblock for women the world over. The recognition of male exploitation must be supplemented with this acknowledgement" (Devi 1995, xxviii). In the footnote to this passage, Spivak draws attention to the passage, through *différance*, from bonded sex labor in India to homeworking in the United Kingdom, and then draws it back again to Devi's own writing on indigenous struggles for cultural and ethnic survival. Her point, which she has pursued elsewhere (Spivak 1990, 1999), is to undo the easy teleology of benevolent organizers and movement fundraisers (I count myself among the latter) through a persistent critique of the structures of internationally divided labor in the home, structures which "we cannot not wish to inhabit." Sheila Allen and Carol Wolkowitz (1987), whom Spivak cites in this same passage, were also concerned about the easy positivism and political positivity pervading discourses of homeworking in the United Kingdom—discourses which erased differences among homeworkers such as "race" as swiftly as they suggested that homework constitutes a "choice" for women among other more or less equal economic "opportunities." Allen and Wolkowitz demystified this kind of political "choice," partially through their own interest in child-care, which highlighted in reverse one of the key issues which concerned me in the last two chapters—that child-care providers are "homeworkers" too![5]

Much more can be said about biopower-centered subjectivities: one part from the point of view of a deconstructive critique that would displace the center onto its sexual and racial margins, as I have been attempting thus far—and another from the point of view of "governmentality." On the latter point, much is being made from an uncritical version of Foucault that centers homework/housework (among other phenomena) in a traditional intellectual struggle for control over worker subjectivities.[6] What this version chooses to forget historically is that beginning in the late eighteenth century, the "spatial fixing" of the European/American home became not only a social strategy for control of laboring subjects, but a state strategy for control of laboring subjects premised on policing sexuality and marriage, and thereby the "biopolitical field" tout court (Ehrenreich and English 1978; Donzelot 1997).[7] At the same time that labor was being commodified throughout the home—especially in the correlated rise of homework and factory production—domestic labor was being coerced, policed and "civilized" into and, then inside, the home. In this respect, Jacques Donzelot was quite clear about the ensuing class divisions (although much less so about gender divisions, and very little about "race" and colonialism). What Allen and Wolkowitz, Tuominen, and others have made clear is that the focus on class-divided homework must also always account for sexual and racial divisions (within migrancy, in particular), if it is to specify the systematic state management (i.e. "biopolitical") forces that find in the home a place not just for divisive control but for class formation and "organizing" as well.

It would be a mistake to read *Discipline and Punish*, on the one hand, and volume three of the *History of Sexuality*, on the other, and deduce that policing was once directed from the outside and then, at a later stage of social development, internalized.[8] One must turn to Foucault's (1979, 1997) texts on "governmentality" to see how social policing became at a certain point instrumental to *self*-policing in the same way, and more or less at the same time, that "the family" became instrumental to government. The relationship of policing to self-policing, in this regard, was an inverted loop or circuit: moral education and training provided by institutional authorities required coercion and compliance, and therefore surveillance, as conditions of their effectiveness. Seeing this movement in relationship to the individual isn't only or merely a question of measurement—i.e. of value in the restrictive economic sense[9]—but rather one of asking where does the individual begin and end in the practice of governmentality. In contemporary telework, for example, surveillance extends from the teleworker to the telework family via the telephone and networking of domestic space.[10] Everyone is at work and under control in this scenario, not least where educational homework and routine testing take on greater social and political engineering significance for the child. This means of course, that we have surpassed neither policing (indeed it is both a more potent and necessary force), nor the family. What it also means is that, since these terms are discursively and politically interrelated, the terrain of governmentality, as Foucault writes, is principled on the ongoing instrumentalization of the family, but through means that aren't only experienced as self-policing; or more narrowly and (presumably) at all times, governmentality is principled on control within the turbulent family.[11] I return to this theme below.

To extend the same critique a bit further, to use Foucault or a Foucauldian analysis in studies of home-based work, requires a displacement onto the terrain of home-based and family-based sexual and gender *identities* in such a way that the use of the term "choice" in the same studies would have to appear differently, although still not entirely within the framework Foucault outlines for the post-Enlightenment political-ethical subject. "Internalized gendering perceived as ethical choice" becomes a technology of the home-based laboring subject, after, for instance subtracting it from the calculus of "governmentality"—or what Gilles Deleuze termed "control society." That is to say, the flow of politicized subjectivity through the self (and in the case of homework through the powerful practice and performativity of the sexual and racial dividing of labor), becomes a successful strategy of *domination* when it succeeds in erasing the linkage to the circuitry of power that is to be found, increasingly throughout the globe, in the multi-face of what many have been otherwise calling "control" inside the network comprised by the homeworker, the local government case manager, the NGO advocate, the organizer, the academic, and the policymaker.

One needs, then, to perform an analysis of homework that links social reproduction, or the possibility of reproduction, to policing which is not reduced to individual or "household strategies," but to something like what Spivak (1990) for a time referred to as the "strategic essentialisms" (which academic theorists typically refuse) of the race- and sex-divided practical politics of "class formation" and various kinds of "organizing." The diffusion of homeworkers throughout social time and space is indeed part of the strategy of the state and individual capitalists, and this could very easily become reflected in the work of the well-meaning NGO or academic expert. Accepting it in analytical terms, and countering with "technologies of the self," serves only to ante-up in a game whose rules are already controlled by the "definitively decisive" victor of the "war of position"; likewise, in the presence of the erasure of these rules, it is to play the game without knowledge of the rules, as working a definition of structuralist research if ever there were one, as Stuart Hall (1986) once put it for British cultural studies.[12]

It is in the spirit of exposing such "regulation" that I now turn to Foucault with a different program in mind, i.e. to re-read the "post-structuralist" Foucault as one invested in a history of the present that doesn't reduce individual being to the individual, that doesn't envision strategy without collective action, and that flows between discourses and practices of the self, rationalization of these and other techniques, and rationalization of the state. This, at least, is how I understand "governmentality." I would stress the importance and appropriateness of such a reading of Foucault, since others in the field of homework studies already have done so with varying intents (Felstead and Jewson 1999; Parrenas 2001; Valsecchi 1999). I intend to try as well to reproduce the specificity of what Foucault theorized as power, ethics, and governmentality, this time for the field of home-based child-care provider organizing in the United States—which it should be emphasized does not stand in for homeworker organizing anywhere or at any time.[13] In this context, one must come to terms with what Foucault meant by power in "specific situations," not because power was his principal concern (possibly it was), but because power inscribes specific "subjects" in such a way that, he argued, one can not avoid power as a reference in the politicized research fields of national history and political theory, crisscrossed as these are by other kinds of "subjects" such as sex and race (Foucault 2003). In a 1984 interview, Foucault remarked:

> . . .we must distinguish between power relations understood as strategic games between liberties—in which some try to control the conduct of others, who in turn try to avoid allowing their conduct to be controlled or try to control the conduct of the others—and the states of domination that people ordinarily call "power." And between the two, between games of power and states of domination, you have technologies of government—understood, of course, in a very broad sense that includes not only the way institutions are governed but also the way one governs one's wife and children. The analysis of these techniques is necessary because it is very often through such techniques that states of domination are established and maintained. There are three levels to my analysis of power: strategic relations, techniques of government, and states of domination. (Foucault 1997, 299)

Foucault's concern for "the subject," over several decades, was explicitly and closely bound to the problem of seeing it in terms other than those given in Enlightenment discourse, i.e. rights, law, the state, etc. Not that the Enlightenment "Subject" wasn't part of the problematic: Foucault was concerned, on the contrary, to show how seeing "the Subject" preeminently as the subject of legal rights was enabled only through the discursive configuration of this subject over against the exclusion, enclosure, domination and subjugation of other historical subjects/figures, e.g. the slave, the prisoner, the insane, the homosexual, and—one might argue given clues from

Foucault's own examples and exclusions—women and children (Hekman 1996).

Even if writers such as Felstead and Jewson were to acknowledge the broader social relations which certainly are interspersed, if not at some points isomorphic, with political and administrative policy governing home-based work, then they still should *want* to see how their categorization of "home-located workers" (i.e. those who are not also employers) into "petty commodity producers" (where they situate "family daycare providers") on one side, and low-wage workers/"homeworkers" on the other side, might function instead as an unacknowledged technology of control in and of "the field."[14] That is to say, such a categorization itself might further disaggregate, "de-classify" and de-politicize these otherwise diversely situated workers, and in so doing forget the social and political dynamics of their grouping, which is part of the very critique brought by Allen and Wolkowitz, among others, that Felstead and Jewson dismiss as too "one-sided." In terms of "re-classifying" (or counter-classifying) home-based work, which analysis of governmentality should help us to accomplish, one might instead situate industrial homeworkers in the same "division" with family daycare providers and personal service homeworkers, even, or especially, from a strictly policy-oriented point of view. From the perspective of these workers, a low-wage is a low-rate is a low-price is a low-income. Technically, the home-based hair cutter is free to start charging more, but she could feel she might lose business and relationships. The same with the child-care provider, only she has less freedom to change prices insofar as the state comes to predominate in the organized demand for child-care. The home-based assembler, never "free" to change piece rates could, and often does, search out other industrial sector employers, as well as other (often home-based) industries, including child-care and hair-cutting (Boris and Prügl 1996; Miraftab 1994).

But even if the "classification" system many homework researchers and advocates are concerned about is altered, and if the decisive issue instead is the controlled relationships of home-based workers *vis à vis* employers and purchasers or contractors of services (including the state), then analysis of what I am calling low-wage homework (such as child-care) reminds us, from the perspective of governmentality, that homeworker "subjectivities" are shaped by a "practice of freedom" which is often in direct conflict with another's practice, to use Foucault's most generic terminology of ethics and power. Felstead and Jewson underestimate this not so much foundational, as ubiquitous, antagonism. Low-wage homeworkers, as we have said, are frequently not paid on time, and occasionally not paid at all. They are by empirical definition "low-paid," although we do certainly know of exceptions to this general rule. In the case that this is not something that an individual homeworker will be able to change in a meaningful way, according to Foucault, what we are seeing are effects of a "state of domination." Within and against the state of domination, we have seen that homeworker/child-care worker organizations utilize an explicit form of "power analysis" to collectively and individually incorporate both transgressive and transformative practices of freedom (Abrams 1999; Tuominen 2002). This is partially what I take from Foucault to be the ethics of the care or technology of the self, at least in terms of the active struggles around home-based work, however broadly or narrowly conceived.[15]

Inside the state of domination, surely, there is another kind of maneuvering room, and here is where, once again, the sexual and racial divisions of labor return (which Felstead and Jewson, to their credit, insist homework researchers must further analyze). But they don't return as though they don't exist outside the home. Felstead and Jewson's politically neutral choice of "household understandings" is helpful to them in one regard: the habitus of sexual distinction, the "androcentric unconscious," and male domination by definition and in practice circulate in and around "comprehensive fields" of social practices and action—concepts appropriate to Bourdieu's (1977) theory of social practice, which Felstead and Jewson cite. Following Bourdieu, "household understandings," are principles of vision, in the most nearly literal sense of that word. One sees a man or woman, a boy or girl, and *immediately* one has already begun dividing space and objects along differential, and in most cases, hierarchical terms (Bornstein 1995). Insofar as "household understandings" intends the kind of divisive negotiations that stereotypically go on in the family/home, they are not incorrect.

The authors of *In Work, at Home* are constrained in their use of "household understandings," however, in a way that is also relevant to a perspective critical of Bourdieu's theory of change in the structure of sexual division, as mine has been implicitly up until now. For if Foucault is correct, if we "distinguish between power relations understood as strategic games between liberties—in which some try to control the conduct of others, who in turn try to avoid allowing their conduct to be controlled or try to control the conduct of the others—and the states of domination that people ordinarily call 'power,'" (Foucault 1997, 299) then, homework researchers must move beyond "habitus" to the technologies of governmentality—i.e. "not only the way institutions are governed but the way one governs one's wife and children" in the telling phrase immediately following this passage—and also be willing to examine how a theory of governmentality may preclude an analysis of what remains outside of domination, what in the context of domestic labor and home-based work one might better understand as "forced labor" *elsewhere*. Thus, even (or especially) where the state wishes to eliminate sexual and other forms of *slavery* and its vestiges (as well as in those places where it lacks the political will to do so), it sees tremendous social promise and economic progress in the massification of subcontracting and very low wage home-based work.

In the European context of public/private promotion and struggle over gender equality, Pierre Bourdieu (2001) acknowledged the productive encounter of self/other struggles with states of masculine domination. As in his much earlier *Outline of a Theory of Practice*, the theory of domination in Bourdieu's later work remained bound both by the circulation of symbolic values—closely tied to both the circular construction of fields, knowledges and distinctive practices—as well as his hallmark notion of habitus—the circulation of social and cultural practices flowing together with subjective cognition, perception, and vision (Bourdieu 1977, 1990). Change in the structure of masculine domination occurs, according to Bourdieu, to the extent that the de-historicization on which masculine domination depends for its permanence is forcibly uprooted, and the erasure of feminine/feminist history and masculine domination themselves are exposed and historicized. Methodologically, this appears to have much in common with Foucault's archaeology of subjugated knowledges, which was also intent on rupturing the hold of dominant discourses by exposing the erasure of minoritarian (and dominant) discourses, as Bourdieu himself noted (Bourdieu 2001, 103).[16]

In the context of First World feminism, the problem of the dehistoricization of the *differential* movements and struggles around value, sex and labor has been repeated (and built upon) many times. One could cite much critical material. Unlike anthropology, much of American and European sociology continues to dismiss variations of "auto-ethnography" in the context of globality as well as inter-nationality, consigning the nomadic subject to the traditional (e.g. anthropological) category of (self-consolidating) Other.[17] Within his own national enclosure, Bourdieu was certainly attentive to "institutional power" (Bourdieu 2001, 85-88). Yet his self-contrasting allusion to Foucault indicates something else: a radical difference in historical object to be sure, but also a note that he is obliged to reiterate about the *History of Sexuality*, namely that the dominant linkage of power to sexuality was always "masculine":

> It follows that the genetic sociology of the sexual unconscious is logically extended into the analysis of the structures of the social universes in

which this unconscious is rooted and reproduces itself, whether it be the divisions embodied in the form of principles of division or the objective divisions that are established between social positions (and their occupants, who are preferentially male or female . . .), the most important of which, from the point of view of the perpetuation of these divisions, is undoubtedly the one which distinguishes the fields devoted to symbolic production. The fundamental opposition, of which Kabyle society offers the canonical form, is 'geared down' or diffracted in a series of homologous oppositions, which reproduce it, but in dispersed and often almost unrecognizable forms . . .These specific oppositions channel the mind, in a more or less insidious way, without ever allowing themselves to be seen in their unity and for what they are, namely, so many facets of one and the same structure of relations of sexual domination. (Bourdieu 2001, 106)

Reading Foucault suggests, often quite explicitly, that it isn't enough—critically—*to see*, as Bourdieu wrote, the "visible changes that have affected the condition of women mask[ing] the permanence of the invisible structures, which can only be brought to light by relational thinking capable of *making the connection between the domestic economy, and therefore the division of labor and powers which characterize it, and the various sectors of the labour market* (the field) in which men and women are involved" (Bourdieu 2001, 106; emphasis in original). Foucault is often quite plain about this: those of us observing the passage of masculine domination from "outside in the academy" need to see how we come to theorize the techniques and apparatuses that allow us—or oblige us—to "see things" and "others" *differently*.[18]

Bourdieu, in a misleading attempt to contrast his work with the *History of Sexuality* (which title, we should remind ourselves, was changed in translation from *The Will to Knowledge*), attempted to "flatten out" Foucault, as Spivak (1993) notes of other prominent readers of Foucault, such as Richard Rorty. Spivak clarifies how Foucault was concerned to show that movements just inside *visible* masculine domination—i.e. the discursive, technical, bodily, and other movements at the *sub-individual* level, at the level of force—*induce* or generate the techniques and apparatuses of truth and power, and ultimately of governmentality, with and through which masculine domination then becomes visible and felt. In this context, of technological "visibility" inside the field of cognition (including *méconnaissance*), the sociologist's power to construct the object is indeed the power to construct the object as *sexual*, holding oneself up as mirror in the process of textualizing the reflexive de-historicization which here constitutes not a mere relation or reflection but a power-laden, governing set of principles in which frame of reference and authority one is to theorize, practice and organize "the sexual." In short, far from a contrast to the *Will to Knowledge, Masculine Domination* succeeds in managing its own truth regime.[19] In the same vein, one might also note Bourdieu's misapprehension at Judith Butler's position on gender performativity in *Gender Trouble*, which he characterizes (much as Alain Lipietz does Antonio Negri's thought) as "voluntaristic." With Butler, one could view what Bourdieu disparagingly labels the postmodern "supersession of dualisms" as the traversing of barriers to social transformation (although one would still have to explain what is meant by supersession). One possible reading of Butler is that heterosexual structuration creates sites of discursive and performative exteriority which function (just) inside the cultural "outside" of the structure. One might think of this exteriority as pure deviations from the norm. In Butler's thinking, the "outside" of this exteriority is the "out-lawed" possibility *within* the cultural. In superseding the binaries—which Bourdieu does not apparently wish to argue is Butler's object—one is obliged to reread structuralism as *prohibition* and its *sites* as sites of resistance and (potential) subversion (Butler 1993).[20]

In the context of work at home as presented by Felstead and Jewson, this kind of resistance might be mundanely simple and extraordinarily subversive: first get together with other homeworkers, next analyze power "diagrammatically,"[21] then act strategically. The contestation of what we are witnessing in the organizing of homeworkers such as child-care providers (and here the language of "witnessing" is itself already discursively positioned in the highly controlled truth-regimes of criminal justice and religious evangelism) remains partially, or perhaps principally, mired in the structuralist metaphor of the legal subject. The prohibition "at work" in home-based labor is that home-based laborers do not—and in the contemporary governmental strategy *cannot*—"get together" with one another, and that if they do it should be only for the purpose of developing those needs which governmental experts dictate (e.g., in the case of the family child-care provider, "professionalization" or training of one highly controlled kind or another). Indeed, it is easy to see in the U.S. case of home-based child-care "provision" that legal prohibitions on collective action are intended to force a greater and greater degree of self-exploitation, or forced giving, of home-based labor. As the Center for Childcare Workforce, the leading national advocacy organization of home-based child-care workers in the United States during the 1990s, noted:

> . . .individual businesses, such as child-care centers and family child-care providers, cannot join together to agree to charge a certain rate, pay a certain wage, or maintain hours of operation. These activities

would constitute price fixing and would violate [ . . .] antitrust laws. Nothing in the law, however, prohibits an individual provider from making her own individual business decisions. (CCW 1999, 35)

From this perspective, the prohibition should extend as well to the child-care worker organization, as in the following: " . . .CCW cannot recommend or suggest that family child-care providers in a community come together and agree to set their fees at a certain rate. We are prohibited from doing so, just as family child-care providers and center directors are . . ." (CCW 1999, 35.) The prohibition is not a meaningless one, even as it is subverted through collective organizing—and indeed CCW was no doubt forced into a certain organizational irony in the particular text I have cited. Unionization efforts of family child-care providers in the state of Illinois *were* preemptively halted through an antitrust suit brought by that state's attorney general some years back. Nonetheless, the Unity Campaign in Virginia and Service Employees Union International Local 880 in Illinois, as well as numerous other organizations (increasingly trade unions) across the country, continue to organize as well as *unionize* home-based child-care workers and home health workers; take over state and local offices; win local and statewide legislation mandating higher rates of reimbursement and employment benefits; and gain due process and grievance procedures in the non-place of home-based care work.

I have taken this detour through Bourdieu, via Foucault, in order to return to "internalized gendering perceived as ethical choice" as a key strategy (alongside the cheapening of labor via structural adjustment) of governmentality today. I have sought to highlight the importance of the discourses and technologies of the state (of which home-based work and the privatization of social welfare in the "globalizing" of domestic economy are prime examples) for the consolidation of normalized "auto-affections" of intersubjective good—a bio- and techno-political process well beyond the need for docile bodies laboring under capitalist self-exploitation (Clough 2000). I have moved in this way to begin to reconnect the circuitry of governmentality, as it were, among the players in the home-based game of technologies of the self and the social, a process which I am suggesting researchers begin viewing more from the perspective of social and biopolitical "organizing" and less from the perspective of either sociological theories of industrial organization or positivist classification.

In one of the few articles examining the organizing experience of home-based child-care workers in the United States, we can see where the resulting differences in approach might begin to emerge. In an article which focuses on the organizing experience of the Center for the Childcare

Workforce, sociologists Cameron Macdonald and David Merrill (2002) argue that if the politics of care work organizing in the United States are to succeed, child-care workers must seek, on the one hand, increasing recognition for their status as professionals givers of care, and on the other, greater "justice" through the redistribution of child-care wages and public subsidies of child-care. They explore some of the tensions—including the misleading "trade-offs"—between seeking institutional (and inter-subjective) recognition for the "labor of love" of child-care work and seeking recognition (and ultimately redistribution) by appealing one way or another to the professional, highly skilled, and demanding work of public child-care provision. They cite the ways in which child-care workers suffer as a result of the degraded status of their work and labor, including the ways in which they continue to care, and continue to give care, even when there is no payment, no respect, no recognition in return. They describe the policy reform-oriented efforts of the Center for the Childcare Workforce to advance institutional recognition and improve the status of child-care workers, as well as increase state distribution of funding for expanded public child-care.

This experience differs in important ways from the home-based child-care organizing campaigns in Rhode Island and Virginia, which learned that far from getting institutional recognition via organizing, what organizing exposed were deeper and thicker layers of sanctioned governmental violence and tactics of control of and inside the home/work place. When McDonnell and Merrill write that "[a]ny attempt to revalue care work must involve not only appeals to redistributive justice, but also to over-coming institutional misrecognition" (Macdonald and Merrill 2002, 73), one must supplement this understanding with the knowledge that, as with Bourdieu's analysis of *méconnaissance* in the context of masculine domina-tion, "institutional misrecognition" almost always follows a path that leads downwards to the dynamics of patriarchal racism and colonization, where the results of "misrecognition" are not merely "a lack of self-esteem" or "poor quality care," as many researchers have pointed out, but the loss of work and home, hunger, untreated illness, imprisonment, destitution, and death.

Such techniques of government continue to mediate between what Foucault termed the "strategic relations" and "power relations" (the "games of power" and "states of domination") implicated by a politics of recognition. Underneath, in the turbulence of the latter, however, emerge a politics (and ethics) that discover in the technologies of government the vio-lent flows of the "way institutions are governed but also the way one gov-erns one's wife and children": a politics of organizing labor in the bodily mode in powerful places like home. Only at that point one would be able not to forget (through historicization) the female worker as a paradigmatic figure of capitalist globality which is constantly being virtualized, hidden, and forgotten. Theorizing and challenging this violence through bottom-up organizing produces a new series of demands, in pathways that circulate now, as much as ever, through the political economy of affective labor, the neoliberal state and home.

As Tuominen (1994b, 242) argues, "to understand the work of child-care, a theoretical framework is needed which reveals gender and race as the fundamental structures by which all child-care work is organized, regardless of its provision in formal or informal markets." In such a framework, one would have to supplement gender and race with internationality in the division of child-care work; and in so doing, one would have to do in theory as in homeworker organizing: i.e., comprehend the networked relations of biopolitical power and capitalist production which both undergird and attempt to destabilize organizing efforts on different sides of the divide(s). In short, we would have to see in "organizing" how the inexorable desire and search for an "expanded textuality of value"—a concept I explore in the next chapter—is crossed by the sexualized, racialized and international-ized governmental violence of what might still be called "primitive capital-ist accumulation," following Maria Mies, or "biopolitics," with practice norming theory, following Foucault.[22] The types and intensity of this vio-lence vary in such a way that any effort to catalog them would have to first acknowledge the epistemic violence in the task.[23] Theorizing labor in the ontological realm of affectivity ("care work" being one such example), as Hardt and Negri (2000) propose, has the virtue of acknowledging the unstable productivity for capital of unwaged reproductive labor, ontologi-cal instability as such in a (capitalist) sociality that requires so much care, thought and affective energy to be reproduced; but waged or unwaged, affective labor is neither the same everywhere, nor does it produce equiva-lent values (or instabilities), in (or for) structurally adjusting global capital, itself a divided subject (which I will not take on for the moment). In the concluding chapter, I take up some of the claims being made for affective and reproductive labor today, in an effort to give time to the place that inspired them.

Chapter Six

# Political Economy and the Unpredictable Politics of Women's Home-Based Work

. . .Rather than the refusal to work of the Jamaican slaves in 1834, which is cited by Marx as the only example of zero-work, quickly recuperated by imperialist maneuvers, it is the long history of women's work which is a sustained example of zero-work: work not only outside of wage-work, but *in one way or another*, "outside" of the definitive modes of production. The displacement required here is a transvaluation, an uncatastrophic *im*plosion of the search for validation via the circuit of productivity. Rather than a miniaturized and thus controlled metaphor for civil society and the state, the power of the *oikos*, domestic economy, can be used as the model of the foreign body unwittingly nurtured by the *polis*. (Gayatri Chakravorty Spivak, *In Other Worlds*)

In chapters one and two, I attempted to show how in explaining the resurgence of homework, one needed to look at the sexual division of labor, and specifically women's unpaid household labor, to see how and why wage-earning work increasingly finds its way into the home—and how this is typically a many-sided strategy. As writers such as Johanna Brenner (2000) have indicated, it is theoretically insufficient and politically mistaken to argue that women's domination and domestication are primarily the effects of ideology. Or rather, that "ideology," if understood only in the domain of consciousness, is insufficient. On the contrary, Brenner argues that sexual "inequality" as measured by pay and hours of work, domestic labor, economic "status," and property ownership, rather than an ideological effect, is an effect of ongoing divisions of labor which practically and materially link women, as sexually divided labor, with biological and social reproduction. One would have to take note of the thousands of popular women's magazine articles on so-called "supermoms," i.e. those with full-time caregiving and income-earning practices, to see how the time and value dilemmas of simultaneous production and reproduction typically get resolved with powerful truisms like, "you don't have to choose between work and family, you can do it all!" Analysis of contemporary women's magazines leads to the unmistakable conclusion that there is no more powerful ideology around than what is "in practice": in the beginning there were women working sixty to seventy hours a week, *then* there were "supermoms."

As we have seen, a corresponding change in the turbulent framework of contemporary capitalism is that in the United States and elsewhere, homework, in an increasing number of sectors, is now positioning women for housework at the site of value-production. Sherry Ahrentzen's (1992) cultural study of home-based work bears this subtle, but eminently "non-ideological" shift out:

> After completing a 2-hour interview, a homeworker hesitated when I got up to leave. "I must tell you," she said, "working at home has made me a housewife." Her husband and teenage children do not see her as "working" since she does not display the exterior signs of professional work, that is, she does not dress up and go out . . .Because her family sees her at home all day, they now expect her to do all the housework. When she tells friends she works at home, they exclaim that she now must be able to get all her household chores done. She complains. (Ahrentzen 1992, 131)

On the other hand, home-based labor studies in South and East Asia, where structural adjustment has increased women's home-based labor and production across the board, find that household labor remains more or less what it used to be before taking up homework, that is to say home-based work in no way diminishes the burden of domestic labor (Balakrishnan 2002). Homework research in general points to this conclusion: that in most cases, homework does not reduce the amount of time spent on housework. Yet, there is still very limited data on just how much time we are talking about, either in paid or unpaid home-based work. The point being that in the structurally-adjusted juxtaposition of housework and homework, paid home-based labor rearticulates domestic labor with capitalist production, and the magnitude of unpaid labor remains more or less immeasurable. Homework, in this context, could be seen as a more direct *valorization* of housework than the patriarchal "family wage" ever was. Of course, this defies the old Marxist critique against viewing domestic labor in terms of surplus value production, which in short maintains that housework cannot obey the law of value in quantitative terms, precisely because in capitalist terms it cannot be measured and therefore has to remain secret in capitalist production (i.e. in the privatized space of the "natural forces of social labor").[1] The corresponding theme in empirical sociological studies of housework is that even when you can measure it, as an increasing number of time-use studies (including some homework studies) are attempting, one is still left with the task of explaining housework in "exchange" terms such as value, that "simple, contentless thing" that still exercises the ghosts of two centuries of political economy.[2] The political implication of much of the work on value in the context of domestic labor, however, bears out the simple, contentless truth that whether or not you understand it to produce value, domestic labor still doesn't constitute a class subject in the restrictive terms of much Marxist political economy.[3]

A more nuanced school of thought on the question of the value of domestic labor, with direct relation to theories of class formation, has loosely gathered around the work of scholars associated with the journal *Rethinking Marxism*. A number of these writers have collaborated to broaden the discussion on class formation as a struggle over time and value—in the home and elsewhere. For this loosely configured school of revisionist Marxism, *class formation* refers less to surplus value and more to the production, appropriation, and distribution of *surplus labor*. In their effort to rethink Marxism, they are obliged to go beyond Marx, who highlighted those class processes in the production and appropriation of surplus labor more or less exclusively in the expanded form of waged, industrial commodity production. That is to say, in Marx's labor theory of value, the sales clerk who earns the minimum wage selling clothing for a profit-making retailer technically was not producing surplus value, while the homeworkers who stitched the garments were. I do not want to lose sight of this methodological distinction, even while shifting theory to value-production in multiple sites of labor, including sites of production and distribution, as the Rethinking Marxism (hereafter RM) group does for the household (Fraad, Resnick and Wolff 1994; Gibson-Graham, Resnick and Wolff 2000).

While they are intent on rethinking class-based politics, the RM writers are equally interested in moving beyond *a priori* theoretical categories, identities and formulations, particularly those related to value and class (Gibson-Graham, Resnick and Wolff 2000, 9–10). While a number of issues are raised by their generally post-stucturalist perspective, two elements of their overall argument about class interest me above all: one, that by focusing on the production and circulation of surplus labor, Marx's labor theory of value can be shifted from a narrow focus on commodity production; and two, that multiple class (domestic, capitalist, communist, feudal, etc.) processes simultaneously co-exist to form an overdetermined social structure (or a "socially structured overdetermination"). The theory of overdetermination, drawn from Freudian psychoanalysis by Althusser in the 1960s and taken up in the decades that followed by a variety of Marxist-inspired cultural studies, suggested that the social and political articulation (or in psychoanalytic terms, the "suturing") of multiple "class" processes (including the social production of race, gender, sexuality, and nation, for example) is more central in terms of arresting and altering social and political change than the traditional class struggle over the industrial wage and control of the work process. That is, capital and labor are not the only, or at times, even the most important, determinants of the complex arrangements of power, contestation, and control in modern societies "structured in dominance" (Hall 1986).

This understanding of class may provide some better understanding of how home-based workers do and don't, will and won't, appear in either traditional or emerging class-based politics. My premise is that in the turbulent order of globalization, the biopolitical control of the sexual, international, and home-based flows of an ever-expanded "textuality of value," to use Gayatri Chakravorty Spivak's (1987b) formulation, becomes the most important task for capitalists seeking class control. The so-called "race to the bottom" in which subcontracted labor is reduced to the lowest possible exchange value is nothing new for capital, which continues to depend on incalculable gifts of time that must appear precisely not as time, or anything measurable, but as duty or, especially in its increasingly financialized form, debt.[4] Whether we think of this as the payment of the claim on future labor, i.e. the debt to capital, or as "labor of love," i.e. the powerfully configured obligation to home, children, loved ones, family, "community," and so on, we are obliged to think through the ethics of the giving of time in the political economy of home-based labor. Focusing on the production, appropriation and distribution of surplus household labor, the RM group draws our attention to the site—both a spatial and temporal "non-place," as we saw in chapter two—of the "invisible" flows of labor that home-based labor researchers, among others, have been documenting over the past two decades.

Drawing on Marx's (1973) distinction between necessary and surplus labor, where necessary labor refers to the labor required to reproduce one's own subsistence (which is already, we have seen, a methodological aporia), the RM group creates an opening to the complex theorizing of class relations and interactions both within households and among households, the state, and capitalist and other enterprises. As some commentators have suggested, it is not clear whether the RM authors' multi-class model of household-state relations altogether succeeds in its account of post-1973 class struggles in the United States.[5] As Spivak hopefully acknowledges, whether the authors fully succeed in the space of that argument doesn't matter so much, since the point of theorizing the "feudal" (or communist) household, as they put it, is not to pin the household to a particular historical mode of production, but to rethink the *approach* to historical modes of production inaugurated by Marx and Engels, the dominant reading of which highlighted a progressive passage from one dominant mode of production to another, more advanced one (Fraad, Resnick and Wolff 1994, ix–xvi). The orthodox mode-of-production reading of Marx and Engels, particularly in the Second International, was inclined to view social and political progress as more or less determined in the modern period by intensified factory worker and party struggle against the state and capital. It was not inclined to see how factory workers might occupy more than one, or sometimes opposed, modes of production (capitalist at work, feudalist at home, for example), nor how the interactions between modes might influence the otherwise privileged, male-centered factory-floor "struggle," itself a metonym for sociality *tout court*. Far from superceding the feudal mode of production, the RM authors theorize the household as a principal site of ongoing class relations in which male wage workers, with the legalistic backing of the state and the normative support of patriarchy, command the surplus labor of housewives: "feudal lords" in an era of capitalism.

Given other powerful Marxist-feminist arguments (e.g. Fortunati 1995) that women's unpaid household labor is indirectly waged labor and therefore constitutes a class relationship between housewives and capitalists mediated by male wage-workers, yet another theory of household labor may appear unnecessary. However, I would agree with commentators that the discussion of multiple modes of production (and, more importantly, their articulation) in *Bringing It All Back Home* shouldn't be read as an alternative explanatory theory or model, good or bad. Rather, I would argue that it accomplishes something that earlier Marxist-feminist theorizing rarely attempted: an alternative theory of class formation based on household surplus labor and the articulation of multiple modes of production. In differentiating the Marxist category of class internally and looking at its total composition in macro-economic analysis, they simultaneously differentiate it externally, suggesting we theorize class beyond the confines of both existing political-economic and cultural categories as well as the "dominant mode of production." Theorizing class in multiple sites of the production, appropriation and distribution of surplus labor as the RM writers variously do—including self-appropriative domestic labor, for example—Marx's distinction between necessary and surplus labor gives way to the turbulent excesses of the flows of value in contemporary global-local society. As Jenny Cameron remarks in *Class and Its Others*:

> . . . the feminine domestic subject is the agent of change bringing about a transformation in domestic class processes . . . To represent women as acting political subjects rather than victims who are acted upon, and households as sites of a diverse range of class processes rather than just a single traditional class process, is to constitute fluidity in the economic and political terrain and to multiply the possibilities for transformation in the domestic situation. (Gibson-Graham, Resnick, and Wolff, 60)

A key element of the challenge of rethinking class along these lines is to collapse class as a category and rewrite it as both a metaphor and process. This deconstructive move has the additional charge of immediately linking class to sex and race. For if the force or power of class derives from the production, appropriation and distribution of surplus labor (including domestic labor) on the one hand, and the articulation of differential modes of production, on the other, then it would be more or less contingent upon us to theorize class differently than in the past, where political economic privileging of the subject of Fordist wage-work and male breadwinning mirrored the burly proletarian struggles in the "streets and in the suites." As Cameron notes, " . . . domestic labor and gendered becomings in households are always already instances of difference." It would come as no surprise if, as representatives of class-as-such, domestic labor and "gendered becomings in households" were to disturb the sleep of the grumpy old men of Marxism and "class struggle" past and present. What would be a surprise, however, is if, while rejecting domestic labor and gendering as stand-ins for class, Marxists somehow managed to keep "class" as a veiled stand-in for domestic labor and gendering.

Such an analysis of household surplus labor offers a tremendous resource in theorizing the flows of value in neoliberal global hegemony. Homework, at the base (but not the end) of the long chains of value production, is rooted in international sexual divisions of labor which simultaneously position women as houseworkers and caregivers, primary income earners, and wage workers, community "servants" and voluntary workers, in the rapid economic deterioration flowing from structural adjustment. The 1970s revolts of women and feminists in the United States and Europe from housework, sexual reproduction, and sexual subordination, were recuperated in Asia, Africa and Latin America with out-migration of domestic servants, child adoption services, and the proliferation of sex tourism, as well as home-based service and industrial labor of all other kinds (Dalla Costa and Dalla Costa 1999; Parreñas 2001).

Thus, like the home-based woman worker, surplus household labor is, *par excellence*, a paradigmatic global figure and phenomenon, the mobilization of which differs widely both between and within the structurally adjusted debtor countries of the South and creditor nations such as the United States. Such differences require international historical analyses that might nevertheless draw on the insights of the specifically *class* analysis presented here. For if the claim on surplus labor, including surplus household labor, is what drives class processes forward, then the articulation of international surplus labor would clearly be on the agenda of an international capitalist class. From a distance, house/homework in South Asia may appear considerably different from home-based child-care in North America. Yet they both rely on one form or another of sexual and ethnoracial division of surplus household labor to position women's time and work at home and produce value for neo-liberal capital—and in ways that home-based workers are not only conscious of (to reference a more ideology-centered discourse of class politics and history), but in ways they are resistant to (Rowbotham and Mitter, 1994). And in this space, consciousness of resistance, and resistance to forgetting, while not the same thing, may be thought of in the (domestic) economy of the same.

The commodification of home-based child-care, and the emerging politics of child-care provider organizing in the United States—the limited but potent example I have presented here—should certainly be understood in the context of (the unacknowledged debt of) massively accumulated wealth in post-industrial societies produced in part, as we have seen, from the home-based production of value flowing from hemispheric South to North. Bracketing this, the question remains of how child-care, once refused as "freely given" or gratuitous time in the wake of its state-controlled commodification, will be politically controlled. From the top of the political structure, emerging policy calls in the United States for universal early childhood education are one step in charting the direction of the future class politics of home-based labor.[6] The experience of the Unity Campaign in Virginia gives some indication, however, of other political openings enabled, in this case, by "bottom-up" organizing. There, child-care providers have refused not only the devalorization of their labor through continuing efforts to increase rates of reimbursement and gain formal employment benefits such as health insurance; they have refused as well many of the elements of the top-down and punitive state control of their work, the political organization of their labor, and their own homes.

In linking their home-based work to worker, community, and ultimately, child education and organizing, the specifically African American
and immigrant child-care providers of the Unity Campaign launch their
labor—understood at least in part as the "call to service" and "love of
children"—into an expanding economy of sometimes violent circulation,
flows and extraction of value. In this respect, I would have to disagree
with otherwise interesting commentators on the political economy of gift-
exchange such as Frow (1997), who argues that the gift is *structurally*
insignificant in late capitalist societies:

> [A] concept of the public good grounded in the category of the inalien-
> able gift cannot be applied in any direct way to the social. The state is
> not a 'gift' domain because its forms of sociability do not involve the
> magical and dangerous ties of personal obligation; obligation at this
> level is an abstract matter. Nor of course is the market a domain of
> the gift, both because it is built on the price mechanism and because,
> like the state, its workings are complex, impersonal, and abstract. In
> any strict sense, the concept of the gift is irrelevant to the structural
> understanding of modern societies, with the exception of the micro-
> level of everyday life. (Frow 1997, 216–17)

As Yang's (2000) political economic study of Wenzhou Province demon-
strates, the market is certainly a domain of the gift; there, ritual expen-
diture of wealth "launches production," in the increasingly capitalist
market-place of "socialism with Chinese characteristics." And somewhat closer to "home," it is not so clear to me that child-care provision
in the United States, especially home-based child-care, is merely a phenomenon at the "micro-level of everyday life," a formulation that has
the nineteenth-century ring of "natural forces of social labor." This is
indeed surprising, given Frow's partial reliance on the anthropologist
Annette Weiner's (1992) work on the gift, in which Weiner understands
the "inalienable possession" of the gift as the power or *mana* produced in
the "enchainment" of the circulating gift (typically a textile produced by
women). Indeed, Frow cites Weiner in this context:

> Here is where we locate women's exclusive role: it is in the ritu-
> als surrounding human reproduction and cloth production where
> women gain control over mana which, in turn, gives them a domain
> of authority and power in their own right. And here, also, we locate
> the source of the 'spirit of the gift.' (Weiner 1992, 50, cited in Frow
> 1997, 113–14)

It is a methodological (if not also political) mistake not to see in organized home-based child-care labor the "spirit of the gift" in which women specifically "gain control over mana," understood as biopolitical power. For is it not the case that the sometimes "magical," sometimes "fierce" love (which we know also to be a labor) of a mother, and a child-care provider, has a certain power in society that extends beyond the micro-level of everyday life? The local and global histories and politics of home-based work—as well as, for example, welfare and reproductive rights in related, but different ways—suggest that they do. Indeed, I am arguing that the "provision" (and here, finally, this term assumes its general economic weight) of child-care—an area of immense biopolitical, and in this sense social and economic, power—is not all-enclosed, or best understood, by relations of exchange and commodification. This, of course, does not imply that all women find in providing child-care "a domain of authority and power in their own right," to cite Weiner, but it does mean that the women who are increasingly struggling over their time will find a place or a situation (in the case I have presented, the local appendages of the ex-welfare state) where control rests not so much on abstract exchange or money, upon which Marx built his analysis, as in the "need *not* to relinquish the things which are the object of most intense desire," including the children in their care.[7] At the point of this powerfully organized and contested desire, the impossibility of the theoretical measure of the "value" of domestic and home-based labor gives way to a "value beyond value," situated in the complex macro and micro-levels of social and biological reproduction (Negri 1999).

## POLITICAL ECONOMY IN THE 21ST CENTURY—THE STORY SO FAR

The specter of women's work haunts capitalism. From women and children being set to work in the nineteenth century by the "invisible threads" of capitalism to today's globalized homeworkers, the "hidden," "invisible," and cyclically forgotten labor of women—derogated by Marx as a natural and thereby "freely appropriated" force of social production—marks a recurring, ghostly passage through history and political economy. The historic appearance of women's work in late twentieth century decrees of the International Labor Organization or the Venezuelan constitution of 1999[8] insistently reminds feminists and critical political economists (undoubtedly in different registers) that cultural, political and social struggles over reproduction, gender, and sexual equality are fully implicated in what is thought today as both neo-liberal economic crisis *and* counter-hegemonic politics. Lurking in the workingman's historic demand for higher wages and a shorter working-day is the paradigmatic figure of the globalized home-based women worker. Class, in this respect, has long been a ghostly appearance of what we have come to think of as gender—and with gender always race.[9]

How are contemporary political economists attending to this aporia? The "autonomist" school of Marxism, particularly the work of Antonio Negri, took its historical cues from the organized mass refusal of capitalist work and restructuring in Italy in the 1960s and 1970s. Negri and others argued that a qualitative leap in global working class struggle had led to something more than the traditional refusal by workers to give alienated labor time in conditions of exploitation.[10] Unlike prior class struggles for shorter hours and higher wages, struggles in the 1960s and 1970s, close in historiographical time to what we now understand as the close of the Fordist period, were at best isomorphic with previous ones. In the more recent period, autonomist Marxists ascribed the antagonistic relationship with capital that constituted the working class to a more extended, if not immaterial laboring body than the stereotypical assembly line worker of the previous era. Rather than the length of the working day or size of the pay packet, it was the communicative and cooperative capacities and the social organization—in short, the highly developed social and affective capacities—of workers that was being struggled over. Indeed, by the 1960s, class struggle in Europe and the United States had expanded well beyond the factory floor and beyond traditional working class demands. The era of the "social factory," as Negri and Mario Tront termed it (Red Notes 1988), saw capital increasingly exploiting labor outside the factory walls, in the substrata of everyday life (in for example the hyper-fashioning of consumer bodies, needs and tastes; the commodification of knowledge and information; the extensive use of subcontracting in a more and more service-oriented economy; and the rise of life-long education). The "social factory" thesis signified that labor increasingly responded in kind by exposing and rejecting what French social theorist Guy Debord termed the "society of the spectacle," and gaining through direct action and political organization reductions in the costs of living and valorization of other aspects of life—gaining in the process what these and other theorists called a "social wage."[11]

While I agree with this analysis, I would also argue that what historically and theoretically modeled the shifts in industrial and post-industrial class power and organization in the latter half of the twentieth century somehow is lodged (hidden) inside the analysis itself. The succession of the era of the "mass worker" by the "socialized worker" was premised on the shift to "a working day so extended as not only to comprise within itself *the relation between production time and reproduction time, as a single whole,* but also and above all to extend the consideration of time over the entire life-space of the labour market."[12] Embedded in this singular transition is the figure whose labor had been "socialized" long before any other—the home-based female worker.

In what follows briefly, I explore the biopolitical transformations of reproductive labor in the twentieth century, changes which have engendered new techniques of production and reproduction, control of bodies and labor power, as well as sites of resistance and refusal. In doing so, I offer, via a critical reading of autonomist Marxism, a theoretical supplement to the Marxist-feminist theoretical revelation of the productivity for capital of unpaid reproductive labor (traditionally conceived "woman's work"). I offer by way of conclusion a "reproductive" labor theory of value that both embraces and critically interrogates the implications of neo-Marxist conceptions of value for understanding social movement and political change today.

As we have seen, studies of home-based work reveal the ways in which homework is both drawn to and, ironically, productive of unpaid labor in the home. Since the early 1970s, Marxist feminists have exposed "domestic labor," the unpaid work of home, as a powerful source of economic value production, class formation, and gendering, among other things. Leopoldina Fortunati's (1995) trenchant analysis of housework, prostitution and social reproduction challenges the obscuring of the sexual division of labor in the political economy built up around the socialized, stereotypical European/ American household. Beginning with Marx's dualistic analysis that work must appear as waged work in capitalism and that value in capitalism is measured by alienated labor time, Fortunati argues that the dialectic which, according to Marx, pervades capital (i.e. the ghost effect of paid/unpaid or necessary/surplus labor in capital), must be held equally to apply to non-wage work such as housework and the physical and affective reproduction of living labor. The reproductive labor of housework, childcare, and sexual reproduction, seen as non-work (because unwaged and engendered), enables capital to interpret "productive labor" as work, in the material-ideological sense, and to exploit it as surplus value-producing labor. Taking this logic to its end, Fortunati insists that housework *must* appear under capitalism as a "natural force of social labor" *in order for* waged work to appear as value-production. Consonant with other Marxist feminists of recent decades, Fortunati recasts the debate over whether women's household labor should appear as simply any other form of productive social labor: "the real difference between production and reproduction is not that of value/non-value, but that while production both *is* and *appears as* the creation of value, reproduction *is* the creation of value but *appears otherwise.*"[13]

Such an understanding radically extends Negri's (1991) brilliant reading of Marx's *Grundrisse*. There Negri asserts that "capital is not just specific exploitation within production, but it *also acquires for itself, gratuitously, social dimensions which are only produced by the living force of labor.*" What is added "gratuitously" is accomplished by a composition of living-labor which "preserves the value of capital as well as . . . which comes to be enriched in the cooperation of large masses, the labor which follows the scientific potential of society *as well as that which results from the simple increase of the population.*"[14] The gratuitousness of the "simple increase of the population" is, I am arguing, one of the ghostly effects of women's home-based work—which in the context of capitalism is also a "nurturing of the political,"[15] as we have seen in the organization of home-based child-care workers in the United States and home-based industrial workers elsewhere.

While classical Marxist political economy understood the extraction of value from surplus labor to produce a measurable profit, which, when reintroduced into productive circulation, became capital, Negri and his co-author Michael Hardt have argued that by the late twentieth century, money (capital's forceful claim on future labor) had broken free of production. Neither exchange value (the wage) nor surplus value (capitalist profit) any longer functions as measure of value. Production time, understood by Marx as the relative and absolute ground of surplus value extraction, no longer adequately measures either the quantity or quality of value-production, which proceeds on an expansive social (i.e. subjectivized but also sub-individual) and global scale. Labor-power has become mobile and cannot be commanded as it had been in the Fordist era. Money, once the expression of a narrowly conceived "regime of exchange between capital and more or less subjectivized labor-power," now launches an entirely new regime of exchange. Money, as capital's "claim on future labor," assumes a more expansive role today, and the labor theory of value has been "transfigured into monetary theory—constructed on the horizon of globalization, organized by imperial command" (Negri 1999, 82).

While Negri goes on to argue that labor no longer operates as the limit or measure of value or productivity but rather as the "living antagonism" within capitalism, he also argues that labor-power "is presented as the social fabric, as population and culture, traditions and innovation, and so forth—in short, its productive force is exploited within the processes of social reproduction."[16] What grounds labor and simultaneously pulls it back from what Negri describes as the "non-place" of value with respect to labor, are forces as much pre-modern as post-modern: population, culture, traditions, etc. Thus labor power in Negri's take on postmodern political economy refers to the biopolitical expansiveness and mobility of the production, appropriation and distribution of what Hardt and Negri (2000) have termed "immaterial labor" (a term which, we will see, is not the same as "reproductive labor"). This is a different, although complementary view of political economy than one finds in the literature on economic globalization. One now expects this story of capital's reply to zero-work: with the slightest hint of social or political turbulence, capital's subcontractors pack up and leave waged "women workers" (long ago socialized or "house-wifized") in a flash, in search of cheaper, more flexible, more cooperative labor-power. What results from combining these two distinct but overlapping perspectives is a spectacular doubling of the ghost of women's work. As we have seen, this has led many researchers of today's homeworking phenomenon to speculate that for labor power exploited in the cycles of global (re)production at the start of the twenty-first century, there is literally "no-place" like home.[17]

As Sassia Sasken, David Harvey and others showed nearly two decades ago, capitalist globalization has reached a non-linear point of more or less instantaneous local and global mobility. The globalization of production has taken the form of an intensification of the social and communal forms of development that modulate and enmesh productive and reproductive forces: for example, massive increases in the educational, information and service sectors (including commodified "women's work" such as childcare) in industrializing and post-industrial economies; the communication and affect-orientation of a greater number of labor sectors in these economies today; and the proliferation via subcontracting and outsourcing of so-called informal, precarious, home-based and other kinds of labor. When Hardt and Negri term this new composition of labor, wholly subsumed in capitalist production, "immaterial labor," one may take pause.[18] By "immaterial," Hardt and Negri ask us to recall in particular Marx's distinction between the *formal subsumption* of labor—when capital encounters labor in so many "alien" forms, with their own distinct rules, traditions and cultures—and the *real subsumption* of labor, when capital has internalized labor in its own specifically capitalist sociality and mode of production. Nevertheless, even though immaterial, the real subsumption of labor does not signify a loss in antagonism for these writers. If capital no longer encounters labor outside itself—as alien to capital—this does not mean that labor is no longer antagonistic to capital. On the contrary, "the social capacity of reproduction, the productive surplus of cooperation, the 'small-scale circulation,' the new needs and desires produced by the struggles," such aspects of the real subsumption of labor have led to a situation where virtually all productive and reproductive work is either directly or indirectly "waged" work. As a result, there is no labor time anymore standing *outside* capital as the external reference or measure for labor time expended within capitalism.[19] Consequently, the objective relationship of antagonism between necessary and surplus labor described by Marx in *Grundrisse* has progressively expanded and intensified. Labor is now *subjectively* and more or less *immediately* antagonistic to capital. We are in a time, as Negri (1991) famously put it, of "Marx beyond Marx," where the struggle over the time and subjectivity of labor has assumed a wholly different speed and texture.[20]

What has transformed the antagonism is both the loss of labor time as measure of value and the displacement of value-production onto what these and other writers term "affect" (Negri 1999). That is to say, in purely spatial terms, the antagonism focused on the factory floor in Fordism has extended to all sites of capitalist sociality: the home, the office, transportation, the internet, health care, education, child-care, popular culture, body culture, morality, political organization, etc. The "moving contradiction," as Marx (1973) termed capital, has extended more deeply into the viscera of life itself. Such a shift does not imply traditional concepts of class, to be sure. There may indeed be new (and old) sectors of stereotypically "affective laborers"—therapists and caregivers are two that come to mind—but that is not what Hardt and Negri mean by affective labor. On the one hand, they mean to highlight the permeability of the line between paid and unpaid labor, and in this way force a rethinking of the phase-shifts between commodification and de-commodification, long noted by homework researcher Ursula Huws (2003), among others.[21] On the other hand, given the tremendous mobility and shifting both within globalization as well as the micro-level of everyday life, value is now being produced more or less everywhere and all the time: from the patenting of genetically modified food, to the shaping of appetites, to the mechanized harvesting of crops, to the marketing of fast food franchises, to take just one example of the production, circulation, and distribution of value today (Thacker 2005).

In relation to this change, we should recall that in the Fordist era of the "mass worker" there was also no abstract or statistical measure of value for specifically *reproductive* labor, other than the workingman's "socially necessary labor," as Marx put it. And this, too, was always limited to a sexually, racially and colonially divided "society of labor." So was the working class being reproduced differently from itself than it is today, as Fraad, Resnick, and Wolff (1994) asked more than a decade ago? Or was the scission of value from measure already "affective" inside the developing states of capitalist sociality—especially as it related to the micro-level of power, on the one hand, and colonialism, on the other? As we saw in previous chapters, there is ample documentation of the changing social norms and governmental forms—the biopolitics—of European and American social policy, beginning in the late eighteenth century. Housing, sanitation, education, philanthropy, child-care, and marriage, to name just a few—were all quantified and measured with a view to modulating social divisions and incipient class formations. As Foucault, Donzelot and others demonstrated so clearly, the *dispositifs* of these fields were always bound to the abstract value-measures of labor, even as they were directly mobilized by and for governmental apparatuses such as "welfare," "security" and "public health." As we noted in chapter two, by the turn of the twentieth century (if not earlier), a robust science of home economics was created around the European and American household, whose explicit purpose was to increase the productivity of domestic labor (Hayden 1981). And throughout the nineteenth and twentieth centuries, there was the violent capitalist accumulation realized in the stark forms of imperialism and colonial genocide.[22]

To suggest today, as Hardt and Negri do, that "affective labor" is *now* hegemonic within the field of class struggle may be correct, but also misleading in a way. As we see briefly in analysis of the ritual economy, where women's gift (of time and other things) must be forgotten—and therefore the supposed prestige, sacrifice, and obligation that were to accompany *her* gift also effaced—so apparently in the theory of value-affect.[23] It bears repeating that "women's work" has long invested "universal" (and now global) wage and value production not only with time and energy, but with affect and subjectivity too.[24] And although Hardt and Negri gesture to the problem, there remains the troubling prospect that the well-educated artisans and biopoliticians of the information economy will not only forget, in the political/policy realm, but continue to exploit, in the affective realm, the gratuitousness of the very complex, "simple increase" in (global-local) population and change in "social fabric" and culture.

And thus, I return to the opening citation of this chapter on women's work as the sustained historical example of "zero-work," work outside waged labor and thus "invaluable," which capital has continuously sought to colonize, discipline and subsume in the sense of the old (but certainly not *passé*) imperialist and patriarchal orders, and which now it seeks increasingly to control in the turbulent expansiveness of global production and value-extraction (e.g. ongoing and wrenching policies of structural adjustment). Today again, there is an opening to contested claims on "affect" (in the form of attention, training, education, "care," and children), on the one hand, as well as to social claims (via material debt and consumption) on future reproductive-productive labor, on the other hand. In both cases, the claims rest on a turbulent recoding of specifically female workers, an increasing number of them home-based, in both old and new class categories and terms.[25]

Such arguments are important for understanding the divides at the heart of contemporary global class politics that studies of home-based labor, among others, imply. They could also be important for understanding the displacements and modulations of the home-based female worker's body in the full assertion of affect and the extended crisis of global capitalism. For once broken out of the circuit of value, either through social organization or violent displacement into the structure of debt, reproductive labor is returned in another ghostly form, marked both by shocks to the system as well as highly focused sexual and racial politics. Agency "from the bottom up" emerges not as the disciplined, organized body of counter-hegemonic struggle, but as indeterminate forces of life both actively circulating gifts of time and energy as well as struggling against neoliberal capitalism's piratical treasuring of them. Indeed, in the twentieth century, the long line of affective labor has come to further change the relationship between production-time and life-time such that, in the words of Hardt and Negri, life

> . . . is now completely inverted with respect to how the discipline of political economy understands it. Life is no longer produced in the cycles of reproduction that are subordinated to the working day; on the contrary, life is what infuses and dominates all production. In fact, the value of labor and production is determined deep in the viscera of life. Industry produces no surplus except what is generated by social activity—and this is why, buried in the great whale of life, value is beyond measure.[26]

For Marxists, the laboring body—and for Marxist-feminists, the racialized female body in particular—has been the placeholder for both value and subjectivity in capitalist sociality. In the post-Fordist period, the identification of the home-based female worker with reproductive labor offers a way to see the emergence of a new figure of overdetermined class politics that is "more or less immediately" antagonistic to capitalist governmentality. In the globalized economy's volatile, unhinged state between order and disorder, however, one sees not so much a subjective identification between productive and reproductive labor as a kind of kinship, a "bio-diversity" of sexual and familial relations, between turbulence—as the emergence of a paradigm of flows and controls of vastly differentiated labor energies and forces which seeks only its own infinite social reproduction— and the new forms of political organization and contestation of the global- ized female homeworker, for example (Parisi and Terranova 2000). Thus, while Marxist-feminists have argued that capital's strategy is premised on the claim on future reproductive labor, others are pointing to the prospect of capital's no longer registering (that is, not registering in the same way or places) whether labor *tout court* does or does not recognize capital's claim on its self or its futurity, much as petty commodity producers ('capitalists' is not the right term historically or politically) did not recognize the claims on their future by a feudal aristocracy in the early modern period.

Given such a thought, strategies of capitalist-state control, as well as approaches to organizing reproductive labor (including home-based workers), do appear more important, and turbulent, than ever. On the shaky ground of the division of reproductive labor, wage labor no longer describes every form of value production, even as most labor, particularly in the service-based capitalist economies, becomes either directly or indi- rectly waged. This has been a tough deconstructive point for traditional leftists and labor organizers to grasp in practical terms. The flows of female labor in the "bodily mode" (e.g. productivity increases imported into the United States from China) and reproductive value mode (e.g. experimenta- tions with biomaterialization and artificial life) are emerging as new sources of valorization as well as new sites of control for global-nationalist class governmentality. Confronted with these (both "pre-capitalist" and emerg- ing) needs for primitive accumulation and free appropriation of forces of nature—including the ghostly woman worker and "life itself" in today's biotech laboratories—how are we to theorize the circumvention, if that is the right word, of the shifting needs of the capitalist class for theft of "Nature" and the treasuring of Nature's "free" gifts (Burkett 1999)?

Missing in this question are the interactions that are undoubtedly occurring between the old "factory-floor" and new "social factory" flows of labor, as well as, in a different way, between the remnants and new configurations of industrial capitalism and the emerging forms of cybernetic capitalism. Surplus value in industrial capitalism is of course still being extracted, most aggressively at the ends and along the edges of the long global commodity chains which home-based labor studies, for one, documents.[27] But the difference between home-based work "at the bottom" and home-based work "at the top" remains important, as capitalism demands disciplined female labor forces in the short-run and controlled reproductive labor/energy in the long run. Home-based work, sexual reproduction, education and child rearing—all with affinities to female labor and reproductive flows, are not the same everywhere you find them. Neither are their controls. Thus, I am arguing that to think of ways in which affective labor in the female worker mode is potentially nurturing the (bio)political—is a good deconstructive move if it is supplemented with a Marxist- and feminist-informed analysis of emergent types of social-organizational power. In this context, one could cite diverse movements such as women-led protection of oil and water "commons" in Africa and Latin America, the formation of home-based and street-based female worker unions and cooperatives around the world, the contestation over state-subsidized care industries in the United States and Europe, and indeed, the inclusion of housewives in the new constitution of Venezuela. Yet how these politics are rendered visible and invisible—how they remain ghostly or not—is a deconstructive question which remains lodged, as Marx indicated, as much in one's approach to political economy, as in today's new (bio)machinery.

As low-wage homeworkers, domestic laborers, and similarly situated workers are made more "visible" through organizing and exposure of all kinds, one can begin to see the intricate governmental relations of social and sexual reproduction on a global scale.[28] Yet who or what will organize (or counter-organize) these expanded and perforce antagonistic armies of reproduction? Class struggle has always been overdetermined as population struggle, as "whole ways of life," "structures of feeling," and nowadays, as "affect economy." Cultural studies have succeeded (rarely unproblematically) in trans-mapping and transfiguring Marxism in and throughout the overlaid critical-theoretical matrices of race, nation, sex, mobility, generation, colony, gender, migration, and location—as well as in challenging the residual economism of restrictive Marxisms, precisely because of (often fleeting) appreciation of this ghostly duty to "give time" prior to and beyond the claim on future labor—that is to say, prior to and beyond the end of capitalism. Being responsible to the worker who labors to produce and reproduce population "gratuitously" is not romanticist, provided it attempts responsibility in the view of the unpredictable class-cultural biopolitics that infuses the micro- and global-local politics of "life itself" in the twenty-first century. And for that, there *is* no place (to end) like home.

# Notes

## NOTES TO THE INTRODUCTION

1. Subsequently renamed Tenants and Workers United in November 2005. Throughout, I refer to the organization by its name at the time period under examination: the Tenants' and Workers' Support Committee.

## NOTES TO CHAPTER ONE

1. Clearly, this formulation should also include the domestic work of servants, nannies, babysitters, housekeepers, maids, cooks, and other paid and often unpaid workers, whose work is conducted in *other* workers' "own homes"; the split between home-based labor studies and domestic work studies must not be papered over, although I admit I am doing little here to make practical connections in terms of a program of research. This remains to be done.
2. Karl Marx, *Capital. Vol. 1* (New York: Vintage Press, 1976), 590.
3. Ibid., 591; emphasis added.
4. The increasing appearance of time-use studies in the home reflects the demographic effort to catch up with the rapidly changing times, a theme and context I return to in later chapters.
5. On one hand, Juliet Schor (1993) and Arlie Hochschild (1997) show how work hours are increasing as well as how the external and internal dynamics of the intensification of work can be linked to a liberal politics of and within the home and family; on the other hand, cultural conservatives such as Robertson (2000) use similar data to draw politically opposed conclusions about what Hochschild calls the "time bind" between home and work. Where liberals see exploitation and false promise in the new sexual division of labor, conservatives see cultural erosion and false hope.
6. See Thompson (1966). For further discussion, see Dangler (1994), especially chapter four.
7. See Moshenberg (2002b).

8. One still thinks of hegemony with Gramsci partially because the paradigmatic class struggle which informed his use of the term came to dominate the historical scene (and historiography) both within and across national borders, and because the cultural, racial, ethnic and sexual struggles which underscored Eurocentric hegemony themselves gradually took on a more hegemonic appearance. See Stuart Hall's *The Hard Road to Renewal: Thatcherism and the Crisis of the Left* (New York: Verso, 1988), where he argues, in the British context, that hegemony has always been up for grabs—and radically re-rooted in racial, sexual and cultural modalities of "class struggle." For a view on hegemony with some thought to the cultural and economic dimensions of home-based (artisanal) production, see García-Canclini (1993). For more on what is meant by "general economy," see Bataille (1991).

9. For a useful analysis and explanation of "overdetermination," see Hall (1986). For a differing take on "overdetermination" inside-out the Eurocentric enclosure, see Spivak (1999).

10. Malaysia being one case where the government renewed controls on foreign capital, and subsequently felt far less of the impact in 1997, earning even the grudging respect of the IMF and U.S. pro-capitalist economic pundits. See Paul Blustein, "Malaysia Survives Dire Predictions," The Washington Post, 19 May 1999, E1.

11. Karen Hansen-Kuhn and Steve Hellinger, "SAPs Link Sharpens Debt Relief Debate. Cologne G-7 Initiative a 'Self-serving Formula,'" *Economic Justice News*, September 1999, Vol. 2, No. 3, (Washington, DC. Fifty Years is Enough).

12. Pam Sparr, "Making the Connections Between Debt, Trade & Gender" *Economic Justice News*, October 2001, Vol. 4, No. 3 (Washington, DC: 50 Years is Enough).

13. See Moshenberg (forthcoming) for further elaboration of this thought in the structurally adjusted field of immigrant occupational health.

14. See Delaney (2004) and Pearson (2004). Homeworkers Worldwide, a network of homework organizations, researchers and advocates created following the demise of Homenet (discussed in chapter three), launched a participatory mapping project of homeworkers in thirty countries, based in large part on the premise that preliminary to organizing, homeworkers need to count themselves and "see that there are others like them."

15. A notable exception is "Bolivarian" Venezuela, where Article 88 of the 1999 Constitution states: "The State guarantees equality and equity between men and women in the exercise of their right to work. The State recognises work at home as an economic activity that creates added value and produces social welfare and wealth. Housewives are entitled to Social Security in accordance with the law." See Global Women's Strike, http://www.globalwomenstrike.net/English2004/Article88Letter.ht for an excellent description of this development and its implications for homeworking women worldwide. I return to this development briefly in chapter six.

16. In addition to those discussed in this section, see Allen and Wolkowitz (1987); Balakrishnan (2001); Boris and Prügl (1996); Hsiung (1996); Lui (1994); and Phizacklea and Wolkowitz (1995).

17. For their methodology and discussion, see chapter six of Benería and Roldán (1987). I am less interested in the statistical findings regarding labor time and income pooling than in the crux of their argument that homework launches a cycle of proletarianization of men by women and subproletarianization of women by men inside and outside the home. Far from being the end of a chain of commodity production and corresponding class formation, homework appears here as a beginning.

18. See Phizacklea and Wolkowitz (1995), chapter three, for more on this point.

19. See Bureau of Labor Statistics, *Career Guide to Industries: Child-care Services* (Washington, DC: Bureau of Labor Statistics, 2002–2003).

20. Ibid., no page reference.

21. I look at this point in detail in chapter four.

22. Prison labor figures somewhat differently here, as it is *constitutionally* "embodied in the state," to borrow Joan Dayan's useful phrasing. See Joan Dayan, "Cruel and Unusual: the End of the Eighth Amendment," *Boston Review* 29:5 (October/November 2004).

23. See UNDP (1995). The UNDP report doesn't include sexual activity, legal or illegal, in its estimation of the monetary value of unpaid labor worldwide.

24. I look at this theoretical impasse in greater detail in Staples (forthcoming).

25. Re-examining Bourdieu's notion of habitus, closely related to Felstead and Jewson's analysis of "household understandings" in the context of home-based production, may be helpful here, once disentangled from the European enclosure which unequally reproduces it. I discuss this at greater length in chapters two and six.

26. For representative texts, see Hartmann (1976); Fortunati (1995); Fox (1980); Fraad, Resnick, and Wolff (1994); Kuhn and Wolpe (1978); and Malos (1980).

27. Various studies of the Women in Informal Employment Globalizing and Organizing (WIEGO) critically document the reports and analysis of these "informal" earnings and distributions. See http://www.wiego.org.

28. With the rise of mass home-based schooling and home shopping in the United States, there re-emerges the specter of a "frontier" population, with some common national and cultural characteristics, who never leave home, even if they do have American Express.

29. The dominant logic applies mostly, but not exclusively, to married women. An unmarried mother who works at home, remains, at best, a "head of household," or "single-earner mother" in today's classificatory schema. In the United States in the early 2000s, reminiscent of an earlier era of welfare provision, this figure remains a prime subject of social control, state-sponsored marriage lessons, and welfare policing.

## NOTES TO CHAPTER TWO

1. Agnes E. Meyer, *Washington Post,* April 10, 1943.
2. Editor's Note, *House of Business,* January-February 2001, 6.
3. Ibid., 6.
4. See OSHA Directive CPL 2–0.125, effective date February 25, 2000. Home-based child-care is not mentioned in the directive, despite being the largest single homeworking sector in the U.S. In the next chapter, I examine some of the consequences of the regulation of the child-care home and child-care worker
5. Helen O'Grady, "An Ethics of the Self," in Dianna Taylor and Karen Vintges, eds. *Feminism and the Final Foucault* (Urbana and Chicago: University of Illinois Press, 2004), 98. O'Grady counsels: "Foucault's insistence on the need to study the constitutive effects of power at the 'microphysical' level of bodies, thoughts, wills, conducts and everyday lives of individuals is apposite here . . . If the microlevel of life is ignored in the push for progressive social change, a range of power relations will remain intact. This points to the importance of addressing power's hold at the intra-subjective level. One strategy for achieving this is to destabilize the idea that self-policing techniques form an inevitable part of identity."
6. For an alternative Foucauldian treatment of home and work see Valsecchi (1999). See also Dangler (1994), Mitter (1986) and Boris and Prügl (1996).
7. For varying Marxist-feminist perspectives on the "domestic economy" see, e.g. Fraad, Resnick, and Wolff (1994); Hartmann (1981); Seecombe (1980); and Spivak (1987a) and (1987b).
8. On housework, see Berk (1985); Oakley (1974); Hochschild (1989). For his use of *méconnaisance,* see Bourdieu (1990).
9. Note the resemblance in formulation to Gayatri Chakravorty Spivak's analysis of gender and prostitution in post-Independence India: "Internalized gendering perceived as ethical choice is the hardest roadblock for women the world over. The recognition of male exploitation must be supplemented with this acknowledgement." See her introduction to Devi (1995, xxviii). I return to examine this insight for home-based labor studies in the final chapter.
10. See Vogel (2000) for a recap of these debates and Himmelweit (2000) for a more extensive review and updating.
11. See Staples (forthcoming) for a more extended discussion of this point.
12. For further discussion and research, see Hsiung (1996) and Pearson (2004). On the unequal gendered outcomes of micro-credit, see (1999).
13. By "nomadological," Casey is referring broadly to Deleuze and Guattari's (1987) notions of smooth versus striated space, as well as regionalism. The implications of these concepts for theorizing large-scale home networking in informational and value-extracting global capitalism hover between the calculable and incalculable. See Deleuze and Guattari (1987, 477–78 and passim).

14. See Thorns (1998) for a discussion of his own and others' sociological treatments.

## NOTES TO CHAPTER THREE

1.  One could make a comparable analysis of elderly care, health care, cleaning, cooking, etc., but here I focus on child-care.
2.  Mike Roberts elaborated this problematic in the context of housing takeovers in San Jose, California, in "Schizo-Space: the Micropolitics of Housing and Homeless Takeovers," a paper presented at the conference of the Midwest Sociological Association, 1995. See also Talmadge Wright, *Out of Place: Homeless Moblizations, Subcities, and Contested Landscapes* (Albany: SUNY Press, 1992).
3.  In 2003, Homenet was formally disbanded and reformed as Homeworkers Worldwide, with non-profit organizational status in the United Kingdom.
4.  The theme of "real subsumption" was usefully developed by Antonio Negri (1988) and taken up at greater length by Hardt and Negri (1994; 2000). I return to some of the implications of this analysis in chapter five.
5.  On "dialectical utopianism," see David Harvey (2000), whose critique of the politically and economically "built" environment curiously tends to overshadow whatever optimism of the will he set out to map. For a dialectical approach that differently acknowledges the circulation of value that my argument intends, see Witheford (1999).
6.  See Prügl (1999, 149–50). See also Cheah, who writes: "Rights are thus not, in the original instance, entitlements of intersubjectively constituted rational agents but violent gifts, the necessary nexuses within immanent global force-relations which produce the identities of its claimants. Yet, they are the only way for the disenfranchised to moblilise" (Cheah 1997, 261).
7.  Rather than "re-routing," Deleuze and Guattari (1987) proposed "reterritorialization." This theme, too, it appears, has been taken up just as effectively by "top-down" organizers.
8.  Percentages exceed 100.0 because of multiple care arrangements. See Smith (2002, 3).
9.  See Administration for Children and Families (1998).
10. See Smith (2002, 16).
11. Poverty figures from Proctor and Dalaker/U.S. Census Bureau (2002).
12. See NCJW (1999) for a profile and Giannarelli and Barsimantov (2000) for an extended study of child-care expenditures.
13. Adapted from Administration for Children and Families (ACF), "A Profile of the Child-care Work Force," (http://www.acf.dhhs.gov/programs/ccb/faq1/workforc.htm). There is a discrepancy in the number of children receiving care between this officials profile and the figures in Smith (2002), a result most likely of disparate counting methods. On a similar note, the Center for the Child-Care Work Force, which may be assumed to have a better on-the-ground sense of the number of providers, reports that there

are at least 2.5 million child-care workers in the United States, a figure that they acknowledge does not take into account turnover among paid relatives and non-relative care providers (as distinct from the known turnover among center-based staff and family providers). See Burton et al. (2002, 17 and passim). There appears to be a basic agreement, however, between the ACF's data on the earnings of child-care workers and earnings reported elsewhere. See Whitebook and Phillips (1999).

14. See Tuominen (1994, 89; 1998, 63–64).

15. Brenner (2000) makes this point more clear in her critique of Michele Barrett on the role of patriarchal ideology in determining women's oppression. For both a theoretical summary and historical perspective, see also Middleton (1988).

16. Gayatri Chakravorty Spivak's formulation of the impossible is instructive: "the structure one cannot not wish to inhabit." See Devi (1995, xxiii–xxix).

17. In this context, one should also cite the elimination of federally funded abortion and gradual erosion of the protection of women's right to abortion in the U.S. and internationally; Reagan/Bush opposition to the Family and Medical Leave Act passed finally in 1994; and weak enforcement of sexual harassment and assault policies, child support and alimony laws, etc.

18. To privatization, one should add correlative expansion of the moral and social policing of the poor, people of color, and children, and the unprecedented increase in incarceration and detention, as elements of increasingly control-oriented structural adjustment policies around the globe. See Garland (2001) and Wacquant (2001) for representative analysis of these historic shifts.

19. I do not write this by way of critique; rather, I wish to draw out the organizing implications of studies of the factors that shape the choices of women in home-based child-care work. Tuominen (2002) does look at the "bottom-up" organization of child-care center workers, who as both private and public employees have had success in unionizing in a number of places and cases.

20. Whitebook and Eichberg (2002) discuss "Teacher Education And Compensation Helps" (TEACH), which at the time was administered in fifteen to twenty states. It offers providers small subsidies to take a number of early education courses, and a corresponding schedule of reimbursement increases, which are generally being reported at around 10%. This means that a home-based provider enrolled in a state's TEACH program, who earns the nationwide average of a little less than $10,000, should, after a year or more of classroom study (and homework of the other sort), make $11,000. The scale of change recommended by the state, in this state, remains powerfully skewed towards further exploitation of a growingly "professional," and thus divided, child-care workforce.

## NOTES TO CHAPTER FOUR

1. "Tenants' & Workers' Support Committee Triennial Report 2002–2004" (Alexandria: VA, 2005, 6). Sheryl Bell was the president of the Unity Campaign, a project of the Tenants' & Workers' Support Committee.

2. Allie Smith, quoted in 2004 TWSC promotional video (Alexandria, VA: Tenants' & Workers' Support Committee).

3. In addition to DARE's Home Day Care Justice Committee, similar campaigns led by autonomous community organizations have been identified in Alexandria, Virginia (Tenants' & Workers' Support Committee), Miami (Miami Workers Center) and Brooklyn, NY (Families United for Racial and Economic Equality). In addition, Alinsky-style campaigns have been developed by the Association of Community Organizations for Reform Now (ACORN) in Los Angeles, New York City, and Chicago. Undoubtedly there are numerous other organizations and campaigns. Of those identified, I look in detail at two of the earliest and most successful efforts so far, the Home Daycare Justice Committee of DARE and the Unity Campaign of the Tenants' & Workers' Support Committee.

4. Home-based workers are required to provide at least $1,800 of services to the state's Department of Human Services within a six-month period to be eligible for the program. The Center for the Childcare Work Force reported that Michigan also has a state-based health insurance program for child-care workers, and that health insurance is a component of several of the state-based TEACH initiatives, although the latter extends exclusively to workers enrolled in TEACH, not to all providers. See Whitebook and Eichberg (2002).

5. Interesting from the perspective of homework, government officials attempted to quell HDJC's effort by arguing that any policy they enacted would have to cover higher-paid, more professionalized center-based child-care workers as well. HDJC's response was that their proposal in no way prevented the state from extending coverage to other workers, which it ultimately did two years after beginning it for home-based providers. Of course, this was not the first effort to divide predominantly non-white, low-wage home-based workers in an effort to maintain a segmented workforce. See Abrams (1999, 17) and Whitebook and Eichberg (2002) on the race- and class-based continuity of struggles over professionalization and center vs. home-based child-care workers.

6. See Jacqueline Salmon, "Va. Providers of Child-care Get Organized," *The Washington Post*, March 14, 2001, A10.

7. Communication with Keith Kelleher, SEIU Local 880, December 18, 2002.

8. The organization's long-term strategy, written in to its mission statement, was to develop forms of community ownership of housing in particular, as a means of protecting the area's increasingly valuable housing stock from gentrifying forces, including both real estate developers and local elected and planning officials.

9. TWSC correspondence, April 30, 1998, emphasis in original.

10. Trigie Ealey, "Day-care Providers Slam Human Services," *The Alexandria Journal*, April 6, 2000, A1.

11. Ibid.

12. See Sarah Godfrey, "Sticks and Bones," *Washington City Paper*, February 8–14, 2002, for a partial account of this story.

13. *Unity News, A Newsletter for Unity Providers*, September 2002 (Alexandria, VA: Tenants' and Workers' Support Committee). See also Trigie Ealey, "Day Care Workers Say Their Licenses Unfairly Revoked," *The Northern Virginia Journal*, August 30, 2002, A1, A9.

14. Jon Liss, personal communication with the author, October 7, 2005.

15. See Foucault (1978, 135–45; 1997, 73–79).

16. I am grateful to Ifeona Fulani for this thought. Cf. Antonio Benitez Rojo's *The Repeating Island. The Caribbean and the Postmodern Perspective* (Durham, NC: Duke University Press, 1992), which views the machinic reproduction of the plantation system in the non-Spanish Caribbean through a Deleuzian framework.

17. One would have to add, "life-management and control of racially marked populations" in *strategic situations of power*, as Foucault (1978) does.

18. Tuominen (1994a, 225). This thought is in part indebted to the first chapter ("Philosophy") of Spivak (1999, 1–111). For a vastly different notion of emergence that further unsettles the dependence on liberal political theory, see the introduction to DeLanda (1997).

## NOTES TO CHAPTER FIVE

1. Family and maternity leave policies, of course, are increasingly important areas of class and gender struggle. Cuba likely has the most advanced regulatory protections for what I am calling "housework" here, although no doubt there are other examples. See Pearson (2000).

2. For discussion of the participatory mapping project of HomeWorkers Worldwide (formerly Homenet), see Delaney (2004) and Pearson (2004). For examples from the policymaking side, see Paul Callister and Sylvia Dixon, "Home work patterns: Evidence from the New Zealand Time Use Survey," paper presented at the 2001 International Association for Time Use Research Conference, Oslo, Norway, October 3-5, 2001; Economic and Social Commission for Asia and the Pacific, "Winning the Support of Policy Makers: Making Unpaid Work Count," paper presented at the Training Workshop on Statistical Aspects of Integrating Unpaid Work into National Policies, Bangkok, Thailand, September 11-15, 2000.

3. The problematic of "regulation of the home" is compounded not so much in the informal sector, where regulations are absent by definition, as in the public political sphere where legal and illegal sexual arousal can and does move mountains. In this context, one would have to cite not only the frequent frenzies around stock market gyrations but also the "feminization of war" in which, as Silvia Federici (2000) has shown, women and children are, once again, the enemies in increasingly "virtual" wars (e.g. the "low-intensity conflicts") of smart missiles, "collateral damage," genocide, and symbolic victories over violated women and children—all alongside ongoing structural adjustment. The problem isn't so much about challenging the rules of war, as about the changing perception of the place of sexual and

domestic violence in warfare. Only in the wake of the Bosnian war was wartime rape criminalized. Prior to that, in the absence of legal, political, and organizational enforcement (which "technologies" have not changed very much), rape in time of war was, at most, *uncivil*.

4. Cf. Gramsci (1971, 238-39) on the transition from "war of maneuver" to "war of position." The latter, Gramsci writes, "demands enormous sacrifices by infinite masses of people. So an unprecedented concentration of hegemony is necessary, and hence a more 'interventionist' government, which will take the offensive more openly against the oppositionists and organize permanently the 'impossibility' of internal disintegration—with controls of every kind, political, administrative, etc., reinforcement of the hegemonic 'positions' of the dominant group, etc. . . .the 'war of position', once won, is decisive definitively." Gramsci's "war of position" hypothesis looks frighteningly accurate from the standpoint of late twentieth-century mass incarceration. If I understand him correctly in these pages, Trotsky, the "political theorist of frontal attack," is the model revolutionary for today's control societies—but perhaps equally so from the side of the state, whose hegemony appears more or less definitively decisive. Hardt and Negri (1994), and autonomist Marxists in general, so terrifically reverse the charge of power in postmodern capitalist society, that one begins to understand how important it is that the state assume the role of its own opposition. "Control" re-opens the possibilities for wars of maneuver, which Gramsci notes, however, are never decisive in hegemonic terms, inside the state itself, and on multiple sides. This leads some in the growing anti-capitalist globalization movement to practice the possibilities for regional or municipal socialisms on ever-expanding scales..

5. See Allen and Wolkowitz (1987, 273), which Spivak (see Devi 1995) also cites in this context.

6. I would cite Felstead and Jewston (1999, 113-19) as a politically dangerous instance of this.

7. This should also be examined in its simultaneity—as Donzelot, for one did not do—with colonial policies of settlement, and the sexualized violence of colonial patriarchy directed at both women and men. Among the many who have done so I would cite Anne McClintock, Rajeswari Sunder Rajan, Ann Stoler, and Robert Young.

8. I am not proposing, then, a literary analysis that would note first off that virtually all of Volume Three concerns texts and practices of the "self" in classical antiquity.

9. On the notion of "restrictive" economy, see Bataille (1991).

10. Heather Menzies (1997) makes these general points much more politically specific in her analysis of the privatization of public communications through women's home-based telework.

11. If anthropologist David Schneider was correct in 1973 in saying that class is the primary cultural characteristic of *family differentiation* in the United States, then it continues to makes sense to return, I would argue, to a (deconstructive) class analysis in the context of sex and race-divided

"family labor" that is attentive to the circuits of governmentality in neoliberal capitalism. See David M. Schneider and Raymond T. Smith, *Class Differences and Sex Roles in American Kinship and Family Structure* (Englewood Cliffs, NJ: Prentice Hall, 1973).

12.  See note 4 above.

13.  One must resist the totalizing impulse in Foucault, especially as it partially makes its way around the world in the critique of "Empire," and be reminded of those who have access neither to neo-liberal governmentality nor to any "indigenous" tradition of "representation." See Gayatri Chakravorty Spivak, "Can the Subaltern Speak," in C. Nelson and L Grossberg, eds. *Marxism and the Interpretation of Culture*, (Urbana: University of Illinois Press, 1986), pp. 271-313.

14.  See Felstead and Jewson (1999, 16). The key here is that child-care providers, like homeworkers, also deliver their product to a "third party," in this case the state. This is not a point about taxonomy, but precisely about how "technologies of the self" are not simply confined to household and "market" practices, unless we say they are.

15.  See Gilles Deleuze's discussion of the "diagram" in *Foucault*: " . . .the diagram, in so far as it exposes a set of relations between forces, is not a place but rather 'a non-place': it is the place only of mutation. Suddenly things are no longer perceived or propositions articulated in the same way" (Deleuze 1986, 85). One might also return again to Hardt and Negri's critical reference to Gramsci's understanding of the relation between civil society and the state. For them, Gramsci's (1971) notion that civil society would itself overcome the state through counter-hegemonic force, i.e. that the political and cultural forces of civil society would engage in a free exchange of power, with State structures progressively and sometimes violently subordinated to the popular will, is a-topic. They argue that the *space* for such struggle no longer exists. "Not the state, but civil society has withered away." More important, the "state doesn't need civil society," its institutions, etc. to practice order. Without completely collapsing the difference between place and space, one can with Deleuze and Foucault nevertheless envision a non-place space where change, a resistant, differential force, does takes spatio-temporal place. See Hardt and Negri (1994, 258-59). Hardt and Negri suggest we think of the latter place in terms of constituent power flowing from immaterial and reproductive labor of all kinds. I suggest we think of it in terms such as "child-care."

16.  There may be other commonalities between Foucault and Bourdieu worth noting. There is certainly the subjective context of colonial history to be looked at, as Ann Stoler has done with regard to Foucault. *Masculine Domination* shuttles repeatedly between Kabylia and Europe. Yet, at least in this text, Bourdieu discusses change in the permanence of the structure of male domination only in the European context, with only brief reference to the passing of the "ideal" conditions for masculine domination in Kabylia (Bourdieu 2001, 56). At very least, this presents a problem of historical imprecision around the notion of "masculine" domination: if change in the

permanence of the structure of male domination or in sexual vision isn't happening in Kabylia, which is precisely what is and is not being said, why not? Do the contemporary Amazigh movements for cultural and linguistic autonomy say and do nothing (anew) about sexual difference? Clearly there are myriad other sources one could turn to for evidence of "change" in the sense Bourdieu outlines. Spivak (1992) has discussed the literature of Algerian novelist Assia Djebar in this meta-context. See Djebar's *So Vast the Prison* (New York: Seven Stories Press, 2001) for an excellent historical-fictional counterpoint to Bourdieu's patronage of Kabylian "permanence."

17. Michael Burawoy suggests such an analysis in the context of a proposal for "global ethnography." See "Introduction: Reaching for the Global" in M. Burawoy et al., *Global Ethnography: Forces, Connections and Imaginations in a Postmodern World* (Berkeley and Los Angeles: Univ. of California Press, 2000).

18. I write this, to reiterate, primarily because Bourdieu's analysis of strategy and habitus in the context of the "household" and sex division of labor partially informs thinking in the field of homework studies.

19. See Bourdieu (1990, 24), where he writes, "...it's impossible not to see that the forms of classification are forms of domination, that the sociology of knowledge or cognition is inseparably a sociology of recognition and méconnaissance, that is, of symbolic domination...", so much so that "... the classificatory structures which organize the whole vision of the world refer, in the final analysis, to the sexual division of labor" for Kabyle society. Isn't Bourdieu a bit too eager to rescue reason here? As Spivak (1993) does very differently with Foucault, we must give Bourdieu in to Derrida. When Bourdieu writes that we should look for change in the "permanence of the invisible structure," he is writing, as it were, *sous rature*. When he suggests we historicize the dehistoricization on which masculine domination relies for permanence, he risks little or nothing. And in the European case of Kabylia, we do not see the resistances which *undergird* the structure, ideal, canonical, or mundane, of masculine domination. Giving Bourdieu in to Derrida, we begin to see how the temporal proximity and spatial separation of selves and others so crucial to the "natural" order of social capital and classification, once inscribed in the foundational sociological text, *shakes* both that text *and* the (enduring, postcolonial) social order it seeks not to historicize but, ultimately, to manage.

20. Gilles Deleuze's reading of Foucault gives Butler's analysis of the "outside" a more definitive, if philosophical, edge: " . . .the final word on power is that *resistance comes first*, to the extent that power relations operate completely within the diagram, while resistances necessarily operate in a direct relation with the outside from which the diagrams emerge" (Deleuze 1986, 89). At the end of this passage, Deleuze cites Mario Tronti, one of Negri's early collaborators. For more of that history, see Red Notes (1979).

21. See note 15 above.

22. On the notion of expanded textuality of value, see Spivak (1987b). I explore in the concluding chapter the possibilities and difficulties within "primitive

capitalist accumulation" of separating home-based workers from the means of their "affective labor" production.

23. The global market in human body parts, including the material of human reproduction, might be thought of as the latest in an updated form of primitive accumulation: separation of owners from their physical means of (re)production. The primitive accumulation process I have foremost in mind, as should be noted throughout, is almost immediately enabled by, and thus (im)possible to distinguish from, institutionally-led structural adjustment programs. How and where these two seemingly remote figures of violence are related and collaborative is not an example of the epistemic violence I refer to, although, no doubt, the members of the World Economic Forum do not wish (us) to see it either. The 50 Years Is Enough Network has been certainly one of the better resources for learning to recognize this from the top down, supplemented by the homeworker organizing examples I have cited as "bottom up."

## NOTES TO CHAPTER SIX

1. This was Paul Smith's argument in the 1970s, at any rate. See Smith (1978). What Smith guessed wrong there, other than that Marx's critique of bourgeois political economy wasn't itself related to the gendered socialist practice of the day, was that there was nothing to pin women's domestic labor to their own wage earning. That is, he forgot or foreclosed the modernist juxtaposition of not only economic and symbolic production (á la Levi-Strauss), but also the modernist juxtaposition of paid outwork and other forms of women's and children's home-based labor with unpaid domestic labor, as Marx described it. I was reminded of this latter point in Moshenberg (2002[b]).

2. For one such sociological survey, see Julie Brines (1993), who in the end opts for a position well short of a theory of value, but well within the orbit of liberal feminism, in which framework it appears sufficient to argue that housework is, in the final analysis, a matter of gender performance. This is quite different from Saba Gul Khattak's analysis (Balakrishnan 2002), in which, citing data from a homeworker study in Karachi, she concluded "there is some logic to women's preference to staying home," because child mortality rates were significantly higher for informal sector workers employed outside the home than for home-based workers. In this instance, value, in one of its most concrete forms, i.e. human survival, is a long (though certainly not unconnected) way from gender performance, since as Khattak continues, "the same study also states that children of home-based women workers have fewer chances of attending school . . . in all probability home-based women workers' children are child workers, assisting their mothers in home-based work." See Saba Gul Khattak, "Subcontracted Work and Gender Relations: The Case of Pakistan," in Balakrishnan (2002, 44).

3. See, for example, Seecombe (1980) for an early iteration of this argument.

4. I make this argument at greater length in an article from which this chapter was derived. See Staples (forthcoming).

5. See "Debating the Marxist-Feminist Interpretation of the Household," in Fraad, Resnick, and Wolff (1994, 42–87).

6. See Whitebook and Eichberg (2002). It should be noted that in Rhode Island, the success of DARE's health insurance campaign for child-care providers was strengthened at least in part by expansion of the state subsidized child-care market by making child-care an income-based entitlement.

7. See Frow (1997, 129). Frow also cites Margaret Jane Radin (1987), "Market-Inalienability," *Harvard Law Review* 100(8): 1849–1937. This article came to my attention too late to address here.

8. Following a concentrated struggle by women's organizations to gain recognition of women's work in the new constitution of Venezuela, an amendment was added that makes this constitution unique in the world. Article 88 of the constitution of Venezuela states: "The State guarantees equality and equity between men and women in the exercise of their right to work. The State recognises work at home as an economic activity that creates added value and produces social welfare and wealth. Housewives are entitled to Social Security in accordance with the law." Several years after its adoption, however, legislation to fulfil the amendment's promise appeared weighed down by the old paternalistic politics of deserving vs. undeserving women.

9. See Fraad, Resnick, and Wolff (1994) for a sustained effort to analyze the displacement of gender into class.

10. See Witheford (2000) for an appreciative analysis of autonomist Marxist writings.

11. See Red Notes (1979).

12. Negri (1988, 219).

13. Fortunati (1995, 8). I agree with Fortunati when she refers to the productive disappearance of reproductive labor as the "line of value" (161). This must be supplemented with further recognition of the international division of (reproductive) labor-value. Reproductive labor is not the same everywhere. Gayatri Spivak, who sees the "line of value" as a "multinational" or even, with much redaction, a "multi-cultural" enclosure, has discussed this point in various ways over many years. For a recent instance, see the chapter on "Culture" in Spivak (1999, 312–421).

14. Negri (1991, 86–87, emphasis added).

15. Biotechnology and its key offshoot, biomaterialization, represent possibly the most powerful of the recent phase shifts in the "biopolitical" economy. Thanks to Patricia Clough for drawing my attention to recent work on this subject, especially Thacker (2005).

16. Ibid., 83.

17. For the thousands of small-scale capitalists roaming the globe in the service of large-scale capitalists as well as their own profit, labor is literally everywhere, or when refused as such, "anyplace but here." For diverse instances of this, see Balakrishnan (2002).

18. Hardt and Negri, *Empire* (2000, 292–93).
19. There certainly will be disagreement over the politics resulting from this perspective, which might be more evident when presented with the utterly contrary view elaborated by Jeffrey Sachs that the billion or more inhabitants of the planet subsisting on less than a dollar a day must become waged for them and capitalism to survive. Such a view begs the question of how people actually are surviving on less than a dollar a day—and what politics this mass survival portends. See George Caffentzis, "Dr. Jeffrey Sachs' The End of Poverty: A Political Review" (July 18, 2005), http://info.interactivist.net/article.pl?sid=05/07/19/0242219&mode=nested&tid=2.
20. See Negri (1991, 69–70); (1999, 82). In an essay entitled "The Constitution of Time," Negri put it somewhat more bluntly: "Does this mean that Marx's theory of value and time should be put out to pasture? The answer is probably yes for a sizeable part of it . . . For now we know that time cannot be presented as measure, but must rather be presented as the global phenomenological fabric, as base, substance and flow of production in its entirety." Antonio Negri, *Time for Revolution* (New York/London: Continuum, 2003), 29.
21. See Ursula Huws (2003), especially chapter ten, for a discussion of these phases.
22. There is an abundant literature one could cite on the formations of biopower and biopolitics. In addition to those cited in chapter two, see also Achille Mbembe, "Necropolitics," *Public Culture* 15 (2003), 11–40.
23. See Weiner (1992).
24. Gayatri Chakravorty Spivak, "Ghostwriting," *diacritics* 25:2 (Summer 1995), 67ff.
25. There is a growing body of literature that documents these claims. See, e.g., Ehrenreich and Hochschild (2002).
26. Hardt and Negri (2000, 365).
27. For a representative sampling, see Boris and Prügl (1996).
28. Among those laboring in this vast and relatively unexplored corner of the global domestic economy, see Parrenas (2001) as well as Ehrenreich and Hochschild (2002).

# Works Cited

ACF. See Administration for Children and Families.

Abrams, Kristi. 1999. *Don't Give Up the Fight. The Story of the Fight for Health Insurance for Family Daycare Providers*. Providence, RI: Direct Action for Rights & Equality.

Administration for Children and Families. 1998. State Spending Under the Child Care Block Grant. HHS Fact Sheet (November 12, 1998), U.S. Department of Health and Human Services, Washington, DC.

Ahrentzen, Sherry Boland. 1992. Home as a Workplace in the Lives of Women. In *Place Attachment*, edited by I. Altman and S. Low, 113–37. New York: Plenum Press.

Allen, Sheila. 1983. Production and Reproduction: the Lives of Women Homeworkers. *Sociological Review* 314:649–65.

———.1989. Locating Homework in an Analysis of the Ideological and Materials Constraints on Women's Paid Work. In Boris and Daniels 1989, 272–91.

Allen, Sheila and Carol Wolkowitz. 1986. Homeworking and the Control of Women's Work. In *Waged Work: A Reader*, edited by Feminist Review, 238–64. London: Virago Press.

———.1987. *Homeworking: Myths and Realities*. London: Macmillan Education.

Aronowitz, Stanley. 2003. *How Class Works: Power and Social Movement*. New Haven: Yale University Press.

Aronowitz, Stanley and Heather Gautney. 2002. *Implicating Empire: Globalization and Resistance in the 21st Century*. New York: Basic Books.

Augé, Marc. 1995. *Non-places: Introduction to an Anthropology of Supermodernity*. London: Verso.

Bachman, S. L. 2000. A New Economics of Child Labor: Searching for Answers Behind the Headlines. *Journal of International Affairs* 53(2): 545–72.

Balakrishnan, Radhika, ed. 2002. *The Hidden Global Assembly Line: Gender Dynamics of Subcontracted Work in a Global Economy*. Bloomfield, CT: Kumarian Press.

Bataille, Georges. 1991. *The Accursed Share. Volume One*. NY: Zone Books.

Beach, Betty. 1989. *Integrating Work and Family Life. The Home-Working Family.* Albany: SUNY Press.

Benería, Lourdes. 1989. Subcontracting and Employment Dynamics in Mexico City. In Portes, Castells and Benton 1989, 173–87.

Benería, Lourdes and Marta Roldán. 1987. *The Crossroads of Class & Gender: Industrial Homework, Subcontracting, and Household Dynamics in Mexico City.* Chicago: University of Chicago Press.

Benton, Lauren. 1990. *Invisible Factories: the Informal Economy and Industrial Development in Spain.* Albany: SUNY Press.

Berk, Sarah. 1985. *Gender Factory: the Apportionment of Work in American Household.* NY: Plenum Press.

Bhatt, Ela. 1987. The Invisibility of Home-Based Work: The Case of Piece Rate Workers in India. In Singh and Kelles-Viitanen 1987, 29–33.

Biehl, João. 2001. Vita. *Social Text* 19(3): 131–49.

Boris, Eileen. 1989. Black Women and Paid Labor in the Home: Industrial Homework in Chicago in the 1920s. In Boris and Daniels 1989, 33–52.

———.1994a. *Home to Work: Motherhood and the Politics of Industrial Homework in the United States.* Cambridge: Cambridge University Press.

———.1994b. Mothers are Not Workers: Homework Regulation and the Construction of Motherhood: 1948–1953. In Nakano Glenn, Chang, and Forcey 1994, 161–80.

———.1996. Sexual Division, Gender Constructions: The Historical Meaning of Homework in Western Europe and the United States. In Boris and Prügl 1996, 19–37.

Boris, Eileen and Cynthia R. Daniels, eds. 1989. *Homework: Historical and Contemporary Perspectives on Paid Labor at Home.* Urbana: University of Illinois Press.

Boris, Eileen and Elisabeth Prügl, eds. 1996. *»Homeworkers in Global Perspective: Invisible No More«.* New York: Routledge.

Bornstein, Kate. 1995. *Gender Outlaw: Of Men, Women, and the Rest of Us.* New York: Vintage.

Bourdieu, Pierre. 1977. *Outline of a Theory of Practice.* Translated by Richard Nice. Cambridge: Cambridge University Press.

———.1990. *In Other Words: Towards a Reflexive Sociology.* Translated by Matthew Adamson. Stanford: Stanford University Press.

———.2001. *Masculine Domination.* Translated by Richard Nice. Stanford: Stanford University Press.

Boydston, Jeanne. 1990. *Home and Work: Housework, Wages and the Ideology of Labor in the Early Republic.* New York: Oxford University Press.

Boyer, Kate. 2003. At Work, At Home? New Geographies of Work and Care-giving Under Welfare Reform in the US. *Space & Polity* 7(1): 75–86.

Brenner, Johanna. 2000. *Women and the Politics of Class.* New York: Monthly Review Press.

Brines, Julie. 1993. The Exchange Value of Housework. *Rationality and Society* 5(3): 302–40.

Bureau of Labor Statistics. 1998. Work at Home in 1997. *Labor Force Statistics from the Current Population Survey.* Washington, DC: Bureau of Labor Statistics.

Burkett, Paul. 1999. Nature's 'Free Gifts' and the Ecological Significance of Value. *Capital & Class* 68: 89–110.

Burton, Alice, Marcy Whitebook, Marcy Young, Dan Bellm, and Claudia Wayne. 2002. Estimating the Size and Components of the U.S. Childcare Workforce and Caregiving Population. Occasional paper of the Center for the Child Care Workforce, Washington, DC.

Butler, Judith. 1990. *Gender Trouble: Feminism and the Subversion of Identity.* New York: Routledge.

———.1993. Critical Exchanges: The Symbolic and Questions of Gender. In *Questioning Foundations: Truth/Subjectivity/Culture,* edited by H. Silverman, 134–69. New York: Routledge.

CCW. See Center for the Childcare Workforce.

Caffentzis, George. 1992. The Work/Energy Crisis. In *Midnight Oil,* edited by the Midnight Notes Collective, 215–71. Brooklyn: Autonomedia Press.

Cameron, Jenny. 1997. Throwing a Dishcloth into the Works: Troubling Theories of Domestic Labor. *Rethinking Marxism* 9(2): 24–44.

Cancian, Francesca M., Demie Kurz, Andrew S. London, Rebecca Reviere, and Mary C. Tuominen, eds. 2002. *Child Care and Inequality: Rethinking Carework for Children and Youth.* New York: Routledge.

Carr, Marilyn, Martha Alter Chen, and Jane Tate. 2000. Globalization and Home-Based Workers. *Feminist Economics* 6(3): 123–42.

Casey, Edward. 1997. *The Fate of Place.* Berkeley: University of California Press.

Center for the Childcare Workforce. 1999. Creating Better Family Child Care Jobs: Model Work Standards. Center for the Childcare Workforce, Washington, DC.

Chang, Grace. 1999. Global Exchange: The World Bank, "Welfare Reform," and the Global Trade in Filipina Workers. In Coontz, Parson, and Raley 1999, 305–17.

Chapman, Tony and Jenny Hockey, eds. 1999. *Ideal Homes? Social Change and Domestic Life.* London: Routledge.

Cheah, Pheng. 1997. Positioning Human Rights in the Current Global Conjuncture. *Public Culture* 9:233–66.

Christensen, Kathleen, ed. 1988. *The New Era of Home-Based Work. Directions and Policies.* Boulder, CO: Westview Press.

Clough, Patricia Ticineto. 2000. *Autoaffection. Unconscious Thought in the Age of Teletechnology.* Minneapolis: University of Minnesota Press.

———.2002. Technoscience: Three Shifts in Critical Theory. Paper delivered at the Humanities Center, University of California at Irvine, January 2002.

———, ed. Forthcoming. *The Affective Turn: Theorizing the Social.* With Jean Halley. Durham, NC: Duke University Press.

Collins, Jane L. 1990. Unwaged Labor in Comparative Perspective: Recent Theories and Unanswered Questions. In Collins and Gimenez 1990, 3–24.

Collins, Jane L. and Martha Gimenez, eds. 1990. *Work Without Wages: Comparative Studies of Domestic Labor and Self-Employment*. Albany: SUNY Press.

Collins, Patricia Hill. 1990. *Black Feminist Thought: Knowledge, Consciousness and the Politics of Empowerment*. Boston: Unwin Hyman.

Coontz, Stephanie, Maya Parson and Gabrielle Raley, eds. 1999. *American Families: a Multicultural Reader*. New York: Routledge.

Crittenden, Ann. 2001. *The Price of Motherhood. Why the Most Important Jobs is Still the Least Valued*. New York: Metropolitan Books.

Dagg, Alex. 1996. Organizing Homeworkers into Unions: the Homeworkers' Association of Toronto, Canada. In Boris and Prügl 1996, 239–58.

Dalla Costa, Mariarosa and Giovanna F. Dalla Costa, eds. 1999. *Women, Development, and Labor of Reproduction: Struggles and Movements*. Trenton, NJ: Africa World Press.

Dalla Costa, Mariarosa and Selma James. 1973. *The Power of Women and the Subversion of the Community*. Bristol, UK: Falling Wall Press.

Dangler, Jamie Faricellia. 1994. *Hidden in the Home: The Role of Waged Homework in the Modern World-Economy*. Albany: SUNY Press.

Davis, Angela. 1981. *Women, Race and Class*. New York: Random House.

DeLanda, Manuel. 1997. *A Thousand Years of Nonlinear History*. New York: Zone Books.

Delaney, Annie. 1996. My Home is My Haven, My Home is My Workplace. *Alternative Law Journal* 21(5): 217–222.

_____. 2004. Global Trade and Home Work: Closing the Divide. *Gender and Development* 12(2): 22–28.

Deleuze, Gilles. 1986. *Foucault*. Translated and edited by Sean Hand. Minneapolis: University of Minnesota Press.

Deleuze, Gilles and Felix Guattari. 1987. *A Thousand Plateaus*. Translated by Brian Massumi. Minneapolis: University of Minnesota Press.

Derrida, Jacques. 1992. *Given Time: I. Counterfeit Money*. Translated by Peggy Kamuf. Chicago: University of Chicago Press.

Desai, Ashwin. 2002. *We are the Poors: Community Struggles in Post-Apartheid South Africa*. New York: Monthly Review Press.

Devi, Mahasweta. 1995. *Imaginary Maps: Three Stories*. Translated and with an introduction by Gayatri Chakravorty Spivak. New York: Routledge Press.

Donzelot, Jacques. 1997. *The Policing of Families*. Translated by Robert Hurley. Baltimore: Johns Hopkins University Press.

Edwards, Linda N. and Elizabeth Field-Hendrey. 1996. Home-based Workers: Data from the 1990 Census of Population. Monthly Labor Review (November 1996), Bureau of Labor Statistics, Washington, DC.

Ehrenreich, Barbara and Deirdre English. 1978. *For Her Own Good: 150 Years of the Experts' Advice to Women*. Garden City, NJ: Anchor Press.

Ehrenreich, Barbara and Arlie Hochschild, eds. 2002. *Global Woman: Nannies, Maids and Sex Workers in the New Economy*. New York: Metropolitan Books.

Elyachar, Julia. 2002. Empowerment Money: The World Bank, Non-Governmental Organizations, and the Value of Culture in Egypt. *Public Culture* 14(3): 493–514.

Engels, Frederick. 1972. *The Origin of the Family, Private Property and the State.* Edited and with an introduction by Eleanor B. Leacock. New York: International Publishers.

Enloe, Cynthia. 1989. *Bananas, Beaches, & Bases: Making Feminist Sense of International Politics.* Berkeley: University of California Press.

European Commission. 1995. *Homeworking in the European Union.* With the Directorate-General for Employment, Industrial Relations and Social Affairs. Social Europe Supplement 2/95. Luxembourg: Office for Official Publications of the European Commission.

Federici, Silvia. 1980. Wages Against Housework. In Malos 1980, 253–61.

———.2000. War, Globalization and Reproduction. *Peace & Change* 25(2): 153–65.

Feldman, Allen. 2001. Philoctetes Revisited: White Public Space and the Political Geography of Public Safety. *Social Text* 19(3): 57–90.

Felstead, Alan and Nick Jewson. 1999. *In Work, At Home. Towards an Understanding of Homeworking.* London: Routledge.

Feminist Review, eds. 1986. *Waged Work: A Reader.* London: Virago Press.

Fernández-Kelly, M. Patricia. 1983. *For We Are Sold, I and My People: Women and Industry in Mexico's Frontier.* Albany: SUNY Press.

Fernández-Kelly, M. Patricia and Anna García. 1989. Hispanic Women and Homework: Women in the Informal Economy of Miami and Los Angeles. In Boris and Daniels 1989, 165–79.

Folbre, Nancy. 2001. *The Invisible Heart. Economics and Family Values.* New York: The New Press.

Fortunati, Leopoldina. 1995. *The Arcane of Reproduction: Housework, Prostitution, Labor and Capital.* Translated by Hilary Creek. Brooklyn: Autonomedia Press.

Foucault, Michel. 1978. *The History of Sexuality. An Introduction. Volume 1.* Translated by Robert Hurley. New York: Random House.

———.1979. Governmentality. *I & C* 6: 5–21.

———.1997. *Ethics: Subjectivity and Truth.* Edited by Paul Rabinow and translated by Robert Hurley et al. New York: New Press.

———.2003. *"Society Must Be Defended." Lectures at the Collège de France 1975-1976.* Translated by David Macey. New York: Picador.

Fox, Bonnie, ed. 1980. *Hidden in the Household: Women's Domestic Labour Under Capitalism.* Toronto: Women's Press.

Fraad, Harriet. 2000. Exploitation in the Labor of Love. In Gibson-Graham, Resnick, and Wolff 2000, 69–86.

Fraad, Harriet, Stephen Resnick, and Richard Wolff. 1994. *Bringing it All Back Home: Class, Gender and Power in the Modern Household.* London: Pluto Press.

Frow, John. 1997. *Time & Commodity Culture.* New York: Oxford University Press.

Fuentes, Annette and Barbara Ehrenreich. 1983. *Women in the Global Factory.* Boston: South End Press.

García-Canclini, Nestor. 1993. *Transforming Modernity: Popular Culture in Mexico.* Austin: Univ. of Texas Press.

Garland, David. 2001. *The Culture of Control. Crime and Social Order in Contemporary Society.* Chicago: University of Chicago Press.

Giannerelli, Linda and James Barsimantov. 2000. Child Care Expenses of America's Families. Occasional Paper Number 40 (December 200), The Urban Institute, Washington, DC.

Gibson-Graham, J. K., Stephen A. Resnick, and Richard D. Wolff, eds. 2000. *Class and Its Others.* Minneapolis: University of Minnesota Press.

Giddens, Anthony. 1991. *Modernity and Self-Identity: Self and Society in the Late Modern Age.* Stanford: Stanford Univ. Press.

Gilder, George. 1981. *Wealth and Poverty.* NY: Basic Books.

Giles, Wenona and Valerie Preston. 1996. The Domestication of Women's Work: A Comparison of Chinese and Portuguese Immigrant Women Homeworkers. *Studies in Political Economy* 51: 147–81.

Gimenez, Martha. 1990. The Dialectics of Waged and Unwaged Work: Waged Work, Domestic Labor and Household Survival in the United States. In *Work Without Wages,* Collins and Gimenez 1990, 25–45.

Glazer, Nona. 1990. Servants to Capital: Unpaid Domestic Labor and Paid Work. In Collins and Gimenez 1990, 142–67.

———.1993. *Women's Paid and Unpaid labor: the Work Transfer in Health Care and Retailing.* Philadelphia: Temple University Press.

Goldsack, Laura. 1999. Haven in a Heartless World? Women and Domestic Violence. In Chapman and Hockey 1999, 121–31.

Gramsci, Antonio. 1971. *Selections from the Prison Notebooks of Antonio Gramsci.* Translated and edited by Quintin Hoare and Geoffrey Nowell Smith. New York: International Publishers.

Gringeri, Christina. 1994. *Getting By: Women Homeworkers and Rural Economic Development.* Lawrence: University of Kansas Press.

Grosz, Elizabeth. 1999. The *Time* of Violence; Deconstruction and Value. *College Literature* 26(1): 8–19.

Hall, Stuart. 1986. The Toad in the Garden: Thatcherism among the Theorists. In *Marxism and the Interpretation of Culture,* edited by C. Nelson and L. Grossberg, 35–57. Urbana: University of Illinois Press, pp. 35–57.

Hansen, Karen. 1992. *African Encounters with Domesticity.* New Brunswick, NJ: Rutgers Univ. Press.

Hardt, Michael and Antonio Negri. 1994. *Labor of Dionysus. A Critique of the State-Form.* Minneapolis: University of Minnesota Press.

———.2000. *Empire.* Cambridge, MA: Harvard University Press.

Hartmann, Heidi I. 1976. Capitalism, Patriarchy, and Job Segregation by Sex. *Signs* 1(3): 137–69, Part 2.

———.1981. The Family as the Locus of Gender, Class, and Political Struggle: The Example of Housework. *Signs* 6(3): 366–94.

Harvey, David. 1990. *The Condition of Postmodernity. An Enquiry into the Origins of Cultural Change.* Oxford: Blackwell.

———.2000. *Spaces of Hope.* Berkeley, CA: University of California Press.

Hayden, Dolores. 1981. *The Grand Domestic Revolution: A History of Feminist Designs for American Homes, Neighborhoods and Cities.* Cambridge, MA: MIT Press.

———.1984. *Redesigning the American Dream: the Future of Housing, Work and Family Life.* New York: W.W. Norton & Co.

Heise, Lori, Jacqueline Pitanguy, and Adrienne Germain. 1994. Violence Against Women: The Hidden Health Burden. World Bank Discussion Papers 255, The World Bank, Washington, DC.

Hekman, Susan, ed. 1996. *Feminist Interpretations of Michel Foucault.* University Park, PA: Pennsylvania State Press.

Heyzer, Noeleen. 1986. *Working Women in South-East Asia: Development, Subordination, Emancipation.* Philadelphia: Open University Press.

Himmelweit, Susan, ed. 2000. *Inside the Household: From Labour to Care.* New York: St. Martin's Press.

Hochschild, Arlie Russell. 1989. *The Second Shift: Working Parents and the Revolution at Home.* New York: Avon.

———.1997. *The Time Bind. When Work Becomes Home and Home Becomes Work.* New York: Metropolitan Books.

Hondagneu-Sotelo, Pierrette. 1996. Immigrant Women and Paid Domestic Work: Research, Theory, and Activism. In *Feminism and Social Change: Bridging Theory and Practice*, edited by Heidi Gottfried, 105–22. Urbana: University of Illinois Press.

hooks, bell. 1990. *Yearning: Race, Gender, and Cultural Politics.* Boston: South End Press.

Huws, Ursula. 2003. *The Making of a Cybertariat: Virtual Work in a Real World.* New York: Monthly Review Press.

ILO. See International Labour Office.

International Labour Office. 1990. *Social Protection of Homeworkers. Documents of the Meeting of Experts on the Social Protection of Homeworkers.* Geneva: International Labour Organization.

———.2001. *Stopping Forced Labor, Global Report under the Follow-up to the ILO Declaration on Fundamental Principles and Rights at Work.* International Labor Conference, 89th Session 2001. Geneva: International Labour Organization.

———.2002. *Women and Men in the Informal Economy: A Statistical Picture.* Geneva: International Labour Organization.

Kempadoo, Kamala and Jo Doezema, eds. 1998. *Global Sex Workers: Rights, Resistance and Redefinition.* New York: Routledge.

Kessler-Harris, Alice and Karen Brodkin Sacks. 1987. The Demise of Domesticity in America. In *Women, Households, and the Economy*, edited by L. Benería and C. Stimpson, 65–84. New Brunswick, NJ: Rutgers University Press.

Kontos, Susan, Carollee Howes, Marybeth Shinn, and Ellen Galinsky. 1995. *Quality in Family Child Care & Relative Care.* New York: Teachers College Press.

Kuhn, Annette and AnnMarie Wolpe, eds. 1978. *Feminism and Materialism: Women and Modes of Production.* London: Routledge and Kegan Paul.

Landry, Bart. 2000. *Black Working Wives. Pioneers of the American Family Revolution.* Berkeley: University of California Press.

Lazo, Lucita. 1996. Women's Empowerment in the Making: The Phillipine Bid for Social Protection. In Boris and Prügl 1996, 259–71.

Leonard, Diane and Sheila Allen, eds. 1991. *Sexual Divisions Revisited*. New York: St. Martin's Press.

Lever, Alison. 1988. Capital, Gender and Skill: Women Homeworkers in Rural Spain. *Feminist Review* 30:3–24.

Lipietz, Alain. 1987. *Mirages and Miracles: The Crisis of Global Fordism*. Translated by David Mace. London: Verso.

Lozano, Beverly. 1989. *The Invisible Work Force: Transforming American Business with Outside Home-Based Workers*. New York: Free Press.

Lui, Tai-Lok. 1994. *Waged Work at Home. The Social Organization of Industrial Outwork in Hong Kong*. Aldershot: Avebury.

Macdonald, Cameron Lynne and David A. Merrill. 2002. It Shouldn't Have to be a Trade: Recognition and Redistribution in Care Work Advocacy. *Hypatia* 17(2): 67–83.

Macdonald, Cameron Lynne and Carmen Sirianni, eds. 1996. *Working in the Service Society*. Philadelphia: Temple University Press.

Malos, Ellen, ed. 1980. *The Politics of Housework*. London: Allison & Busby.

Markusen, Ann R. 1980. City Spatial Structure, Women's Household Labor, and National Urban Policy. *Signs* 5(3): S23-S44.

Martin, Deborah. 2002. Constructing the 'Neighborhood Sphere': Gender and Community Organizing. *Gender, Place and Culture* 9(4): 333–50.

Marx, Karl. 1973. *Grundrisse*. Translated by Martin Nicolaus. New York: Vintage Press.

———.1976. *Capital. A Critique of Political Economy. Vol. 1*. New York: Vintage Books.

Massey, Doreen. 1996. Masculinity, Dualisms and High Technology. In *BodySpace: Destabilizing Geographies of Gender and Sexuality*, edited by Nancy Duncan, 109–26. London: Routledge.

Mattera, Phil. 1985. *Off the Books: The Rise of the Underground Economy*. New York: St. Martin's Press.

McClintock, Anne. 1995. *Imperial Leather: Race, Gender and Sexuality in the Colonial Contest*. New York: Routledge.

McDowell, Linda. 1999. *Gender, Identity, and Place: Understanding Feminist Geographies*. Minneapolis: University of Minnesota Press.

McGee, T. G., Kamal Salih, Mei Ling Young, and Chan Lean Heng. 1989. Industrial Development, Ethnic Cleavages, and Employment Patterns: Penang State, Malaysia. In Portes, Castells, and Benton 1989, 265–78.

Menzies, Heather. 1997. Telework, Shadow Work: The Privatization of Work in the New Digital Economy. *Studies in Political Economy* 53:103–23.

Middleton, Chris. 1988. The Familiar Fate of the *Famulae*: Gender Divisions in the History of Wage Labour. In *On Work: Historical, Comparative & Theoretical Approaches*, edited by R. E. Pahl, 21–47. Oxford and New York: Basil Blackwell.

Midnight Notes Collective, eds. 1992. *Midnight Oil: Work, Energy, War, 1973–1992*. Brooklyn: Autonomedia Press.

Mies, Maria. 1986. *Patriarchy and Accumulation on a World Scale: Women in the International Division of Labor*. London: Zed Books.

Mink, Gwendolyn. 1998. *Welfare's End*. Ithaca, NY: Cornell University Press.

Miraftab, Faranak. 1994. ReProduction at Home: Reconceptualizing Home and Family. *Journal of Family Issues* 15(3): 467–90.

Mitter, Swasti. 1986. *Common Fate, Common Bond: Women in the Global Economy.* London: Pluto Press.

———.1994. On Organising Women in Casualised Work: a Global Overview. In. Rowbotham and Mitter 1994, 14–52.

Moody, Kim. 1997. *Workers in a Lean World: Unions in the International Economy.* London: Verso.

Moshenberg, Daniel. 2002a. Of Empire in the Absence(s) of Colonialism. *Voice of the Turtle Reviews.* http://www.voiceoftheturtle.org/show_article.php?aid=204.

———.2002b. Sweating Modernity: Womenworkers in Textual and Textile Industry. *Rethinking Marxism* 14(4): 1–26.

———.Forthcoming. Occupied Territories: Occupational Health, and Citizenship, in the Fifteenth Department, U.S.A. *Interventions.*

Mullings, Leith. 1997. *On Our Own Terms. Race, Class, and Gender in the Lives of African American Women.* New York: Routledge.

NCJW. See National Council of Jewish Women.

Nakano Glenn, Evelyn. 1992. From Servitude to Service Work: Historical Continuities in the Racial Division of Reproductive Labor. *Signs* 18(1): 1–43.

Nakano Glenn, Evelyn, Grace Chang, and Linda Rennie Forcey, eds. 1994. *Mothering. Ideology, Experience, and Agency.* New York: Routledge.

Naples, Nancy. 2002. Activist Mothering and Community Work: Fighting Oppression in Low-Income Neighborhoods. In Cancian et al. 2002, 207–21.

National Council of Jewish Women. 1999. *Opening a New Window on Childcare: A Report on the Status of Child Care in the Nation Today.* New York: NCJW.

Negri, Antonio. 1988. *Revolution Retrieved: Selected Writings on Marx, Keynes, Capitalist Crisis & New Social Subjects 1967–83.* London: Red Notes.

———.1991. *Marx Beyond Marx: Lessons on the Grundrisse.* Edited by Jim Fleming. Translated by Harry Cleaver et al. Brooklyn: Autonomedia Press.

———.1999. Value and Affect. *Boundary 2* 26(2): 77–88.

Nelson, Margaret K. 1990. Mothering Others' Children: the Experiences of Family Day-Care Providers. *Signs* 15(3): 586–605.

New Jersey State Department of Labor, Division of Workplace Standards. 1982. *Study on Industrial Homework.* Trenton: New Jersey Department of Labor.

Oakley, Ann. 1974. *The Sociology of Housework.* New York: Pantheon Books.

Panitch, Leo and Colin Leys. 1999. *Global Capitalism Versus Democracy.* New York: Monthly Review Press.

Parisi, Luciana and Tiziana Terranova. 2000. Heat-Death. Emergence and Control in Genetic Engineering and Artificial Life. *Ctheory,* a084 http://www.ctheory.net/articles.aspx?id=127.

Parreñas, Rhacel Salazar. 2001. *Servants of Globalization: Women, Migration and Domestic Work.* Stanford, CA: Stanford University Press.

Pearson, Ruth. 2000. All Change? Men, Women and Reproductive Work in the Global Economy. *European Journal of Development Research* 12(2): 219–37.

____. 2004. Organising Home-Based Workers in the Global Economy: an Action-Research Approach. *Development in Practice* 14(1–2): 136–48.

Petersen, Hanne. 1996. *Home Knitted Law: Norms and Values in Gendered Rule-Making*. Aldershot, UK: Dartmouth Press.

Phizacklea, Annie, ed. 1984. *One Way Ticket. Migration and Female Labour*. London: Routledge and Kegan Paul.

Phizacklea, Annie and Carol Wolkowitz. 1995. *Homeworking Women: Gender, Racism and Class at Work*. London: Sage Publications.

Piore, Michael J. and Charles F. Sabel. 1984. *The Second Industrial Divide: Possibilities for Prosperity*. New York: Basic Books.

Portes, Alejandro, Manuel Castells, and Lauren A Benton, eds. 1989. *The Informal Sector. Studies in Advanced and Less Developed Countries*. Baltimore: Johns Hopkins Univ. Press.

U.S. Bureau of the Census. 2002. Poverty in the United States: 2001. Current Population Reports P60–219 (September 2002), U.S. Bureau of the Census, Washington, DC.

Pratt, Geraldine. 2004. *Working Feminism*. Philadelphia: Temple University Press.

Prügl, Elisabeth. 1999. *The Global Construction of Gender. Home-based Work in the Political Economy of the 20th Century*. New York: Columbia University Press.

Rabinbach, Anson. 1990. *The Human Motor. Energy, Fatigue, and the Origins of Modernity*. NY: Basic Books.

Rahman, Aminur. 1999. Micro-credit Initiatives for Equitable and Sustainable Development: Who Pays? *World Development* 27(1): 67–82.

Redclift, Nanneke and Enzo Mingione, eds. 1985. *Beyond Employment: Household, Gender and Subsistence*. New York: Blackwell.

Red Notes. 1979. *Working Class Autonomy and the Crisis*. London: Red Notes and CSE.

Robertson, Brian C. 2000. *There's No Place Like Work: How Business, Government, and Our Obsession with Work Have Driven Parents from Home*. Dallas: Spence Pub.

Romero, Mary. 1992. *Maid in the U.S.A*. New York: Routledge.

Rowbotham, Sheila. 1993. *Homeworkers Worldwide*. London: Merlin Press.

———.1998. Weapons of the Weak: Homeworkers' Networking in Europe. *The European Journal of Women's Studies* 5: 453–63.

Rowbotham. Sheila and Swasti Mitter, eds. 1994. *Dignity and Daily Bread. New Forms of Economic Organising Among Poor Women in the Third World and the First*. London: Routledge.

Rybczynski, Witold. 1986. *Home: the Short History of an Idea*. New York: Viking Press.

Salmon, Jacqueline L. 1999. For Many Children, Nowhere to Go. High Demand, Low Wages Put the Squeeze on Child-Care Providers. *Washington Post*, September 19, 1999, A10.

Sassen, Saskia. 1988. *The Mobility of Labor and Capital: A Study in International Investment and Labor Flow*. Cambridge: Cambridge University Press.

———.2000. Women's Burden. Counter-geographies of Globalization and the Feminization of Survival. *Journal of International Affairs* 53(2): 503–24.

Saxton, Alexander. 1990. *The Rise and Fall of the White Republic: Class Politics and Mass Culture in Nineteenth-Century America*. London: Verso.

Schor, Juliet. 1993. *Overworked American: The Unexpected Decline of Leisure*. New York: Basic Books.

Seecombe, Wally. 1980. The Expanded Reproduction Cycle of Labour Power in Twentieth-Century Capitalism. In Fox 1980, 217–66.

Sengupta, Somini. 1999. Openings Go Unfilled as City Officials Plan How to Spend Day-Care Money. *New York Times*, October 30, 1999, B1.

Serres, Michel. 2000. *The Birth of Physics*. Translated by Jack Hawkes. Manchester, UK: Clinamen Press.

Siegel, Reva. 1998. Valuing Housework: Nineteenth Century Anxieties about the Commodification of Domestic Labor. *American Behavioral Scientist* 41(10): 1437–52.

Silver, Hilary. 1989. The Demand for Homework: Evidence from the U.S. Census. In Boris and Daniels 1989, 103–29.

Silver, Hilary and Frances Goldscheider. 1994. Flexible Work and Housework: Work and Family Constraints on Women's Domestic Labour. *Social Forces* 72(4): 1103–19.

Silverman, Hugh, J., ed. 1993. *Questioning Foundations: Truth/Subjectivity/Culture*. New York: Routledge.

Singh, Andréa Menefee and Anita Kelles-Viitanen, eds. 1987. *Invisible Hands: Women in Home-Based Production*. New Delhi: Sage.

Smith, Joan, Immanuel Wallerstein, and Hans-Dieter Evers, eds. 1984. *Households and the World Economy*. Beverly Hills, CA: Sage Publications.

Smith, Kristin. 2002. Who's Minding the Kids? Child Care Arrangements: Spring 1997. Current Population Reports P70–86 (July 2002), U.S. Bureau of the Census, Washington, DC.

Smith, Neil. 1993. Grounding Metaphor: Towards a Spatialized Politics. In *Place and the Politics of Identity*, edited by Michael Keith and Steve Pile, 67–83. London: Routledge.

Smith, Paul. 1978. Domestic Labor and Marx's Theory of Value. In Kuhn and Wolpe 1978, 198–219.

Spivak, Gayatri Chakravorty. 1987a. Critical Theory and Feminism. In *In Other Worlds: Essays In Cultural Politics*, by Gayatri Chakravorty Spivak, 77–92. New York: Methuen Press.

———.1987b. Scattered Speculations on the Question of Value. In *In Other Worlds: Essays In Cultural Politics*, by Gayatri Chakravorty Spivak, 154–75. New York: Methuen Press.

———.1990. *The Post-Colonial Critic. Interviews, Strategies, Dialogues*. Edited by Sarah Harasym. New York: Routledge.

———.1992. Acting Bits/Identity Talk. *Critical Inquiry* 18: 770–803.

———.1993. More on Power/Knowledge. In *Outside in the Teaching Machine*, by Gayatri Chakravorty Spivak, 25–51. New York: Routledge.

———.1999. *A Critique of Postcolonial Reason*. Cambridge, MA: Harvard University Press.

Stall, Susan and Randy Stoecker. 1998. Community Organizing or Organizing Community? Gender and the Crafts of Empowerment. *Gender and Society* 12:729–56.

Staples, David. Forthcoming. Women's Work and the Ambivalent Gift of Entropy. In *The Affective Turn: Theorizing the Social*, edited by Patricia Clough. Durham, NC: Duke University Press.

Sudbury, Julia. 1998. *'Other Kinds of Dreams': Black Women's Organisations and the Politics of Transformation*. London: Routledge.

Tate, Jane. 1994. Homework in West Yorkshire. In Rowbotham and Mitter 1994, 193–217.

———.1996. Making Links: The Growth of Homeworker Networks. In Boris and Prügl 1996, 273–89.

Thacker, Eugene. 2005. *The Global Genome: Biotechnology, Politics, and Culture*. Cambridge, MA: The MIT Press.

Thompson, E. P. 1966. *The Making of the English Working Class*. New York: Vintage Books.

Thorns, David C. 1998. Home, Home Ownership and the Search for Ontological Security. *Sociological Review* 46(1): 24–47.

Tiano, Susan. 1994. *Patriarchy on the Line: Labor, Gender and Ideology in the Mexican Maquila Industry*. Philadelphia: Temple University Press.

Tuominen, Mary C. 1994a. *The Conflicts of Care-Giving: Gender, Race/Ethnicity and the Changing Political Economy of Child-Care Labor*. PhD dissertation, University of Oregon.

———.1994b. The Hidden Organization of Labor: Gender, Race/Ethnicity and Child-Care Work in the Formal and Informal Economy. *Sociological Perspectives* 37(2): 229–45

———.1997. Exploitation or Opportunity? The Contradictions of Child-Care Policy in the Contemporary United States. *Women & Politics* 18(1): 53–80.

———.1998. Motherhood and the Market: Mothering and Employment Opportunities Among Mexicana, African-American and Euro-American Family Day Care Workers. *Sociological Focus* 31(1): 61–79.

———.2002. Where Teachers Can Make a Liveable Wage': Organizing to Address Gender and Racial Inequalities in Paid Child Care Work. In Cancian et al. 2002, 193–206.

Trinh, T. Minh-Ha. 1989. *Women, Native, Other: Writing Postcoloniality and Feminism*. Bloomington: Indiana University Press.

UNDP. See United Nations Development Program.

United Nations Development Program. 1995. *Human Development Report*. New York: United Nations.

Uttal, Lynet. 2002. *Making Care Work. Employed Mothers in the New Childcare Market*. New Brunswick, NJ: Rutgers University Press.

Valsecchi, Raffaella. 1999. Surveillance and Self Discipline: the Sociological and Theoretical Implications of Foucault's Theoretical Framework for Social Research on Homeworking. http://www.tryoung.com/journal-grad.html/3coates/Rafaella.htm.

Van Raaphorst, Donna L. 1988. *Union Maids Not Wanted. Organizing Domestic Workers 1870–1940*. New York: Praeger.

Vogel, Lise. 2000. Domestic Labor Revisited. *Science & Society* 64(2): 151–71.

Wacquant, Loic. 2001. Deadly Symbiosis. *Punishment & Society* 3(1): 95–134.

Waring, Marilyn. 1988. *If Women Counted: Worth and Value in the Global Economy*. San Francisco: Harper & Row.

Weiner, Annette. 1992. *Inalienable Possession: The Paradox of Keeping-While-Giving*. Berkeley: University of California Press.

Whitebook, Marcy and Abby Eichberg. 2002. Finding a Better Way: Defining and Assessing Public Policies to Improve Child Care Workforce Compensation. Paper 2002–002, Center for the Study of Childcare Employment, Berkeley, CA.

Whitebook, Marcy and Deborah Philips. 1999. Child Care Employment: Implications for Women's Self-Sufficiency and for Child Development. Working Paper Series, Foundation for Child Development, Washington, DC.

Wigley, Mark. 1992. Untitled: The Housing of Gender. In *Sexuality & Space*, edited by Beatriz Colomina, 327–89. New York: Princeton Architectural Press.

———.1993. *The Architecture of Deconstruction: Derrida's Haunt*. Cambridge, MA: MIT Press.

Witheford, Nick. 1994. Autonomist Marxism and the Information Society. *Capital & Class* 52:85–126.

———.1999. *Cyber-Marx. Cycles and Circuits of Struggle in High-Technology Capitalism*. Urbana and Chicago: University of Illinois Press.

Wong, Sau-Ling C. 1994. Diverted Mothering: Representations of Caregivers of Color in the Age of "Multiculturalism." In Nakano Glenn, Chang, and Forcey 1994, 67–91.

Wrigley, Julia. 1995. *Other People's Children*. New York: Basic Books.

Yang, Mayfair Mei-hui. 2000. Putting Capitalism in Its Place. *Current Anthropology* 41(4): 477–510.

# Index

For Product Safety Concerns and Information please contact our EU
representative  GPSR@taylorandfrancis.com
Taylor & Francis Verlag GmbH, Kaufingerstraße 24, 80331 München, Germany